ITALY
TRAVELBOOK™

2001 EDITION

AAA

President and CEO: Robert Darbelnet
*Executive Vice President, Publishing and
Administration:* Rick Rinner
Managing Director, Publishing: Alan Borne
*Managing Director, GIS/Cartography and
Administration:* Bob Hopkins

Director, Product Development: Bill Wood
Director, Publishing Operations: Susan Sears

Managing Editor: Margaret Cavanaugh
Development Editor: Greg Weekes
Cover Design: Mike McCrary
Cover Photo Research: Diane Norden,
Patricia Nasser

Manager, Design: Mike McCrary
Manager, Pre-Press: Tim Johnson
Manager, Product Support: Linda Indolfi
*Manager, Publishing Communications and
Marketing:*
Josette Constantino
Manager, National Publications Sales: Robert
Foley
Manager, Retail Sales – Travel Store:
Sharon Edwards

Published by AAA Publishing, 1000 AAA
Drive, Heathrow, Florida 32746

The contents of this book are believed to be
correct at the time of printing. The
publishers are not responsible for changes
that occur after publication.

The *AAA Italy TravelBook* was created and
produced for AAA Publishing by AA
Publishing, Basingstoke, England.

Written by Sally Roy
Managing Editor Jackie Staddon
Page make-up by Anton Graphics Ltd.

Cover photos
Main photo: Dolomites
© Manfred Mehlig/Stone Images
Cover inset: Masked woman
© Geostock/PhotoDisc
Spine: Leaning Tower of Pisa
© PhotoLink/PhotoDisc

ISBN 1-56251-444-X

Cataloging-in-Publication Data is on file
with the Library of Congress.

Color separations by Leo Reprographic
Ltd., Hong Kong

Printed and bound in Italy by G. Canale &
C. S.P.A., Torino, Italy

Carnival time in Venice

FOREWORD

Welcome to the AAA Italy TravelBook!

If you're planning an Italian vacation, this book will help you discover the real Italy. We've selected not only the great cities, but the best of the towns and stunning countryside that will give a true taste of the diversity of this beautiful land. You'll experience historic city centers packed with world-class sights and museums, breathtaking landscape, and some of Europe's most beguiling small towns and villages. Discover the glories of Rome, Italy's capital; enjoy the unsurpassed artistic treasures of Florence; and delight in the unique beauty of Venice, a city built on water. You'll find there's more to dynamic Milan than industry and designer-name shopping, while the vibrant southern cities of Naples and Sicily's capital, Palermo, offer a superb contrast to the well-ordered northern centers.

Outside the cities there's a varied and welcoming country, the beauty of its landscape offering the perfect backdrop for the cities. Northern Italy butts up to the ragged peaks of the Alps; east, the glorious Italian lakes give way to the dramatic scenery of the Dolomites; and the Apennines – Italy's "backbone" – extends southward almost the entire length of the peninsula. You'll find bustling ports like Genoa, cities of art such as Siena and sun-and-sand resorts like Rimini. We've also included some of Italy's prettiest small towns and villages, enabling you to put together a varied and memorable trip, while suggested walks and drives will help you get the most out of your Italian experience.

Dip into this book to get your initial taste from the informative text and evocative photographs, then use it for more solid planning. There's practical information to smooth your way, from tips on getting around to suggestions on where to stay. We've included maps to help you find your way, ideas for eating, drinking and shopping, and descriptions of what to see. The insider advice offered by our specialist author will help you get the most out of this enchanting country.

ITALY TRAVELBOOK™

CONTENTS

Contents

One of the graceful statues that
adorn Piazza della Signoria in
Florence

Introduction to Italy

INTRODUCTION TO ITALY

*" **A** COUNTRY whose beauty and art are more than matched by its people's charm and style is rich and blessed indeed. "*

TIMELINE 22
SURVIVAL GUIDE 24

Fishing boats drawn up at Sorrento on the lovely coast south of Naples

ITALY

Beautiful Italy (*bella* Italia) has much to offer – varied and lovely scenery, a treasure trove of art, history and culture, and a population that truly understands the value of enjoying life. An Italian vacation means different things to different people, and therein lies its magic. Whether you're looking for heady days in the great outdoors, beaches to laze on, stunning art and culture, stylish cities, prosperous towns or picturesque villages, you'll find it here. You'll also find warm and sincere people, delicious food, splendid wine and a relaxed way of life that will enchant you. Whether you're here by chance or design, whether this is your first visit or your fiftieth, Italy will live up to your expectations and leave you ready for more.

Italians have a sense of style

Above: Clear waters lap a cove on the Monte Argentario peninsula

Right: Tuscany's tiny Renaissance city of Pienza

The Shape of the Land

From top to toe, Italy is scenically heart-stopping, with contrasting landscapes of varied beauty. The great Alpine massifs of the north, snow-topped even in summer, give way to mist-laden plains and to a rolling, fertile heartland, the classic landscape of grape and olive, and the dry and desolate beauty of the sun-baked south.

Italy's long coastline snakes around the country, encompassing everything from misty lagoons through pine-clad white cliffs to curving golden sands, all fringed with azure and turquoise waters. The country is predominantly mountainous, with the northern Alps and Dolomites (Dolomiti) forming a natural barrier with Italy's neighbors.

The long spine of the Apennines (Appennini) runs almost the whole way down the country, in some areas stretching virtually from coast to coast. Throughout Italy, much of this upland area is wooded, with huge tracts of

natural forest and great stands of beech, oak and chestnut, which once played a vital part in the economy. The northern plains of the Po river valley are immensely fertile and intensively farmed, as is the rolling, serene countryside of central Italy.

Farther south, there are more mountains. Here, the land is harsher, the country less fertile, the climate truly southern Mediterranean. Italy's coastal waters are dotted with islands, ranging in size from true land masses like Sicily and Sardinia to tiny and sometimes uninhabited outcrops.

Hot, Cold, Wet, Dry

Italy's long narrow shape jutting into the Mediterranean makes for plenty of climatic variety and year-round temperature differences between the north and south. The popular perception of a country bathed in perpetual sunshine couldn't be further from the truth; Italy has weather, not climate. With the possible exception of July and August, when thunderstorms break the heat and hailstones reach the size of tennis balls, it can drizzle, rain and downpour.

Winter brings cold and snow to north and central Italy, but in the south, it's confined to the high tops. Sun and showers punctuate spring, until gradually the heat intensifies, the showers dry up and glorious early summer arrives with warm days and cool, restful nights. Summer ushers in heat, humidity, mosquitoes and storms. This is the time to head for the coast, where the sea is cooling, and the air is fresh and clear.

Rain returns in September, heralding a mini-spring, with fresh growth and a flush of autumn flowers. Temperatures drop, more and more rain falls, and chilling fog floats in the plains and valleys. By November, the first snow falls.

The State of the Nation

Italy has a long history, but it's only been one country since 1870, making it far younger than the United States. The country has been a republic since 1946; the 21 regions enjoy a large degree of self-government, with some, such as Sicily and Sardinia, being semi-autonomous. Since World War II, Italy has lurched politically through more than 50 governments. The great scandals of the 1980s and 1990s, when the real depths of corruption came into

Sunflowers add a splash of extra sunshine to the fertile countryside

the open, still cause repercussions at every level. Surprisingly, these turmoils seem to have had little effect on the economy, one of the most successful in Europe. It's sometimes hard to remember how much has been achieved in just 50 years, as Italy has moved from being a peasant-based, largely agricultural country to one of the world's leading industrial nations. Early entry into the European Union aided economic development.

There is a very real economic and cultural division in the country. The north is richer, more advanced and more successful than the arid and impoverished south, from where the majority of American Italians emigrated. For the north, foreign markets are closer, the climate is better for agriculture and energy sources, and raw materials are near at hand. Vast sums have been poured into the south during recent years, but the gap remains, with southerners still traveling north to look for work, and northerners still resenting what they see as a drain on their hard work and effort.

Towns and Villages

Italy's history and culture have left a superb legacy. Towns and villages are packed with fine churches, civic buildings and works of art. Every settlement, no matter how large or small, retains its central piazza, with churches and municipal buildings grouped around it. Italians have a strong tradition of living in villages and towns. Even in rural areas, the tradition has been to go out from the village to work in the fields. Nevertheless, there's a huge – and historically rooted – gulf between the urban and rural population, with large numbers of peasants still working the land in traditional ways.

The middle class was a late arrival in Italy, only emerging in the decades following World War II, and still growing fast in some areas as the economic boom continues. Increasing affluence has led to much development in urban areas. You'll see spreads of unattractive industrial zones and dismal apartment blocks on the outskirts of countless towns.

Milan's Gothic-style church of Santa Maria delle Grazie

The Italian emphasis on family, sociability and *bella figura* is always present in small-town life

The People

Italy's complex history, more a story of a collection of separate states than the history of a nation, has left an indelible mark. Cavour's famous statement after the 1870 unification, "We have made Italy, now we must make Italians," still holds true. There is no such thing as "an Italian." Ask an Italian where he's from and the answer will never be "from Italy." Italians see themselves as primarily Roman, Sicilian, Tuscan or whatever. Everything about them – their outlook, character, attitudes and prejudices – stems from their native region and its history. So the work-driven Milanese fail to understand the turbulent Neapolitans, and the rational and conservative Tuscans have little in common with the abrasive Romans.

It is precisely these regional differences that give Italy its appealing diversity, which was strengthened by the huge numbers of regional dialects until well into the 20th century. With widespread literacy and the growth of television, the Italian language has come to prominence. Modern Italian derives from Tuscan, a medieval dialect used by Dante and Petrarch and firmly based on Latin. It's a beautiful, elegant, musical and expressive language, a joy to listen to whether you understand it or not.

Italian Style

Figuring out what makes Italians tick will add to the pleasure of your trip. You're bound to have your own ideas on what is typical – peasant farmer, Latin everyday Italian life. The tradition of the evening *passeggiata*, when everyone's out on the streets in their smart clothes, combines many of these elements; here is the *bella figura*, the chance to be with other people doing the same thing, enjoying one of life's simple pleasures. Watch Italian TV, and you'll see how many truly dreadful game shows there are. The content may be bad, but they're perfect for showing off.

Italians mean well and want to be well thought of; they'll go out of their way to solve small problems, and outbursts of anger are quickly over and forgotten. They make a good deal of noise, but voices are rarely harsh with ill-temper.

Family Life

Family values are still important – to see them in action, have lunch in any restaurant on a Sunday to observe the 20-strong family groups catching up on the news. Despite having the lowest national birth rate in the world, family ties are still very close, with the mother's role being of paramount importance. It's said that the reason behind Italian men's constant philandering is a desperate search for a woman who will live up to the perfections of *mamma*.

Parents provide lavishly for their children, who reward them by living at home well into their 30s, then expecting *mamma* and *babbo* to provide the first marital home. Such largesse makes you look good – *bella figura* in action. There's genuine thoughtfulness in the treatment of the very young and very old. Italy is still a country where people value the experiences of older adults. There are few other countries where the coolest teenage boy will go out of his way to admire a baby. Transparent and simple on many levels, Italians are fundamentally lovable people.

lover, pasta-cooking mamma – but beware of stereotypes. For every one that conforms, there's another that proves the exception. But a few points may hold true. Italians are social animals who abhor solitude and are happiest doing what everyone else is doing.

The *bella figura* – looking good – means a lot, whether it applies to clothes, cars or homes. Italians have an innate sense of style and are expert at putting themselves together to the best advantage. Their outlook on life is balanced, with an aptitude for hard work going hand-in-hand with natural spontaneity and a sensuous enjoyment of life's pleasures. Natural kindliness is tempered with a certain detachment; many seemingly deep emotions are fairly superficial. As you travel around, you'll observe these characteristics in

Introduction to Italy

Pleasures and Pastimes

Italians enjoy all the same things that people in developed countries worldwide appreciate, though often with a distinctly Italian twist. Talking, eating and drinking – activities that allow for maximum attention to appearance and involve a group of people – are high on the list. Shopping is very popular for men and women, as everyone likes to have the newest styles as fast as possible. Italian men are real "peacocks," and you'll notice that men's stores often outnumber women's stores in the smartest areas of town. Both sexes visit their hair stylist regularly; it's an ideal opportunity for more talk.

On the whole, Italians are not big on the great outdoors. Skiing, hiking and sailing are as much about showing off designer outfits as exercising. The top two sports in Italy are soccer and cycling, with the Sunday sports schedules devoted to these two. Around 4 p.m. on Sunday, you'll notice men everywhere with tiny radios glued to their ears; they're tuning out the gossip and into their team's match.

Despite 97 percent of the population being baptized Catholic, only about 10 percent attend church regularly, with the attendance figures among young people falling disproportionately. Movies, music and nightclubs attract this age group.

With their innate sense of style, Italians stage excellent exhibitions of every type, so keep an eye open for one that might be of interest.

A Major Pleasure

Food is a major Italian pleasure. Cooking is immensely varied, with each region, province, town and village having its own specialties and recipes. Dishes are simple and rely on the superb quality of ingredients. Frozen food is virtually nonexistent, so menus are dictated by the seasons, with a rich procession of dishes punctuating the calendar. This makes for great variety, especially if your trip covers several regions. One of Italy's pleasures is the arrival of the "first" – the first Sicilian citrus in the fall, the first *cavolo nero* (black cabbage) from Tuscany and the first raspberries from the cool north.

If you're food shopping, look for the label *nostrano* on fruits and vegetables, proudly proclaiming they are grown locally. Different regions serve up

Below: Peaceful Tuscany is popular with anglers
Right: Hands are as important as voice in many Italian conversations

Introduction to Italy

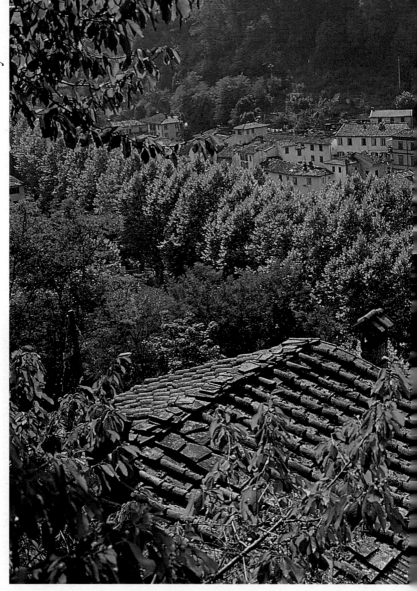

The peaceful spa town of Bagni di Lucca in northern Tuscany – Italians enjoy taking a water cure

different types of food, and each thinks its own is best. Northerners fill up on *polenta* (cornmeal) and rice, while southerners couldn't imagine life without the daily mound of pasta. Tuscans eat beans and plain meat. Sicilians love pepper, chili and odd sweet-and-sour Arab-influenced flavor combinations. Rich cheese and cream appear in mountain recipes, truffles in

those from Piedmont (Piemonte) and Umbria. Vegetable sauces, not meat, dominate the *cucina povera* (poor kitchen) of the south. Enjoy it all and emulate the Italians, who think nothing about driving to the coast to eat fish or lobster. Why plan your trip solely around great pictures and historic towns when you could plan it around white truffles, artichokes and red wine?

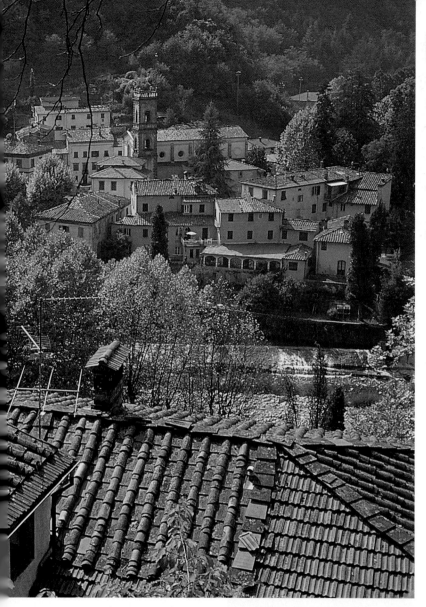

Getting Around

Traveling in Italy is easy. The excellent toll *autostrada* (freeway) network covers the whole country, with the option of driving on good highways if you're not pressed for time. Side roads, particularly in the mountains, can be twisting and steep, and country roads are not always surfaced very well.

If you're using public transportation, the train system is cheap, punctual and efficient. All towns have a railroad station, but cross-country routes can be slow and complicated. It makes sense to stick to more direct inter-city services when traveling by train. If you want to get off the beaten track, you'll find even the tiniest places are served by buses. Driving will be different from back home, but once you're accustomed to the style, you should have no problems. Bear in mind: speed limits are much

Above: The good things of life on show in a Milan shopping center

Left: An appreciative eye from the *carabinieri*

higher than in the United States and Italians tend to drive fast and aggressively but safely.

All major cities have an airport, with frequent flights between cities. Hotel standards vary throughout the country, but all hotels are inspected and rated annually by regional authorities, and, whatever the price range, will be spotlessly clean. Air-conditioning is becoming more widespread but is by no means universal. Buildings can be stifling during summer. By law, heating in hotels and public places is not turned on until November 1.

Tourism is a major industry, so English is widely spoken in hotels and

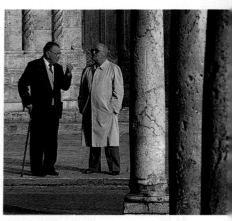

Renaissance and medieval buildings fill the Piazza del Popolo, Áscoli Piceno

and you'll get more from your vacation if you do a bit of homework. Check what you'd like to see and do, read a few recipes, watch a few movies. Consider writing ahead to tourist boards in the areas you'll be visiting for information on attractions and sights.

The Internet

Much information is available on the Internet, but the quality of data varies, and some sites are only writtten in Italian. But it's fun to browse before you go. Here are some sites you may like to visit:

Official Italian State Tourist Board *www.enit.it*
Second Italian State Tourist Board *www.piuitalia2000.it*
New York office of the Italian State Tourist Board *www.italiantourism.com*
General information *www.travel.it*

You also can access all the regional sites in Italy, which will have full tourist information, though not always in English, by visiting *www.regione.nameofregioninitalian.it*

restaurants in major tourist areas, though hardly at all off the beaten path. Tourist offices and the level of information they provide vary hugely, ranging from excellent, with up-to-the-minute books and maps in English, to very poor. Do try a few words of Italian, the effect it has is well worth the effort, and it will add a whole new dimension to your Italian experience. Above all, be flexible. Don't be surprised to find transportation schedules that mysteriously change, museums closed when they should be open and major attractions shrouded in scaffolding overnight – this is Italy.

Before You Go

Planning and researching your trip should be fun. There's a wealth of literature on every aspect of Italian life,

TIMELINE

3000–1800 BC	First traces of migratory peoples in peninsula.
800 BC	Phoenicians and Carthaginians appear, establishing colonies in southern Italy.
700–300 BC	Etruscan federation, centered on present-day Tuscany and Lazio, exists alongside emerging Roman republic.
509 BC	Roman republic established, Etruscan power gradually diminishes.
264–146 BC	Punic Wars against Carthage; Rome emerges as master of the Mediterranean.
44 BC	Julius Caesar assassinated.
AD 200–400	Decline of the Roman Empire.
410	Rome is sacked by Barbarians.
550–770	Peninsula fragmented with different areas under Byzantine, Papal, Lombard and Frankish influence.
800	Charlemagne crowned Holy Roman Emperor. North torn between Pope and emperor for next 400 years.
827	Arab conquest of the south.
1000s	Norman invasions in south; Palermo becomes capital of Norman kingdom.
1300–1400	Emergence of the city-states in north; prosperity is founded on trade and commerce. First stirrings of Renaissance era.
1442	South unified under Spain and remains in Spanish hands until 18th century.
1494	French invade the north.
1500–1848	Peninsula is fragmented under foreign domination.
1848–61	Struggle for unification, led by Giuseppe Mazzini, Camillo Cavour and Giuseppe Garibaldi, with brief republic established in 1848; kingdom of Italy proclaimed in 1861.
1870	Unification completed by annexation of Rome and the Papal States.
1915–18	Italy sides with Allies during World War I.
1921–25	Rise of Benito Mussolini in post-war social and economic chaos. Mussolini comes to power as dictator.
1929	Mussolini signs Concordat with Vatican, which establishes the Vatican as an autonomous church-state within Italy.
1940	Italy enters World War II on Axis side.
1943	Fall of Mussolini and armistice with Allies. Germany then

reinstates him as head of puppet republic. Allies invade from south and struggle north.

1944   Rome is liberated.

1945   Mussolini shot near Milan.

1946   The Italian Republic is established.

1950   Establishment of Cassa del Mezzogiorno, an agency to fund development of southern Italy.

1957   Treaty of Rome; Italy becomes founding member of European Community, economy starts to boom.

1960–85   Period of social and political confusion, inflation and terrorism. Despite this, the population prospers.

1985   Economy steadies, political confusion and scandal continue. Corruption is rife, but Italy flourishes while desire for political and institutional reform grows.

1990s   Government drive, led by Giuliano Amato, against the Mafia following murders of anti-Mafia judges Giovanni Falcone and Paolo Borsellino.

1992–96   Tangentopoli crisis; thousands of political figures are implicated and arrested for bribery and corruption. Public swings against established political parties.

1997   Giulio Andreotti, former prime minister, on trial for Mafia connections.

1999   Italy becomes one of the first European Union entrants to adopt single European currency (the euro).

THE NORMANS IN SICILY

In AD 827, the Arabs invaded and conquered the island of Sicily, heralding a period of economic growth and political stability. To help maintain their power, the Arabs used mercenaries, frequently Normans from France, who were quick to realize Sicily's rich potential. In 1061, Roger Hauteville seized Messina, and by 1072, Palermo had become the capital of the Norman Kingdom of Sicily. The kingdom lasted little more than a century, but in that time five kings left a legacy of incomparable art and architecture, while at the same time excelling in administration, religious tolerance and justice.

Roger I and his son, Roger II, were among Europe's most successful medieval monarchs, expanding their kingdom to include southern Italy, Malta and parts of north Africa. They were followed by William I, William II and William III, who was ousted by the Hohenstauffen emperor, Henry VI. The Normans' artistic influence can be seen all over Sicily and the south, while their genetic legacy lingers in redheaded and blonde Sicilians, with straight Norman noses and blue eyes. Echoes of their language survive in the dialects of remote villages.

Introduction to Italy

SURVIVAL GUIDE

- Inevitably, Italy's star attractions in Rome, Venice and Florence and the other major centers become packed during the summer, as do many coastal resorts. Italians, too, are on vacation. Sightseeing can be exhausting in the heat, and big-city restaurants and shops are often closed while their owners take a break. It makes sense to visit in the spring, late fall or winter, when it's quieter and cooler. May and September are peak months in terms of international visitors.

- One of the chief pleasures of Italy is the *passeggiata* (the early evening parade), when the streets are crowded with strolling and chatting locals. It occurs the length and breadth of Italy, in big cities and tiny villages, so be prepared for the streets to become packed for a couple of hours beginning at 6. By 8:30, they'll be deserted.

- Much of Italy closes down from around 12:30 until 4:30 or 5 while people eat lunch and have a siesta. So plan your day around this, remembering that museums, churches, galleries and shops will all be shut for several hours. You'll enjoy your sightseeing more if you do as the locals do and take a midday rest, with shops staying open until 8 or 9 in towns and later in beach resorts.

- Generally, museums and art galleries throughout Italy are closed on Mondays. So if sightseeing is your main aim, plan to do your traveling on Mondays. That way, you won't waste valuable time while everything's closed.

- Italians spend much time and effort on their appearance, always showering and changing their outfits for the evening *passeggiata*. They will appreciate it if tourists also make the effort, so try and look appropriately smart. Shorts are not acceptable city wear in Italy, and you will not be allowed into churches if too much arm or leg is showing – it's considered disrespectful.

- Meal times are different from those in the United States; it is unusual to eat dinner before 7:30 or 8; lunch is served starting at 12:30. Some restaurants offer fixed-price menus, but you may want to choose some of the local specialties. Vegetarianism is considered odd, but there are plenty of pasta and side dishes that are suitable. Check with the waiter on the ingredients. Italians sometimes think salami, prosciutto and meat stock don't count as meat. Children are genuinely welcome in all restaurants.

- Italians enjoy wine, which they drink at all meals, but the concept of the cocktail hour is alien, as they associate alcohol with food. For this

Lunchtime at one of the upscale restaurants in Milan's elegant Galleria Vittorio Emanuele

reason, if you order a pre-dinner drink in a bar it will always be served with potato chips, nuts or canapés. In Italy, inebriation is a serious social taboo.

- Bars are much more than the name suggests; open from dawn till midnight or later, they offer coffee, tea, soda, snacks, sandwiches and pastries as well as alcohol. They are brightly lit, immaculately clean and efficiently run for speedy service. Italians rarely sit down, and you will be charged extra if you do, as it involves waiter service. All bars have public telephones, restrooms and newspapers, useful for weather maps on the back pages.
- Smoking is common in public places throughout the country.
- One of the joys of Italy is shopping in little local stores, with their wonderful personal service, and at the colorful street markets. Italy has very few department stores except in the cities, and even these bear little

resemblance to what you're used to back home. There are virtually no shopping malls. Shop and market prices are fixed.

- If you buy goods to take home, remember to inquire about tax-free shopping. Many stores and outlets offer this, particularly those catering to tourists. If a purchase is a gift, tell the sales person. It will be beautifully and artistically wrapped and ribboned.
- In summer, be sure to drink enough water. With high temperatures, dry heat and little air conditioning, it's important to keep fluid levels high. Caffeinated and alcoholic beverages will further dehydrate you. Drinks in Italy are rarely served with ice. Italians think too much ice is bad for the stomach.
- Facilities for people with disabilities are improving, but are still not as good as those back home. If you need help, check ahead with the local tourist offices.

THE NORTHWEST AND EMILIA ROMAGNA

"THE Northwest's Alpine peaks, coastline and dynamic cities set an interesting contrast to the wide flat plains, intensive agriculture and historic small cites of Emilia Romagna. "

Color-washed houses are reflected in the tranquil waters of Portofino's tiny harbor

The Northwest and Emilia Romagna

THE NORTHWEST AND EMILIA ROMAGNA

The huge swath of the northwest and Emilia Romagna sweeps from coast to coast across the top of Italy, a region packed with rich and major cities, historic towns and pretty villages. Its fine landscape encompasses the Alps, sparkling lakes, stunning coastal scenery, and the great Po river valley with its intensive agriculture. Prosperous and forward-looking, the entire area gives a taste of the true diversity of modern Italy, where the past has shaped the present against the background of a traditional way of life, and tourism is only part of the whole picture.

The Shape of the Land

Much of the northwest is either hilly or mountainous, with the major exception of the Po river valley, a huge, flat and intensively cultivated plain that stretches almost two-thirds of the way across Italy from south of Milan to the Adriatic. The Po valley lies in Lombardy and Emilia Romagna, Italy's two richest regions.

Lombardy (Lombardia) also boasts the Italian Lakes, celebrated for centuries for their great natural beauty and entrancing mix of water, mountains, woodlands and charming villages. Emilia Romagna is mainly flat, its fertile farmland giving way to a long stretch of sandy coast on the Adriatic, a favorite holiday destination for families from all over Europe.

In the west lie the regions of Piedmont, Valle d'Aosta and Liguria, where you'll find some of Italy's most beautiful coastline and glorious mountain scenery. Piedmont is surrounded on three sides by the Alps; to the west and south the Maritime Alps straddle the border with France and to the north the Monte Bianco chain penetrates down through the Valle d'Aosta.

Aosta is splendid, with scything valleys, rushing torrents and soaring peaks. It has true wilderness country in some parts. Liguria, too, has mountains, which run behind the coast from the French border as far as the north of Tuscany. The shelter they provide has created a microclimate along this stretch, where subtropical vegetation flourishes and cold weather is rare.

The Past

The history of this part of Italy is, as all over the country, one of fragmentation until the 19th-century process of unification. During the Middle Ages, the developing cities were largely independent, Milan being particularly important, while the Renaissance saw ruling families establish brilliant courts at their power bases in cities such as Mantua and Ferrara. On the west coast, Genoa was one of Europe's great

maritime republics, while in Emilia Romagna, Bologna became home to one of the Continent's oldest and most prestigious universities.

After the French invasions at the end of the 15th century, political power lay for centuries in the hands of outsiders; at various times the Spanish, the French and the Austrians all held Milan, Turin and other major centers. The House of Savoy, which ruled Piedmont, came to be a firm backer of the cause of unification; Victor Emanuel of Savoy became the first king of a united Italy, and the capital was, for a short time, Turin. This background has produced the common Italian tendency to make local rather than regional or national loyalties the

The Northwest and Emilia Romagna

The Castello di Sarre in the scenic Valle d'Aosta is backed by majestic mountains

strongest. People are passionately proud of their city, town or village, but not necessarily of Italy as a whole.

Modern Prosperity

The northwest, while scenically beautiful, is also work-driven and extremely prosperous, with a much faster pace of life than that in central or southern Italy. Milan is a major industrial and technological center, and has more in common with northern Europe than southern Italy. Turin is a major automobile manufacturing city, the home of Fiat and Lancia. Italy's industrial revolution began in Genoa, which is still Italy's largest port, while Bologna's present-day wealth comes from its computer-associated industries.

The lesser towns, too, have solidly based and thriving industries. Agriculture is still important, with rice, corn and tobacco thriving in the fertile Po river valley, and extensive vineyards in the hillier areas. Development has brought much new construction in its wake, and you'll find parts of the area pretty built-up, with many lovely old towns surrounded by ugly modern industrial zones and stretches of new housing. The region has never been poor or isolated, and this long-established sense of security is evident in the open friendliness and politeness of most of the people.

Exploring the Region

If you're interested in a combination of great scenery, vibrant cities and historic towns, head for this area's western section, where there's the bonus of a superb coast. From the foothills of Piedmont there's easy access into the Alpine valleys, and you can hike or drive in clear mountain air surrounded by spectacular scenery. Lombardy, in the center, has a bit of everything, from the frenetic pace of Milan to the delights of lovely old Bergamo, while the beauties of Lakes Maggiore, Lugano and Como lie within easy reach to the north.

Farther east, in Emilia Romagna, the flat plains are liberally sprinkled with the historic towns of Cremona, Ravenna and Ferrara, all packed with artistic treasures. Independent travel is easy in this thoroughly modern region with its excellent infrastructure and good roads. A rental car makes sense for your explorations, but if you're spending time in Milan, Turin or Bologna, arrange to pick up your car either before or after your visit; driving and parking can be difficult in any of these cities. It is possible to explore

Sunflowers are grown for oil all over Italy

using public transportation, an option that works well if you're concentrating on towns. If you're planning to spend time in the mountains, however, a rental car gives you the chance to go as you please.

When To Go

Spring, early summer and fall, before or after the hordes of European vacationers, are the best times to come. Summer in the Alps is lovely, but you'll be sharing the mountains and hotels with what will seem like half of Europe. September and October, with the spectacular autumn foliage at its best, are the perfect months. While winter brings its own charms, an off-season trip here is not recommended. Winter can be long and harsh in the mountains, city pollution is often at its worst, and the plains can be shrouded for days in penetratingly cold mist and fog. The only area to escape to is the western coastal strip, but the delightful villages here are primarily summer resorts, and winter facilities for visitors are few.

The Northwest and Emilia Romagna

MILAN

Noisy, dynamic Milan (Milano) is like no other Italian city. The driving force behind northern Italy's booming economy, it lacks the easy-going charm and relaxed pace you find elsewhere. The atmosphere has far more in common with the countries north of the Alps than with the Italian peninsula. Don't expect a beguiling city, but sample Milan as a vital element in modern Italy.

Seeing the City

Milan is well-endowed with museums, churches and galleries. In addition to the big sights, there's a host of smaller museums and historic churches, a couple of large parks and fantastic shopping at every price level. Don't neglect areas like Navigli and Ticinese to the south; these are arty and attractive districts with interesting shops, good bars, clubs and restaurants. They provide fine antidotes to the frenetic city center. Pick up a copy of *Milano – Where, When, How* from the tourist office; it's packed with general information and listings that will help make the most of your stay.

Getting Around

Milan is a big and sprawling city, its main streets radiating out from the Piazza del Duomo and crossed by three concentric roads. Most of what you'll want to see lies in a relatively small central area and you should be able to walk for much of the time. Streets can be packed, so you may want to take the subway to a central point near several main sights, then proceed on foot. Or you could take a city tour; these run daily Tuesday through Sunday, last about three hours and have an English commentary.

Eating

Milan restaurants can be very expensive; but there are more fast-food eateries than in any other Italian city, and plenty of good moderately priced places. Milan has its own specialties, the best-known is probably *cotoletta alla milanese* (wiener schnitzel) and *risotto alla milanese*, the simplest and most delicious risotto. Carbohydrates come in the form of *polenta*, a type of cornmeal-based porridge, nowadays trendy throughout Europe. The nearest wine zones to Milan are San Colombano and Oltrepò, though wine lists in restaurants are often extensive.

Shopping

Fashion and design are Milanese obsessions, so it's hardly surprising that shopping here is taken very seriously. The area to head for is the Golden Quadrangle (Quadrilatero d'Oro). Here, the world's best in high fashion and accessories line the elegant streets, and the customers are as eye-catching as the shops.

Other expensive shops cluster in the Galleria Vittorio Emanuele, while nearby La Rinascente, on the Piazza del Duomo, is a slightly cheaper alternative, a major department store that's a Milan institution. For interesting smaller shops and antiques, head for the Navigli district. Milan also has a number of discount stores selling high-fashion designer clothes.

Entertainment

Opera fans will probably want to make arrangements to attend a performance at La Scala (see page 35). There are other chances of enjoying classical music around the city, as well as live theater and movies in English. Milan is known among the young as Italy's hippest nightlife center, with a plethora of every type of club, jazz and rock concerts.

The Northwest and Emilia Romagna

MILAN

 TOURIST INFORMATION
•Via Marconi 1, ☎ 02 7252 4301/2/3;
e-mail apt@netitalia.it
•Stazione Centrale ☎ 02 7252 4360/370
•City tours ☎ 02 8645 0433

 URBAN TRANSPORTATION
Milan's public transportation system is a
well-integrated and efficient
combination of trams, buses and subway. The
subway is fastest, easiest and most useful, and
consists of three lines, the red (MM1), the green
(MM2) and the yellow (MM3), which converge at
four main hub stations. You can pick up a map at
the information offices at either the Duomo or
Stazione Centrale subway stations. Tickets are
valid throughout the different systems; buy them at
bars, tobacco shops or subway stations, either

singly or in books of 10; 24- and 48-hour tourist
tickets are also available. They are valid for 75
minutes from the journey's start and may be used
for one subway ride plus an unlimited number of
tram and bus rides. Taxis are available at key
points throughout the city, or you can telephone
☎ 02 6767, 8383, 3100 or 5353.

 AIRPORT INFORMATION
Milan has two airports, Linate
(☎ 02 748 5220, toll-free from within Italy
800 337 337; website www.sea-aeroportimilano.it),
4 miles from the city center, and Malpensa (☎ 02
748 5220, toll-free from within Italy 800 337 337;
website www.sea-aeroportimilano.it), 28 miles
away. Each airport handles domestic and
international flights, and each has a bus service to
Milan and the other airport.

CLIMATE – Average highs and lows

JAN.	FEB.	MAR.	APR.	MAY	JUN.	JUL.	AUG.	SEP.	OCT.	NOV.	DEC.
6°C	8°C	13°C	16°C	21°C	25°C	28°C	27°C	24°C	18°C	11°C	7°C
43°F	46°F	55°F	61°F	70°F	77°F	82°F	81°F	75°F	64°F	52°F	45°F
-4°C	-2°C	-1°C	4°C	10°C	13°C	15°C	15°C	12°C	6°C	0°C	-4°C
26°F	27°F	34°F	40°F	50°F	55°F	59°F	59°F	54°F	43°F	32°F	25°F

The Northwest and Emilia Romagna

MILAN SIGHTS

Key to symbols

➕ map coordinates refer to the Milan map on page 33;
sights below are highlighted in yellow on the map
✉ address or location ☎ telephone number
🕐 opening times 🍴 restaurant on site or nearby
🚇 subway station 🚌 nearest bus or tram route
🎟 admission charge: $$$ more than L5,000, $$ L3,000
to L5,000, $ less than L3,000 ℹ information

ACCADEMIA BRERA

By far the most prestigious of Milan's art
galleries, the Accademia Brera (Brera
Academy) houses a huge collection. It
may be best to concentrate on the
highlights or your own particular
interests. The gallery's emphasis is firmly
on Italian painting, with the core dating
from the Renaissance. You'll be struck by
the incredible perspective of Mantegna's
Cristo Morto – a foreshortened view of
Christ's dead body from the pierced soles
of his feet. It's a fine contrast to the
almost contemporary *St. Mark Preaching*
by Gentile Bellini, packed with turbaned
men and eastern animals – there's even a
camel and giraffe. Venetian art is
represented by Veronese's action-packed
Supper in the House of Simon and
Carpaccio's lovely *Presentation of the
Virgin*. The enigmatic Florentine Piero
della Francesca is represented by the
Brera's most outstanding work, his
austere, balanced and compelling
*Madonna with Angels, Saints and Federigo
di Montefeltro*, all grays and subdued tones
with shafts of intense color.
➕ B3 ✉ Via Brera 28 ☎ 02 722 631 🕐 Tue.–Fri.
9–9, Sat. 9 a.m.–midnight, Sun. 9–8, Apr.–Oct.;
Tue.–Sat. 9–5, Sun. 9–8, rest of year 🚇 M2 Lanza,
M3 Montenapoleone 🎟 $$$

CASTELLO SFORZESCO

The huge red-brick structure of the
Castello Sforzesco (Sforza Castle) is one
of Milan's most striking landmarks, rising
above the chaotic traffic whirling around
the Foro Buonaparte. The first version of
the castle was built by the then-ruling
family, the Viscontis, destroyed in 1447 by
rebels, and rebuilt by the Visconti

successors, the Sforzas. It became one of
Europe's most glittering courts, powerful
and cultured – Leonardo da Vinci was
among the artists patronized by the
family. Milan fell to the French in 1499
and the castle was used as barracks until
the late 19th century. Today, it houses a
series of museums; among them, the
Museo d'Arte Antica (Ancient Art
Museum), where you can see
Michelangelo's last unfinished *Pietà*, and
the Pinacoteca del Castello (Castle Art
Gallery). The most striking picture here
has to be the bizarre *Primavera* by
Arcimboldo, a portrait of a woman
entirely composed of flowers, 16th-
century surrealism at its best.
➕ A3 ✉ Piazza del Castello ☎ 02 6208 3940
🕐 Tue.–Sun. 9–5:30 🚇 M1 Cairoli, M2 Lanza 🎟 Free

DUOMO

The Duomo (Cathedral), Italy's largest
Gothic building and the third largest
church in Europe (after St. Peter's in
Rome and Seville Cathedral), should be at
the top of your sightseeing list. Work
started in 1386 and finally finished in
1813, when the last details were added to
the riot of stone carving and tracery on
the facade. The best place to appreciate
the incredible complexity of the spires,
sculptures and turrets is by strolling
around the roof – where you'll have the
bonus of wonderful city views. Inside, dim
light filters in through the stained-glass
windows to illuminate the soaring marble
columns and the crucifix suspended above
the high altar, which contains the
cathedral's most precious relic, a nail from
Christ's cross.
➕ B2 ✉ Piazza del Duomo ☎ 02 8646 3456
🕐 Museo del Duomo: Daily 9:30–12:30 and 3–6;
Treasury and Crypt: 9–noon and 2:30–6; Baptistery:
10–11:45 and 3–5; Roof: 9–5:45, Mar.–Oct.; 9–4:15, rest
of year 🍴 Bistrot Duomo, see page 199 🚇 M1, M3
Duomo 🎟 Museo del Duomo $$, Roof $$

GALLERIA VITTORIO EMANUELE

Emerging from the cathedral, head across
the Piazza del Duomo to the Galleria
Vittorio Emanuele, a splendidly opulent,

19th-century, covered shopping gallery – the father of modern malls. The lofty cruciform structure was designed in 1865 by Giuseppe Mengoni, who was killed in a fall from the roof before the gallery even opened. It still serves its original purpose and is constantly busy with shoppers and patrons heading for the smart – and expensive – restaurants and cafés.

✚ B2 ✉ Galleria Vittorio Emanuele 🍴 Savini, see page 200 🚇 M1, M3 Duomo

LA SCALA

Walk through the Galleria Vittorio Emanuele and you emerge on the Piazza della Scala, the site of Milan's world-famous opera house, La Scala. It first opened in 1778 and is still the cultural center, with tickets both expensive and hard to come by. You can glimpse the interior by visiting the museum, which is packed with opera memorabilia, including plaster casts of the hands of conductors who have appeared here. From the square, Via Manzoni, one of Milan's most fashionable streets, runs toward the high-class shopping area known as the Quadrilatero d'Oro (Golden Quadrangle). It's the site of the Museo Poldi-Pezzoli, a varied assortment of paintings and jewelry assembled by a 19th-century collector.

✚ B2 ✉ Piazza Scala 🕾 Opera house 02 7200 3744; museum 02 887 9473 🕐 Museum: daily 9–noon and 2–5, May–Sep.; Mon.–Sat. 9–noon and 2–5, rest of year 🍴 Savini, see page 200 🚇 M1, M3 Duomo 🎫 $

Museo Poldi-Pezzoli ✚ B2 ✉ Via Mazoni 12 🕾 02 794 889 🕐 Tue.–Sun. 10–6 🚇 M3 Montenapoleone 🎫 $$

SANT'AMBROGIO

Milan is rich in churches, and there's none lovelier than Sant'Ambrogio, founded in the fourth century and dedicated to St. Ambrose, the city's patron saint. Today's structure, a superb Romanesque basilica reached through the colonnaded quadrangle, dates from the 11th century. The glittering apse mosaics are contemporary, as is the fine pulpit, intricately carved with ferocious wild animals. St. Ambrose's remains lie buried

The glass-domed Galleria Vittorio Emanuele

in the crypt; his fifth-century portrait is in the chapel near the sacristy.

✚ A2 ✉ Piazza Sant'Ambrogio 15 🕾 02 8645 0895 🕐 Daily 9–noon and 3–6 🚇 M2 Sant'Ambrogio

SANTA MARIA DELLE GRAZIE

The refectory attached to the church of Santa Maria delle Grazie draws more visitors than almost any other site in Milan, for here you can see Leonardo da Vinci's ghostly masterpiece, *The Last Supper*. Painted between 1495–97, this breathtaking composition captures the moment when Christ announces he will be betrayed by one of his disciples. Despite lengthy restorations, the fresco is in a bad and fragile state, its colors faded, much of its detail lost. This is chiefly due to da Vinci's technique; he scorned traditional wet-plaster methods and applied oil and tempera to dry plaster. Within five years the work had started to deteriorate. Matters were not helped by primitive restoration attempts and even whitewashing. Napoleonic troops used the painting as a target when they billeted here, and virtually the whole building around it was destroyed by a 1943 bomb.

✚ A2 ✉ Piazza Santa Maria delle Grazie 🕾 02 498 7588 🕐 Reservations are required (🕾 02 8942 1146) 🚇 M1, M2 Cadorna 🚋 Tram 24 🎫 $$$

The flamboyant facade of Milan's huge cathedral dominates one of the city's busiest squares

WALK: THE TICINESE DISTRICT

Refer to route marked on city map on page 33.

This walk takes about three hours and leads you away from the most fre-quented sights and through the city to the Ticinese district, by day a peaceful area with attractive shops, by night the scene of some of Milan's best nightlife.

Take Via Torino out of Piazza del Duomo. At Piazza Santa Maria Beltrade, cross Via Torino and take Via delle Asole on the right to Piazza San Sepolcro.
Behind the church on the piazza, you'll find the Pinacoteca e Biblioteca Ambrosiana (Ambrosian Library and Art Gallery). Commissioned in 1607 by Cardinal Borromeo, this was one of Europe's first public libraries and contains more than 35,000 manuscripts, among them a copy of Virgil once belonging to Petrarch and the Atlantic Codex, a collection of notebooks and drawings by Leonardo da Vinci. The art gallery, too, has some real treasures; look out for a cartoon by Raphael for the *School of Athens* in the Vatican, and Caravaggio's tactile *Basket of Fruit*, the first Italian still life.
Take Via Zecca Vecchia, turn right into Via San Maurilio, then left on Via Santa

Marta. Follow Via Circo and Via Lanzone to Piazza Sant'Ambrogio, with its wonderful ninth-century church (see page 35). Leave Piazza Sant'Ambrogio on Via San Vittore, then branch left onto Via Olona and left again down Via Edmondo de Amicis. This leads to Corso di Porta Ticinese, where you'll find the entrance to the Basilica di San Lorenzo.
This is one of Milan's most important early churches, a central-plan basilica surrounded by three small octagonal chapels. Look for the row of columns outside; these are some of the few reminders of Roman Milan.
Turn right down the Corso di Porta Ticinese to the Piazza Sant'Eustorgio. After visiting this 12th- to 15th-century church, explore the canalside areas of Ticinese and Navigli.
The canals and the basin known as the Darsena were part of Milan's port system from the 15th century up to the 1950s. The northern Italian plain was once networked with canals linking the river systems, giving inland cities easy trade access with each other and the sea. The Corso di Porta Ticinese is packed with off-beat shops and the surrounding streets are the venue for the secondhand and antique markets on the last Sunday of the month. This is one of Milan's most desirable residential areas and has some of the city's best restaurants.

The graceful exterior of La Scala opera house

The elegance of the Milanese

A DAY IN MILAN

Most Milanese have daily schedules similar to those of people in the United States and northern Europe – but with an Italian twist. The day starts early, with many workers commuting into the bustling city from the network of suburban subway stations. Many people drive, and the daily struggle to park lends a certain excitement to the day. As all over Italy, breakfast is often eaten in a bar; the time taken by the busy Milanese to drink a cup of coffee and eat a pastry is around five minutes maximum.

The Working Day

Office employees work to the same timetable as London, Paris or New York. There is no stop for a long lunch, and siesta. People even go so far as to eat at their desks – which is unheard of in the rest of Italy. If people go out for lunch, it will be a quick sandwich from a bar or fast-food counter, unless they are entertaining clients. Most offices work until 6 or 7 p.m.

The Family Day

Many married Milanese women work outside the home; this is a city where Italian women's equal rights really mean something, and women often hold down key positions. But there are still plenty of old-fashioned wives and mothers who spend their mornings cleaning, shopping and preparing a traditional lunch to welcome the kids home from school at 2:30. Italian children have mounds of homework, and mothers often supervise them before chauffering the kids to sports events and extracurricular activities. Dinner is around 8 or 9. Sunday lunch is the big family event

The Sybaritic Day

There are many seriously rich people in Milan. They are the patrons of the smart art galleries, the exhibitions and the auctions. Women will spend hours at the hairdresser, and shopping is pursued with an obsessive attention to the finest details of personal appearance. Domestic help is common, so rich women need not worry about household chores.

The Evening

Milan has a wonderful nightlife, with great restaurants, bars and clubs, and a huge range of cultural events. The young will party mid-week, but for older people Friday and Saturday evenings are the traditional nights out.

REGIONAL SIGHTS

Key to symbols

⊞ map coordinates refer to the region map on page
28; sights below are highlighted in yellow on the map
✉ address or location ☎ telephone number
🕐 opening times 🍴 restaurant on site or nearby
🚌 nearest bus or tram route
🎫 admission charge: $$$ more than L5,000, $$ L3,000
to L5,000, $ less than L3,000 ℹ information

ALBA

Wine and food enthusiasts will love Alba,
home of two of Italy's most splendid
culinary treats, Barolo wine, "King of
Italian Reds," and truffles, the world's
most expensive food. You'll find both in
the tempting local food stores – head for
the bustling Via Vittorio Emanuele,
Alba's main street. Wonderful shops burst
with local products – wine, truffles,
cheese, cakes, biscuits and mounds of
aromatic fungi in autumn. The famous
white truffles *(tartufo bianco)* are in season
in November and December, but available
in different preserved forms all year. Wine
is everywhere, and many of the
surrounding hill villages such as Barolo,
Grinzane di Cavour and Annunziata have
wineries offering tastings and *vendita
diretta* (direct sale). The reds are mainly
made from the Nebbiolo grape; the
astonishing range of flavor and depth is
dictated by the soil conditions in the
different areas around Alba. Alba is a
place for a lengthy gastronomic lunch, and
perhaps a peek at its lovely late-Gothic
Duomo (Cathedral) with its fine inlaid
Renaissance choir stalls.

⊞ B2
Tourist information ✉ Piazza Medford ☎ 0173 35
833 🕐 Tue.–Fri. 9–noon and 3:30–6:30, Sat. 9–noon

AOSTA

Heading into Italy through the Alps from
France, the spectacularly scenic Valle
d'Aosta leads to Piedmont. This is border
country, with Alpine meadows and a
chain of castles, where names are both
French and Italian and the population is
at home in both languages. Aosta, the
capital of this beguiling region, is a

Snow-capped mountains form the perfect
backdrop for Aosta's stone spires

historic and pleasant town with a
wonderfully spacious central piazza and
attractive streets. Founded by the Romans
in AD 25 as a border camp, it makes an
ideal base for exploring the Gran Paradiso
(see pages 46–47) and the Monte Bianco
areas. The fine Porta Pretoria dates from
Roman times when it was the town's
main gateway; there are other Roman
remains in the shape of the Arco di
Augusto (Augustus' Arch) and the Teatro
Romano (Roman Theater). The
Cattedrale (Cathedral) has a good Gothic
interior behind its dull facade; be sure to
see the presbytery floor mosaics and the
wonderfuly carved choir stalls, a riot of
saints, birds and beasts. Sant'Orso is
another interesting church, with
10th-century frescoes hidden up near the
roof and a tiny and charming
Romanesque cloister.

⊞ A3
Tourist information ✉ Piazza E Chanoux 8
☎ 0165 236 627 🕐 Daily 9–1 and 3–8, Jun.–Sep.;
Mon.–Sat. 9 –1 and 3–8, Sun. 9–1, rest of year
Teatro Romano ✉ off Via Porta Pretoria
🕐 Daily 9–7, May–Sep.; 9:30–noon and 2:30–4:30,
rest of year
Cattedrale ✉ Piazza Giovanni XXIII 🕐 Daily 9–7
Sant'Orso ✉ Via Sant'Anselmo 🕐 Mon.–Fri. 9–6:30,
Sat. and Sun. 9–noon and 2–5

One of the many fortified castles to be found at strategic points in the Valle d'Aosta

The Northwest and Emilia Romagna

Bérgamo's lovely Cappella Colleoni in the heart of the old town

ASTI

Asti's famous "bubbly," Asti Spumante, is enjoyed all over Europe, and this little town is the capital of Italy's sparkling wine industry.

In medieval times it rivaled Milan in importance; today it's a low-key and sedate town with fine towers, churches and palaces along or near its main street, the Corso Vittorio Alfieri. The 14th-century Duomo (Cathedral) has a checkered red-and-white facade, but the church of San Pietro in Consavia, with its little 12th-century circular baptistery, is far more alluring. San Secondo, behind Asti's pretty arcaded main Piazza Alfieri, was founded in the second century; nothing that old remains, but the delicate crypt dates from the sixth century. Asti bursts into life in September, when its annual Palio is held. This bareback horserace around the Campo del Palio is similar to Siena's, though far less known.

🞥 B2

Tourist information 🖂 Piazza Alfieri 🕿 0141 530 357 🕔 Mon.–Fri. 9–12:30 and 3–6, Sat. 9–12:30 🛈 The Palio is held on the third Sun. in Sep.; details from the tourist office

San Pietro in Consavia 🖂 Corso Alfieri 2 🕔 Tue.–Sat. 9–noon and 3–6, Sun. 10–noon. Ring the bell for the *custode* (guardian) if the church isn't open

San Secondo 🖂 Off Piazza Alfieri 🕔 Daily 7–noon and 3:30–7

BÉRGAMO

Lovely Bérgamo, clinging to the hills above the plain of Lombardy, is divided into two distinct parts, Bérgamo Bassa and Bérgamo Alta. You'll want to head straight for Bérgamo Alta, a beautiful old hill town with gated walls and architectural and artistic delights. The Venetians ruled Bérgamo for over 350 years until 1796, leaving a legacy of beautiful buildings and their lion symbol adorning walls and fountains everywhere. The old town centers around the Piazza Vecchia, a harmonious mélange of architectural styles, dominated by the medieval Palazzo dell Ragione (Palace of Reason), a Venetian-Gothic structure. Next to it looms the Torre della Civica (Civic Tower); its ancient bell still chimes a 180-peal curfew every night. Nearby, on the Piazza del Duomo you'll find both the Duomo (Cathedral) and the glorious Santa Maria Maggiore, a Romanesque church whose interior is a riot of fantastic gilded baroque fantasy. Flanking this is the Cappella Colleoni (Colleoni Chapel), a Lombard Renaissance gem, designed for Bartolomeo Colleoni, who made his fortune as a Venetian mercenary. For views of the town, walk up the hill to the old military stronghold of the Cittadella. Leave time to visit the Accademia Carrara, one of northern Italy's least-known – yet most important – art galleries. The collection is outstanding, with luminous portraits by Botticelli, soulful virgins by Bellini, and Venetian canal scenes by Canaletto and Guardi.

🞥 C3

Tourist information 🖂 Viale Papa Giovanni XXIII 110 🕿 035 242 226 🕔 Mon.–Fri. 9–12:30 and 3–5:30 **Torre della Civica** 🖂 Piazza Vecchia 🕔 Sun.–Thu. 9–noon and 2–8, Fri. and Sat. 2–11, Apr.–Sep.; Sat. and Sun. 10–noon and 2–6, Oct.–Feb.; daily 10–noon and 2–6, Mar.

Santa Maria Maggiore 🖂 Piazza del Duomo 🕔 Mon.–Sat. 8–noon and 3–6, Sun. 9–1 and 3–6 **Cappella Colleoni** 🖂 Piazza del Duomo 🕔 Daily

9–noon and 2–6, Mar.–Oct.; Tue.–Sun. 9–noon and
3–5, rest of year
Accademia Carrara ✉ Piazza dell'Accademia 82/a
☎ 035 399 643 🕐 Tue.–Sun. 9:30–12:30 and
2:30–5:30 🅱 $

BOLOGNA

Beautiful, historic and booming Bologna
is the capital of Emilia Romagna. It's an
old-brick city known for its wealth, its
ancient university, its left-wing politics
and its cuisine. Surrounded by sprawling
suburbs housing the computer-associated
industries its modern prosperity derives
from, the inner historic core is
surprisingly compact, a series of stunning
porticoed streets radiating from the two
main squares, Piazza Maggiore and
Piazza del Nettuno. The latter is named
after the great Neptune Fountain,
sculpted by native-born Giambologna in
1556. It's the focal point of this lovely
square and its medieval civic buildings,
including the Palazzo Comunale and the
Palazzo Re Enzo.

The Neptune Fountain is the focal point of one of
Bologna's central squares

The nearby Piazza Maggiore is
dominated by the church of San Petronio,
a huge 14th-century Gothic church
originally intended to be double its
present size. It houses some lovely
paintings and a splendid astronomical
clock where a shaft of sunlight striking a
brass meridian line tells the time.

Bologna's other attractions cluster near
the two main squares. Head first to the
university district, taking in Via
Clavatura, with its mouthwatering food
shops and market stalls, en route. The
oldest university structure is the
Archiginnasio, built in 1565 when the
university itself was already several
hundred years old. In this quarter, too,
you'll find the Due Torre (Two Towers),
the only survivors of the hundreds the city
contained in the Middle Ages. You can
climb the Torre degli Asinelli; it's a good
way to get an overview of the city.

South from the Archiginnasio stands
San Domenico, built in 1251 to house the
relics of St. Dominic. These are enclosed
in the Arca di San Domenico, a superb
piece of 15th-century sculpture with figures
by Pisano and the young Michelangelo.

Bologna has some fine museums. The
Pinacoteca Nazionale (National Art
Gallery) has some excellent paintings,
while the Museo Civico Archeologico
(Archeological Museum) is strong on
Roman and Etruscan antiquities. For
something different, take in the Museo di
Anatomia Umana, a bizarre and highly
idiosyncratic collection of anatomical
waxworks used in medical demonstrations
at the university until the 19th century.
Above all, leave time for simply
wandering the city's lovely arcaded streets
and squares, sitting in cafés, window-
shopping and enjoying memorable meals.
➕ D1

Tourist information ✉ Palazzo d'Accursio, Piazza
Maggiore 6 ☎ 051 239 660 🕐 Daily 9–7
San Petronio ✉ Piazza Maggiore 🕐 Daily 8–12:30
and 3–6
Torre degli Asinelli ✉ Piazza di Porta Ravegnana
🕐 Daily 9–7 🅱 $
San Domenico ✉ Piazza San Domenico 🕐 Daily
8:30–noon and 3–6
Pinacoteca Nazionale ✉ Via Belle Arti 56
🕐 Tue.–Sat. 9–2, Sun. 9–1 🅱 $$
Museo Civico Archeologico ✉ Via
dell'Archiginnasio 2 ☎ 051 233 849 🕐 Tue.–Fri. 9–2,
Sat. and Sun. 9–1 and 3:30–7 🅱 $$
Museo di Anatomia Umana ✉ Via Irnerio 48
☎ 051 244 467 🕐 Mon.–Fri. 9–1

The Northwest and Emilia Romagna

CINQUE TERRE

A string of idyllic coastal villages, crouching beneath precipitous hills running straight into the sea, spreads along the coast of Liguria just north of the port of La Spézia. These are the Cinque Terre, the Five Lands, one of the most alluring clusters of seaside settlements anywhere in the peninsula. Each village is little more than a picturesque jumble of color-washed houses assembled around a tiny fishing harbor – though today the fishing boats share space with yachts and pleasure craft. Stony paths, crisscrossing through woods, mountains and coastlines, used to be the only link between the villages. The surrounding steep cliffs, carpeted with springtime flowers and planted with olives and grapes, plunge into the crystal-clear sea.

For centuries, the easiest route between the villages was by sea, and you can still take a boat trip; it's a wonderful way to admire the superb scenery. The railroad arrived in the 19th century and links all the villages; trains run frequently and it's only a few minutes between stops.

From north to south, Monterosso is the biggest, with a good-size beach and more accommodations than elsewhere. South lies Vernazza, a huddle of houses with a tiny beach, and then there's Corniglia, the smallest of the five. Manarola is the pick of the bunch, the quintessential Mediterranean charmer, with a sliver of beach, pretty houses and a busy little harbor. Riomaggiore, the farthest south, is a little larger with an allure all its own.

All the villages have romantic waterfont restaurants where you can sample the white wine produced from the vines clinging to the hills behind. This coast is the perfect place to relax for a few days, but it's popular with Italians in summer, so be sure to book ahead. You could base yourself in Lévanto, a small coastal town just to the north. It has a laid-back holiday atmosphere and plenty of accommodations. You can explore the Cinque Terre from there; it's only a few minutes away by train.

Lévanto ✚ C1

Tourist information ✉ Piazza Cavour 12 ☎ 0187 808 125 🕐 Mon.–Sat. 9:30–12:30 and 3:30–6:30, Sun. 9:30–12:30, Apr.–Oct.; Mon.–Fri. 9:30–12:30 and 3:30–5:30, rest of year

A clifftop view of Vernazza, one of the main villages along the stunning coastline of the Cinque Terre

CREMONA

Stradivari and his violins draw visitors to Cremona, an unpretentious, prosperous, provincial town that was once the home of the world's greatest-ever violin maker. Here, in 1566, Andrea Amati established the world's first violin-making workshop, passing down his secrets to his son Nicolo and his pupils, Stradivari and Guarini. There are still more than 80 violin makers and an internationally famous school of violin-making in Cremona. The oddly shaped Piazza del Comune marks the town's center; it's surrounded by the pretty red-brick Loggia dei Miltia and the Palazzo del Comune. You can climb the 13th-century Romanesque Torrazzo in the northeast corner for great views before popping into the Duomo (Cathedral). Music lovers should first head upstairs in the Palazzo del Comune where some of Cremona's most treasured violins are kept.

The cathedral overlooks the intimate heart of prosperous Cremona

Time is also well spent in the Museo Stradivariano, a fascinating museum devoted to violin-making, with an enlightening English-language video to fill you in. Before you leave town, buy some of Cremona's famous *mostarda di frutta*, a deliciously piquant, mustard-enhanced, candied-fruit condiment.

✚ E2

Tourist information ✉ Piazza del Comune 5 ☎ 0372 23233 🕐 Mon.–Sat. 9:30–12:30 and 3–6
Palazzo del Comune ✉ Piazza del Comune 8 🕐 Tue.–Sat. 8:30–5:15, Sun. 9:15–12:15 and 3–6 📖 $$ 🔔 Guided tours only (in Italian)
Museo Stradivariano ✉ Via Palestro 17 ☎ 0372 461 886 🕐 Tue.–Sat. 9:15–12:15 and 3–6

FERRARA

Peaceful Ferrara, surrounded by fruit orchards, makes a good stopover if you're heading northeast from Bologna to Venice. It's hard to believe that this lovely and little-visited town was once a major player on the Renaissance political scene, its court was one of the most dynamic in Europe. Its ruling dynasty was the d'Este family, whose palaces and monuments scatter the city and whose members married into Italy's most powerful ruling families. It was d'Este money that paid for

the artistic treasures you see today. Their seat of power was the Castello d'Estense, a bulky late 14th-century structure worth visiting for the decorated apartments and spooky dungeons.

Another d'Este palace, the Palazzo Schifanoia, has delightful frescoes by Cosimo Tura in the Sala dei Mesi (Room of the Months), complete with lively court and hunting scenes. You might also want to visit the Palazzo Diamante, the home of the Pinacoteca Nazionale (Art Gallery), and the Duomo (Cathedral), with its magnificent facade and small museum packed with treasures. A major Ferrara pleasure is to simply wander. The medieval tangle of streets around Via delle Volte provides a rich contrast to the restrained elegance of the later Renaissance palaces.

✚ E2

Tourist information ✉ Corso Giovecca 12 ☎ 0532 209 370 🕐 Mon.–Sat. 9 -1 and 2:30–7, Sun. 9–1
Castello d'Estense ✉ Piazza della Repubblica 🕐 Tue.–Sun. 9:30–12:30 and 2:30–8 📖 $$
Palazzo Schifanoia ✉ Via Scandiana 23 ☎ 0532 641 178 🕐 Daily 9–7 📖 $$
Pinacoteca Nazionale ✉ Corso Ercole d'Este 21 ☎ 0532 205 844 🕐 Daily 9–7 📖 $$
Duomo and Museo del Duomo ✉ Piazza Cattedrale 🕐 Daily 8–1 and 3–6 📖 $

The Northwest and Emilia Romagna

GÉNOVA

Génova's (Genoa) greatest days were the Middle Ages, when the city was one of Italy's five maritime republics with territories stretching from Syria to North Africa. Christopher Columbus was born here, but the bankers wouldn't back him and he had to turn to Spain to fund his voyages. Italy's industrial revolution, based on steel and ship-building, began in Genoa, and, despite the decline of its industry and docks, it's still the country's main maritime city. The port lies at the heart of the city and is backed by an eclectic quarter of medieval streets.

Behind the port, this confusing city will require perseverance as it sprawls over the coastal hills with different levels linked by public elevators and cog railroads. You shouldn't miss a stroll down Via Garibaldi, an imposing stretch of Renaissance palaces built by rich bankers in the 16th century. Two now house galleries, the Palazzo Bianco and the Palazzo Rosso. The Palazzo Bianco has the finer collection – look for Flemish masterpieces, including the sensuous *Mars and Venus* by Rubens. The Palazzo Rosso would be worth a visit for the sumptuous interior decor alone, though the paintings shine here, too.

South from here is Genoa's cathedral, San Lorenzo; its black-and-white Gothic facade was constructed by French workmen. It has some fabulous precious metalwork in its treasury. Just up the street lies Piazza Matteotti, the medieval heart of the city. The huge striped building is the Palazzo Ducale, the last in a line of buildings erected for Genoa's ruling Doges from 1384 to 1515. Streets lead down to the revitalized waterfront, a pleasant place to spend time and perhaps take the elevator up the Grande Bigo, Renzo Piano's visual centerpiece of the port's Expo 1992 regeneration. The views of the city are superb. Down here, too, lies the Aquarium, a major crowd-pleaser with sea creatures from all the world's major habitats. Boat trips around the harbor leave from here.

➕ B1

Tourist information ✉ Palazzina Santa Maria, Via al Porto Antico ☎ 010 248 711 🕐 Mon.–Fri. 8–1 and 3–6:30, Sat. 8–1

Palazzo Bianco ✉ Via Garibaldi 11 ☎ 010 291 803 🕐 Wed. and Sat. 9–7, Tue., Thu., Fri., Sun 9–1 💰 $$

Palazzo Rosso ✉ Via Garibaldi 18 ☎ 010 282 641 🕐 Wed. and Sat. 9–7, Tue., Thu., Fri., Sun. 9–1 💰 $$

Cattedrale di San Lorenzo ✉ Via San Lorenzo 🕐 Daily 8–noon and 3–6; Treasury: Tue., Thu. and Sat. 9:30–11:45 and 3–5:45

Grande Bigo ✉ Molo Vecchio 🕐 Tue.–Sat. 11–1 and 3–6, Sat.–Sun. 11–1 and 2–8 💰 $

Aquarium ✉ Ponte Spinola 🕐 Tue., Wed., Fri. 9:30–7. Thu., Sat., Sun. 9:30–8:30 💰 $$$

LAGO DI GARDA

The largest of all the Italian lakes, Lago di Garda (Lake Garda) has become a summertime honeypot for visitors from all over Europe. People are attracted by its range of scenic beauty and lovely climate. Its southern end is fringed by gentle hills, its central area is lush with olives, grapes and citrus, and its north is squeezed by craggy mountains.

Northern Riva del Garda is the best-known resort; lively and crowded, it's packed throughout the season. Head down the west side to escape the crowds, perhaps detouring

The harbor of the great and historic port of Génova

Idyllic Sirmione and its castle jut out into the southern end of Lago di Garda

into the scenic backroads in the hills behind Limone sul Garda before a stop at elegant Gardone Riviera. Heading along the south side you'll come to exquisite Sirmione, gem of the lot, with its beautifully sited castle. Northeast lies Punta di San Vigilio; with its cypress-filled gardens, white beaches and grand views, it's probably the lake's prettiest spot. Farther on, pleasing Malcésine gives access via cable car to the summit of Monte Baldo. In the mountains, there's superb hiking amid carpets of wild flowers. If you've got kids head for Gardaland, Italy's biggest theme park, with more than 2 million annual visitors.

🚩 D2

Riva del Garda tourist information ✉ Giardini di Porta Orientale 8 ☎ 0464 554 444 🕐 Mon.–Sat. 9–noon and 3–6:30

Gardone Riviera tourist information ✉ Via della Repubblica 37 ☎ 0365 20 347 🕐 Mon.–Sat. 9–12:30 and 3–6, closed Thu. afternoon

Sirmione tourist information ✉ Viale Marconi 2 ☎ 030 916 245 🕐 Daily 9–12:30 and 3–6, Apr.–Oct.; Mon.–Fri. 9–12:30 and 3–6, rest of year

Malcésine tourist information ✉ Via Capitanato ☎ 045 740 0044 🕐 Daily 9–1 and 3–6:30

Monte Baldo Cable Car 🕐 Every half-hour 8–5:45, Apr.–Oct.; 8–4:45 rest of year 🖐 $$$ ℹ️ Expect long lines in summer

Gardaland ✉ Castelnuoo del Garda ☎ 045 644 9777 🕐 Daily 9 a.m.–midnight, Jul.–Aug.; 9–6, Apr.–Jun. and Sep. 🖐 $$$

LAGO MAGGIORE

When exploring Lago Maggiore (Lake Maggiore) you'll need to be selective as some stretches are marred by factories and industry. Stresa is the best stop, an elegant lakeside town with good transport links along the lake. From here you can take a boat to the Isole Borromee (Borromean Islands), an exquisite archipelago famed for the baroque gardens on the Isola Bella. Ferries run on to the Ìsola dei Pescatori (Fishermen's Island), a favorite of Ernest Hemingway. Back on the western shore, garden lovers shouldn't miss the 20,000 plant species in the gardens at Villa Táranto, created in the 1930s. Cannobio, a charming village that combines a lakeside position with a tangle of stepped alleys, is worth a visit. The eastern shore has peaceful and pretty spots such as Cannero Riviera and Angera.

🚩 B3

Stresa tourist information ✉ Via Principe Tomaso ☎ 0323 30 150 🕐 Mon.–Sat. 8:30–12:30 and 3–6:15

Ìsola Bella tourist information ☎ 0323 30 556 🕐 Daily 9–noon and 1:30–5:30, mid-Mar.–Sep. 🖐 $$$

Villa Táranto ✉ Via Vittorio Veneto 111, Pallanza 🕐 Daily 8:30–7:30, Apr.–Oct. 🖐 $

A glimpse of the cathedral from the colonnade of
Mántova's vast Palazzo Ducale

MÁNTOVA

You'll have to penetrate some pretty grim
outskirts to reach Mántova's (Mantua's)
stunning medieval core, circled by three
tranquil lakes, but it's well worth it. The
Gonzaga family, another of the great
Renaissance dynasties, built the
astounding Palazzo Ducale, a huge
complex with 500 rooms, and once the
largest palace in Europe. You can take a
tour here that includes the Camera degli
Sposi, a room that contains masterful,
intimate and tender frescoes by the 15th-
century artist Mantegna, showing the
Gonzaga Marquis Ludovico with his
family and much-loved dog.

Across town lies the family's summer
residence, the lavish Palazzo Te, one of
the finest Mannerist ensembles anywhere,
frescoed throughout by Giulio Romano.
This palazzo is a must-see, from the
portraits of the Gonzaga's favorite horses
to the excesses of the topsy-turvy world of
the Sala dei Giganti (Room of the
Giants). Elsewhere in town, take a look at
Alberti's facade for the church of
Sant'Andrea, before spending time in the
cobbled central Piazza dell'Erbe.

➕ D2

Tourist information ✉ Piazza Mantegna 6

☎ 0376 328 253 ◷ Mon.–Sat. 9–1 and 3–6
Palazzo Ducale ✉ Piazza Sordello ☎ 0376 320 283
◷ Tue.–Sat. 9–1 and 2:30–6, Sun.–Mon. 9–1 ▯ $$$
ℹ Guided tours only (in Italian though occasionally
in English) lasting around 90 minutes
Palazzo Te ✉ Vial Te ☎ 0376 323 266 ◷ Tue.–Sun.
9–6, Mon. 1–5:30 ▯ $$
Sant'Andrea ✉ Piazza Mantegna ◷ Daily 8–1
and 3–6

MÓDENA

Módena is a quintessential northern town
– quietly prosperous, its medieval core a
delight, its industrial outskirts thriving.
Ferrari and Maserati build their cars
nearby, and its most famous modern
citizen is the great tenor, Luciano
Pavarotti. The historic center is a ring of
tight medieval streets around the Piazza
Grande; sprinkled with shops and serious
restaurants, this area is a delight. The
town's main artistic sight is its 12th-
century Duomo (Cathedral), a
Romanesque masterpiece with a lurching
campanile, the Torre Ghirlandina. The
west facade, its portal supported by stately
lions, and the south side have very fine
stone relief work, while the serene and
lofty interior has more fine wall sculpture.
Five minutes walk from here along Via
Emilia, Módena's museums are housed in
the Palazzo dei Musei. The best of these
is the Galleria Estense, a pleasing
collection amassed by the d'Este family,
who left Ferrara (see page 43) for Módena
in 1598.

➕ D2

Tourist information ✉ Piazza Grande 17 ☎ 059 206
660 ◷ Mon.–Sat. 8:30–1 and 3–7, Sun. 9:30–1
Duomo ✉ Piazza Grande ◷ Daily 9–1 and 3–6
Galleria Estense ✉ Piazzale Sant'Agostino 5
☎ 059 222 145 ◷ Tue., Fri., Sat. 9–7, Wed., Thu. 9–2.,
Sun. 9–1 ▯ $$

PARCO NAZIONALE DEL GRAN PARADISO

The Parco Nazionale del Gran Paradiso
(Gran Paradiso National Park) is a
spectacular reserve around the Gran
Paradiso massif, the only peak over 13,000
feet solely in Italy. You can explore it by
driving up any of the three valleys west of

The majestic icy splendor of the Parco Nazionale del Gran Paradiso

the Valle d'Aosta, perhaps combining your drive with cable-car rides and hiking. The park was once a royal hunting zone where the Savoys pursued game; around 1920 they bequeathed it to the state to become Italy's first national park. The variety of scenery is stupendous, ranging from glaciers and snowy mountains to forests and Alpine meadows.

The little town of Cogne makes a good base. From here you have access to great walks, while the high tops are served by cable car. Nearby, at Valnontey, you'll find the Giardino Botanico (Botanical Garden), at its best in June when there are splendid spreads of native Alpine flora. But for the true experience, take to the hills to see the chamois, ibex and birds in profusion.

➕ A2

Cogne tourist information ✉ Piazza Chanoux 36, Cogne ☎ 016 574 040 🕐 Mon.–Sat. 9–12:30 and 3–6, Sun. 9–12:30

Giardino Botanico ✉ Above Valnontey 🕐 9–noon and 2:30–6, May–Sep. 🎫 $

PARMA

There's much more to Parma than *prosciutto* (Parma ham) and *parmigiano* (parmesan cheese), as you'll soon discover on arrival in this affluent provincial town.

Most sights lie east of the Parma river, though music lovers might want to visit Casa di Toscanini (Toscanini's birthplace) and stroll in the lovely 18th-century gardens of the Parco Ducale across the river. In the old center you'll find the beautiful 11th-century Lombard-Romanesque Duomo (Cathedral), whose interior has works by both Corregio and Parmigianino. The cathedral's 12th-century baptistery, four stories of sculpted pink marble, deserves more than a cursory glance before you head for the massive Palazzo della Pilotta. Built as a Farnese palace in the 16th century and restored after World War II bombing, it houses the Galleria, with its collection of massive Renaissance paintings. Parma is also noted for its opera – the Teatro Regio has a reputation that rivals Milan's La Scala.

➕ D2

Tourist information ✉ Piazza Duomo 5 ☎ 0521 234 735 🕐 Mon.–Fri. 9–12:30 and 3–6, Sat. 9–12:30

Casa di Toscanini ✉ Borgo Tanzi 13 ☎ 0521 285 499 🕐 Mon.–Sat. 10–1

Duomo and Baptistery ✉ Piazza del Duomo 🕐 Daily 9–noon and 3–7, Apr.–Sep.; 9–noon and 3–5, Nov.–Mar.

Galleria Nazionale ✉ Palazzo della Pilotta 15 ☎ 0521 233 617 🕐 Tue.–Sat. 9–2, Sun. 9–1 🎫 $$

Teatro Regio ✉ Via Garibaldi 16a ☎ 0521 218 678 ℹ Book well in advance for good seats at the opera

The Northwest and Emilia Romagna

DRIVE: MOUNTAINS AND LAKES

Duration: 3½ to 4 hours

This drive takes you around Lago di Como (Lake Como), the most beautiful of the Italian lakes, a dream of water, mountain peaks, lush vegetation and gracious buildings.

The route is straightforward, though for some stretches you'll have the option to take either the older, more scenic route along the lake shore, or the new fast route higher up the slopes through numerous tunnels. En route you'll have a chance to explore some of the lakeside towns and villages, enjoy some breathtakingly lovely gardens, take steamers up or down the lake, or spend time at one of the beaches along the water's edge. Lake Como's proximity to Milan means huge crowds on weekends and in July and August, so bear this in mind when planning your trip.

The drive starts in Como, the main town at the lake's southern end.

Como's main industry is silk manufacture, and the revamped old town center has plenty of outlets where you can buy locally made scarves and fabrics. The town's locale is lovely, but it's always crowded with visitors and the industrial outskirts don't add to its

The red-roofed houses of Menággio

charm, so don't linger – though the cathedral is certainly worth more than a cursory glance.

Take the SS340 up the west shore of the lake, heading for Argegno.

En route you'll pass Cernobbio, a pleasant lakeside village that is the starting point for a 130-kilometer (80-mile) hiking trail through the mountains, the Via dei Monti Lariani. Argegno is a medley of old houses with wooden eaves, steep and narrow streets, and an appealing array of lakeside cafés. Boats run from here to the Isola Comacina, Como's only island, a wild little place that's the home of a small artists' colony.

Continue along the SS340 to Tremezzo.

Look for signs to Mezzegra; the Villa Belmonte there was the scene in 1944 of the execution of Mussolini and his mistress Clara Petacci by the partisan leader Walter Audisio.

Elegant Tremezzo, with its villas and hotels, has a distinctly fin-de-siècle air. It's worth stopping here to visit the Villa Carlotta, a lavish neoclassical pink-and-white villa built by a Prussian princess and now filled with 18th-century statuary. Its main attractions are the gardens, 14 acres of beautifully tended grounds renowned for camellias, azaleas and rhododendrons. These shrubs flower between January and July and are a glowing range of reds, pinks, whites and yellows. They're at their peak around Easter.

Continue along the lake, passing through bustling and lively Menággio, to

Lovely villas and fertile gardens border the Lago di Como at Bellágio, the jewel of the lakeside towns

*Gravedona, an old lakeside town.
At the northern tip of the lake, cross the
River Mera, then head down the east fork
on the SS36. If time is short, you have the
option of taking this higher, faster road or
sticking to the old scenic route along the
water's edge. Both roads are extremely
busy on weekends.*

Varenna makes a good stopping point along this shore, a pretty and relaxed place with two more outstanding gardens, Villa Cipressi and the Villa Monastero. South from here you'll be heading down Como's east fork, a fjord-like stretch with huge granite ridges rising behind the water.

At Lecco pick up the SS583 to Bellágio.
Standing on the tip of land separating Como's two forks, Bellágio has to be one of northern Italy's loveliest towns. Its oleander-planted waterfront, cobbled streets and gracious hotels and villas make it a great place for a stopover. There are more horticultural treats at the Villa Serbelloni, or you might simply want to relax by taking a steamer trip down the lake.

*From Bellágio take the
SS583, which runs along the
east shore of the lake's left
road back to Como.*

Como tourist information
✉ Piazza Cavour 17 ☎ 031 265 244 🌐 Mon.–Sat. 9–12:30 and 2:30–6
Bellágio tourist information
✉ Piazza della Chiesa 14 ☎ 031 950 204 🌐 Mon.–Fri. 8:30–noon and 2:30–6

PAVIA

Only half-an-hour by train from Milan, Pavia makes a nice excursion. It's one of those small and enjoyable northern towns whose sum more than equals its parts, and whose chief pleasures lie in a leisurely stroll through narrow streets past towers and piazzas. Its zenith was more than a thousand years ago when it was capital of the kingdom of the Lombards; its two major churches, San Pietro in Cield'Oro and San Michele, both date from the 11th to 12th centuries. There's a 14th-century fortress, the Castello Visconteo, which houses the local museum, and a big, cobbled central square adjacent to the cathedral. Pleasant enough, but for a real treat drive the 10 kilometers (6 miles) to the Certosa di Pavia (Carthusian Monastery), one of Europe's most impressive monasteries. It was built for the Milan Viscontis in the 15th century as a mausoleum and is dazzlingly rich in Renaissance and baroque art. You can tour the church, cloisters and refectory, then stop off and purchase some chartreuse at the monastery shop, still made by Carthusian monks who live here.

➕ C2

Tourist information ✉ Via Fabio Filzi 2
☎ 0382 22 156 🕐 Mon.–Sat. 8:30–12:30 and 2–6
Castello Visconteo and Museo Civico ✉ Via le XI Febbraio 🕐 Tue.–Sat. 9–1:30, Sun. 9–1 💰 $$
Certosa di Pavia ✉ Certosa di Pavia ☎ 0382 925 613 🕐 Daily 9–11:30 and 2:30–5, Mar.–Oct.; 9:30–12:30 and 2:30–4, rest of year 🎫 Guided tours only, led by a monk; almost always in Italian

PIACENZA

If you enjoy low-key, prosperous small towns, Piacenza, near the Lombardy border, merits a stop. The Roman town marked the end of the Via Emilia, one of the big consular roads, and Piacenza's street plan still adheres to the old Roman grid pattern. The main square, Piazza dei Cavalli, gets its name from the splendid bronze equestrian statues on either side – they're the work of a pupil of Giambologna and were cast in the 17th century. The red-brick Palazzo del Comune dates from 1280, the same period as the nearby church of San Francesco. The cathedral is a grand Lombard Romanesque structure dating from the 1220s, much altered over the centuries – the interior is particularly lovely. Piacenza's Museo Civico (Civic Museum) houses the odd bronze known as the *fegato di Piacenza* (Piacenza liver). This liver-shaped object, covered with inscriptions, dates from Etruscan times and was used to divine the future. The museum building itself was built in the 16th century.

➕ C2

Tourist information ✉ Piazzetta dei Mercanti 7
☎ 0523 329 324 🕐 Daily 9–12:30 and 4–6:30, closed Thu. afternoon
Museo Civico ✉ Piazza della Cittadella 29
☎ 0523 328 270 🕐 Tue., Wed., Fri. 9–12:30 and 3:30–5:30, Thu. 9–noon and 3–6, Sat. 9:30–noon and 3:30–6:30 💰 $$

RAVENNA

The finest Byzantine mosaics in the world (other than Istanbul's) are found in Ravenna, an appealing small town near the Adriatic coast, with a gentle pace of life and pleasing atmosphere. In 402, the Emperor Honorius moved the capital of the rapidly declining Roman Empire to Ravenna, an easily defensible marshland town near the important Roman port of Classis. Until it fell to the Goths in 476, it was the imperial capital and continued to thrive under first barbarian, then later Byzantine rule.

We owe the wondrous sixth-century churches and their mosaics to the last Romans and the Byzantine rulers, notably Theodoric and Justinian. San Vitale, a typical Byzantine-style basilica richly decorated with glowing mosaics, was begun in 525. The mosaics show biblical scenes, while the walls portray the Emperor Justinian and his wife, Theodora, an unattractive character who was a prostitute and circus performer. Across from the basilica you'll find the tiny and jewel-like Mausoleo di Galla Placidia (Tomb of Galla Placidia), whose interior walls glitter with lustrous blue-and-gold mosaics. Nearby there's Ravenna's Museo Nazionale (National

The plain exterior of Ravenna's Basilica di San Vitale hides some of Europe's finest Byzantine mosaics

The Northwest and Emilia Romagna

Museum), worth a quick look. From here head across town to Sant'Apollinare Nuovo, another mosaic-rich sixth-century church. The mosaics here run each side of the nave, with stately processions of martyrs bearing gifts for Christ and the Blessed Virgin.

On the way to Sant'Apollinare, you'll pass through the main Piazza del Popolo, an enticing 15th-century square with plenty of cafés. Also en route is Dante's Tomb, a small 18th-century building housing the great poet's remains; he died in Ravenna in 1321 after having been exiled from his native Florence. Ravenna's other Byzantine masterpiece, the great church of Sant'Apollinare in Classe, lies just outside the city near the remains of Roman Classis. Perhaps the most evocative of all Ravenna's churches, Sant'Apollinare's interior is spacious and beautifully proportioned, with glittering gold mosaics.

✚ E1

Tourist information ✉ Via Salara 8/12 ☎ 0544 35 404 🕐 Daily 9–1 and 3–6 🛈 Ask the tourist office about entry tickets valid for all Ravenna's main sights

San Vitale ✉ Via Fiandrini ☎ 0544 34 266 🕐 Daily 9–4:30

Mausoleo di Galla Placidia ✉ Via Fiandrini 🕐 Daily 9–4:30 💷 $$

Museo Nazionale ✉ Via Fiandrini ☎ 0544 34 424

🕐 Daily 9–4:30 💷 $$

Sant'Apollinare Nuovo ✉ Via Roma ☎ 0544 39 081 🕐 Daily 9:30–4:30

Tomba di Dante ✉ Via D Alighieri 9 ☎ 0544 30 252 🕐 Daily 9–noon and 2–5

Sant'Apollinare in Classe ✉ Romea sud ☎ 0544 527 004 🕐 Daily 9–5

RIMINI

Big, brash and glitzy, with miles of sandy beaches and baking summer sun, Rimini is the archetypal seaside town, a successful combination of family resort and a buzzing center for the best of European nightclubs. It can be noisy and sleazy, but it's never tacky. If you're looking for an Italian taste of the European club scene, this is the place to come. The downside to this is Rimini's wide reputation for an active prostitution scene for all lifestyles.

Rimini, with its satellite resorts, stretches for 20 kilometres (12 miles) along the coast. The other face of Rimini can be seen inland; here you'll find the old town, well worth a morning's wander. Its high spot is the Tempio Malatestiana, designed by the famous Renaissance architect Alberti in 1450 to honor Rimini's ruler, Sigismondo Malatesta. It's a bizarre and pleasing building, whose interior houses a Giotto crucifix and a

Summer swimmers frequent one of the Riviera di
Levante's picturesque villages

fresco portrait of Sigismondo by Piero
della Francesca.

✚ E1

Tourist information ✉ Piazzale Federico Fellini 3
☎ 0541 51 101 🕓 Daily 8–8, Jun.–Sep.; Mon.–Sat.
8–2, rest of year 🚌 An all-night bus, the Blue Line,
runs during the summer between Rimini's clubs
Tempio Malastestiano ✉ Via 4 Novembre
🕓 Mon.–Sat. 7–noon and 3:30–7, Sun. 8–1 and 3:30–7

RIVIERA DI LEVANTE

The stretch of coast southeast of Genoa
(see page 44) is known as the Riviera di
Levante, a chain of fishing villages and
resorts backed by mountains and cliffs
with pines and aromatic maqui. The finest
section is the Cinque Terre (see page 42),
but if you're looking for an alternative
there are several choices. Down the coast
from Genoa is Camogli; quieter than
some villages, its steep streets are lined
with colorful houses clustered around a
tiny harbor. Rapallo makes a good
contrast. Built in gentle Edwardian times,
it's a pleasing mix of elegance and fun,
with a lively cultural season in summer.
Beautiful and picturesque Portofino to the
west is synonymous with sophisticated
dolce vita, a classy and exclusive resort
heaving with the rich and famous and

prices to match. For much the same type
of village and atmosphere, but less
expense, you can head down the coast to
Portovenere, just south of the Cinque
Terre. You can explore the coast from
here, or take a trip to the lovely and
relatively unspoiled island of Palmária just
off the coast.

✚ C1

Camogli tourist information ✉ Via XX Settembre 33
☎ 0185 771 066 🕓 Mon.–Sat. 8:30–noon and 3:30–6,
Sun. 8:30–noon
Rapallo tourist information ✉ Via Daz 9 ☎ 0185
545 73 🕓 Mon.–Sat. 9–12:30 and 3–7, Sun. 9–12:30
Portofino tourist information ✉ Via Roma 35
☎ 0185 269 024 🕓 Daily 9:30–1 and 1:30–6:30
Portovenere tourist information ✉ Piazza Bastreri 1
☎ 0187 790 961 🕓 Mon.–Sat. 9–noon and 3–7, Sun.
9–noon

TORINO

A fitting capital to Piedmont, Italy's
second-richest region, Torino (Turin)
stands on the banks of the Po river. Turin
is a sprawling industrial city with an
elegant baroque heart. Its still-discernible
French flavor arrived with the ruling
house of Savoy in 1574; three centuries
later they teamed up with the
Risorgimento's liberal politician, Camillo
Cavour, to lend credibility to the
unification movement.

In 1860 Turin became the first capital
of Italy, and 10 years later its Savoy
monarch, Vittorio Emanuele, became
king of the united country. During the
20th century Turin became the
headquarters of Fiat, whose owners, the
immensely powerful Agnelli family, are an
undisputed force throughout Italy.

The elegant Via Roma, all designer
stores and classy cafés, bisects the city-
center grid plan, and most of what you'll
want to see lies around here. First stop
should be Turin's two main museums, the
Museo Egizio (Egyptian Museum) and
the Galleria Sabauda (Sabauda Gallery),
housed in the same building. The
Egyptian collection is superb. Don't miss
the tomb of Kha and Mirit; a 1400 BC
architect, Kha was buried with his wife
and everything they would need in the
afterlife. The Sabauda's artistic base is the

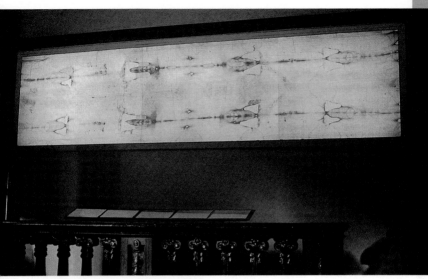

A replica of the Holy Shroud is exhibited in the cathedral in Torino

Savoy private collections, particularly strong on Dutch and Flemish schools, though you shouldn't miss Pollaiuolo's wonderful *Tobias and the Angel*, a taut and colorful 15th-century masterpiece.

Nearby, visit the Museo Nazionale del Risorgimento, devoted to Turin's role in unification, with a fascinating section on Garibaldi. Piazza Castello is home to the incredibly opulent Palazzo Reale (Royal Palace), the more restrained Palazzo Madama and the Armeria Reale (Royal Armory), one of the world's great museums of arms and armor. Off Piazza Castello, is the Duomo (Cathedral), whose best-known treasure is the Holy Shroud (Sindone). This length of linen contains what many Christians believe to be the imprint of the face and body of Christ. Many people contend the shroud was used to wrap Jesus' body after the crucifixion.

From the cathedral, head toward the river and walk down to the Parco del Valentino, a large park humming with life in the evenings. Here you can visit the Borgo Medioevale, an attractive synthesis of Piedmont's best medieval buildings, constructed in 1884. Farther along the river, automobile fans will enjoy the Museo dell'Automobile (Automobile Museum).

➕ A2

Tourist information ✉ Via Roma ☎ 011 535 181 🕐 Mon.–Sat. 9–7:30

Museo Egizio ✉ Via Accademia delle Scienze 6 ☎ 011 561 7776 🕐 Tue.–Sat. 9–7, Sun. 9–2 💲 $$$

Galleria Sabauda ✉ Via Accademia delle Scienze 6 ☎ 011 547 440 🕐 Tue.–Sat. 9–2 💲 $$

Museo del Risorgimento ✉ Via Accademia delle Scienze 5 ☎ 011 562 1147 💲 $$

Armeria Reale ✉ Piazza Castello 191 ☎ 011 543 889 🕐 Tue. and Thu. 2:30–7:30, Mon., Wed., Fri., Sat. 9–2 💲 $$

Duomo ✉ Via XX Settembre 🕐 Daily 7:30–noon and 3–6

Borgo Medioevale ✉ Parco del Valentino 🕐 Daily 8–8

Museo dell'Automobile ✉ Corso Unità d'Italia 40 ☎ 011 677 666 🕐 Tue.–Sat. 10–6:30 💲 $$

The Po river cuts through the heart of Torino

A TASTE OF THE NORTH

In the prosperous regions of the north, you'll find some of the best cooking in all Italy. It features a rich cuisine based on superb-quality fresh ingredients and a range of local specialties. Many of these are either imported or imitated in the United States, but make a point of sampling them on their home ground, where cheese is made from unpasteurized milk, and hams, wild mushrooms and wine have had to travel only a few miles from their point of origin. You'll taste the difference.

Valle d'Aosta and Piedmont

These regions display close links with France, so it's not surprising that there are French overtones in local food. Butter, cream and cheese are freely used, and you should try *fonduta*, a melted cheese dish similar to fondue. Piedmont's prize food is the white truffle, in season in the fall from the hills around Alba (see page 39). With an intensity of flavor impossible to describe, this is one extravagance you should indulge in for a once-in-a-lifetime experience. Wild mushrooms are less expensive and another culinary treat; the best variety are *porcini*, a meaty-textured and robustly flavored woodland giant often served grilled. The full-bodied wines from the region, such as the fabulous Barolo and Barbarino, could have been invented as an accompaniment. They go equally well with roasted sweet chestnuts. Much sparkling wine is made in Asti (see page 40), while worldwide favorite vermouths like Martini and Cinzano are made near Turin.

Lombardy

Piedmont's neighbor, Lombardy, has its own gifts. This is a region where the staple is either rice or *polenta*, not pasta. *Polenta* is cornmeal, stirred and boiled for 40 minutes or so, then served as it comes or cooled and used to accompany different meats and sauces. Rice, mainly the firm and plump-grained *arborio*, ideal for risotto, is grown in the Ticino area. The classic risotto is the seemingly simple *risotto alla Milanese*, which uses veal

juices, saffron and butter. Milan was the birthplace, too, of *osso buco*, a slow-cooked dish of veal shanks; it is rich and deep-flavored.

Lombardy, one of Italy's biggest cheese-making regions, is the home of *gorgonzola, mascarpone* and *Bel Paese*. If you've enjoyed a light, vanilla-scented *panettone* cake at Christmas, remember that this, too, originates in Milan.

Liguria

With Liguria's long shoreline, fish is inevitably a treat, and you'll find it on menus everywhere. The most wonderful local ingredient has to be basil, and you may be lucky enough to see – and smell – a whole field of this heavenly herb as you travel in Liguria. It's used to make the ubiquitous *pesto* and many other dishes – even as a flavoring for ice cream. Its aroma is complemented by the wines from the

Left: Ingredients for Liguria's famous pesto sauce
Below: Rice, the basis for intensely flavored risotto

Cinque Terre (see page 42). Dry and clean-tasting, the wines have a light and flinty bouquet that goes well with the local pizza variant, *focaccia*.

Emilia Romagna

Across the country in Emilia Romagna, there's more rich, smooth cooking. Many Italians freely admit that you eat better here than almost anywhere else in Italy (except their own region, of course). Parma, the home of *prosciutto di Parma* (Parma ham) and *parmigianino* (parmesan cheese), lies in this region. Much local produce is of a quality and flavor to live up to these two culinary superstars. Balsamic vinegar is produced here; buy a precious bottle to bring life to your cooking, just a few drops will go a long way. Pasta, usually made with eggs and stuffed with meat, cheese and herb combinations, is enjoyed here.

Lambrusco is the great local wine; wine snobs may look aghast, but try a DOC (Denominazione di Origine Controllata) variety, which guarantees the origin and quality, and you'll be amazed at its dark, deep nose.

THE NORTHEAST

"THE beauty of Venice, the grandeur of the Dolomites and the quiet serenity of the hinterland with its splendid towns draw countless visitors to the northeast."

The Grand Canal, lined with superb buildings, is Venice's main highway

The Northeast

THE NORTHEAST

Many visitors to the northeast never discover the immense variety of this diverse region. Made up of Veneto, Trentino-Alto Adige and Friuli-Venezia Giulia, the area encompasses some of Europe's finest mountain scenery and a clutch of Italy's most alluring towns. Add to this the economic prosperity brought by the region's industry and a long tradition of agriculture and wine-making, and the attractions of this tucked-away corner of Italy become clear.

Shaping of the Northeast

The region of the Veneto forms this area's core; this was the heartland of independent Venice, the mainland territories ruled by the Venetian Republic from the 14th to the 18th centuries. Historically settled and prosperous, the Veneto is very much a part of mainstream Italy.

North of the Veneto, the situation changes in the Trentino-Alto Adige, a multicultured hybrid of a region made up of Italian-speaking, mainly rural Trentino, and the German-speaking Alto Adige, also known as Sudtirol.

The Alto Adige was ceded to Italy at the end of World War I, having previously been part of the Austro-Hungarian Empire. Ethnic differences here have caused tension and an undercurrent of terrorism over the years, but a large measure of autonomy has, on the whole, kept the lid on nationalist ambitions.

Friuli-Venezia Giulia borders Austria and Slovenia. This area has quite a mixture of cultures, languages and allegiances. It straddles the hazy bridge between the Mediterranean world and that of Teutonic and Slavic central Europe. Becoming part of Italy after World War I, its final border disputes with Yugoslavia were not settled until the 1970s.

The Northeast Today

Although industrialization has marred some of the region's scenic beauty, it has also brought prosperity. The flat coastal plains are scattered with light industry and modern housing. The vast industrial complex around Marghera is best avoided. But agriculture is still vital, with arable farming in the lowlands and extensive wine-producing areas in the lower hills. Tourism is important throughout this region; apart from Venice itself, Verona and Padua draw the crowds, while the mountain splendor of the Dolomites draws skiing and hiking enthusiasts year-round.

On the whole, vacationers here are Italian, and, outside Venice itself, you won't encounter the vast numbers of visitors to be found in other regions. You'll notice more than a touch of Teutonic efficiency in some parts, while the general affluence is striking. Well-dressed people, smart shops and expensive cars catch the eye. There's a good balance between traditional ways and the 21st century, making this corner a real Italian microcosm.

European Influences

Throughout the Veneto, people are polite, friendly, efficient and hard-working, but without the relentless drive of their neighbors nearer Milan. Like all Italians, they live life to the fullest in a less dramatic and passionate way to that so evident farther south. Accustomed to dealing with international visitors, they know what people expect in the way of facilities. In the service industries, you'll find English widely spoken. In the main towns and cities, the siesta is not as important, which means longer hours for museums and churches.

In the Trentino-Alto Adige, you'll immediately notice the Teutonic influences. The area is completely

Mellow sunlight in a peaceful corner of Treviso

The Northeast

bilingual, with German the dominant language in many places. Teutonic efficiency reigns and mixes delightfully with typical Italian pleasures. The cuisine, in particular, pays homage to its northern roots, with dumplings and sauerkraut, wiener schnitzel and apple strudel often on the menu.

Similar culinary links exist in Friuli-Venezia Giulia, but here the accent is middle European with a strong café culture, cream cakes, goulash and more dumplings. Friuli-Venezia is more ethnically jumbled, comprising a cocktail of Italian, Slavic and middle European cultures. You'll see evidence of this in the bilingual street signs throughout the region; the dialect here is *friulano*.

Appreciating the Northeast

Venice is one of the world's most enticing cities, but there's much more to the area. If you make the trip this far north, take time to explore. You should see Verona, as beautiful now as when Shakespeare set *Romeo and Juliet* there, while Vicenza, with its tight-knit center and Palladian architecture, should also be high on your list. Padua, though less immediately appealing, has unrivaled artistic treasures. These three can be tackled individually as day trips from Venice, though they deserve an overnight stay to appreciate them fully.

In Trentino-Alto Adige, Bolzano and Merano have great charm, but the real attraction is the Dolomites. These magnificent mountains can be enjoyed

Scenic grandeur surrounds many of the upland villages in Italy's northeast corner

by rail or car, though to get the best out of them you should try to fit in some skiing or hiking. Farther east, Friuli-Venezia Giulia offers immense variety, from the Alps and the limestone plateau known as the Carso, to alluvial plains and stretches of varied coastline.

Trieste has an atmosphere all its own, while the charms of Cividale dei Friuli and Aquiléia are on a par with far-better-known areas. Getting around is easy, with good roads, public transportation and plenty of accommodations. To get the most out of a Dolomite trip it really needs a car rental; although if you're a nervous driver, the dramatic mountain roads might be better avoided.

When To Go

If you enjoy winter sports, you could combine skiing with a Venice trip; December and January, when the city is virtually empty of tourists, are the best times to visit. The weather then can be sparkling clear and bitterly cold or romantically mist-shrouded. If seeing Venice in sunshine is your goal, wait until late spring; May and June are the optimum months. This is also a splendid time for the mountains, when the snows are retreating and the Alpine meadows spread with wildflowers. It's best to avoid the peak summer months (July and August), when you'll have to battle with crowds and the heat can be unpleasant for sightseeing.

The Northeast

VENICE

The city built over water, Venice (Venezia) never fails to enchant. Familiar from a thousand pictures, the city's magical blend of stone and water with all its sounds and scents will be a highlight of your Italian experience. It may be crowded and expensive, crumbling and shabby, but this treasure-packed city will win your heart no matter how often you return. It's a dream waiting to come true.

Picturesque Surroundings

If money is no object, the optimum place to stay is one of the luxury hotels along the Grand Canal, but there are many other options, often in quieter but just as picturesque surroundings. The *sestiere* (city areas) of Dorsoduro, San Marco, Castello and San Polo are perhaps the nicest parts. Avoid the area around the railroad station where it is less pleasant, though there's plenty of accommodations here for late arrivals. Don't stay in Mestre, a polluted industrial sprawl across the causeway.

Take time daily to work out your itinerary; Venice can be slow to move around in and shortcuts through the maze of streets can save valuable time. You'll be doing a huge amount of walking as you negotiate the bridges; come prepared with comfortable, well broken-in shoes. Main through-city routes are marked by yellow signs above head height. The tourist office publishes a bilingual monthly guide to Venice, *Un Ospite di Venezia* (Venetian Guest), which has everything you'll need to know.

Try to allow three to four days at least to see Venice; there are enough sights to keep you busy for months. Start by getting a feel of the place before venturing into the crowded visitor areas. A good way to ease yourself in is by taking a *vaporetto* boat; number 1 down the Grand Canal or 51

Gondolas

The elegant gondola is a shallow-draft vessel propelled by a single oarsman standing at the back of the boat. Their shape and depth make them ideal for penetrating even the narrowest and shallowest canals. A ride in a shiny-black gondola is an essential experience for many visitors, but they are very expensive and normally follow a set route.

or 52, the *Giracittà* (Round the City) are both good bets. Take a boat trip to some of the lagoon islands; public transportation is more fun than a tour. Or simply wander.

Dining Out

It's worth paying a little extra to enjoy typical Venetian dishes. Starters include delicate plates of mixed seafood and *sarde in saor*, sardines cooked with vinegar, and pasta dishes range from *spaghettie alle vongole* (with clams) to various rice dishes. Venetians eat a lot of fish but some can be expensive, and you often pay for the weight of your portion. Liver and onions *(fegato alla veneziana)* is another local dish.

Tiramisu, now found everywhere, is a Venetian dessert. Made from coffee-soaked spongecake and sweetened *mascarpone* cheese, its name means "pick-me-up." Most wine comes from the Veneto region on the mainland; wines to look out for include Soave, Valpolicella, Bardolino and the excellent Bianco di Custoza. Be sure to try a glass of dry sparkling *prosecco* as an aperitif; mixed with fresh peach juice, it becomes a Bellini. An essential city experience is relaxing over a drink at Florian's or Quadri's, Venice's smartest cafés, situated on either side of Piazza San Marco.

VENICE

0   200   400 m
0   200   400 yards

N

Gesuiti (Santa Maria Assunta)

FONDAMENTE NUOVE

Rio dei Gesuiti

Rio dei Mendicanti

Santa Maria Mirácoli

Rio di San Ghistina

Monumento Colleoni

CAMPO SANTI GIOVANNI E PAOLO

Santi Giovanni e Páolo

San Francesco della Vigna

CAMPO SANTA MARIA FORMOSA

Santa Maria nosa

Palazzo Querini-Stampália e Pinacoteca

CASTELLO

San Giórgio dei Greci

Scuola di San Giórgio degli Schiavoni

Rio della Pietà

Basilica di San Marco

San Zaccaria

CAMPO SAN ZACCARIA

CAMPO BANDIERA E MORO

Arsenale

Palazzo Ducale   Prigioni

RIVA DEGLI SCHIAVONI

San Martino

Santa Maria della Pietà

San Giovanni in Brágora

Museo Stórico Navale

Ponte dei Sospiri

San Biágio

di Marco

Canale di San Marco

San Pietro di Castello

Isola di San Giórgio Maggiore

San Giórgio Maggiore

D   Teatro Verde   E

Venetian Craftware

The main stores are clustered along the Calle dei Fabbri, the Frezzeria and the so-called Merceria, a network of streets connecting Piazza San Mark's with the Rialto. Here the best of the Murano glass manufacturers have their showrooms. Artisan shops selling imaginative craftware are found in the oddest corners, while another temptation comes in the shape of stunning silk and velvet fabrics. Marbled paper and exotic papier-maché masks are another good souvenir. You can even buy a gondolier's shirt or hat – try Emilio Ceccato, near the Rialto.

Entertainment

Carnival, when thousands of people wearing costumes and elaborate masks parade the city streets, lasts for 10 days before the start of Lent. The main summer festival is the feast of *La Sensa*, when the mayor and his entourage sail out in the state barge and enact a symbolic marriage to the waters. This is followed in July by the *Festa del Redentore*, a festival of thanksgiving for deliverance from a plague. A pontoon bridge is built across the Giudecca canal to the great Redentore church, and the feast culminates in a spectacular fireworks display. During the *Regata Storica* in September, there are races of decorated craft manned by crews in period dress. Year-round entertainment includes classical concerts, theater, football games and the casino. *Un Ospite di Venezia* carries full listings of what's going on.

ESSENTIAL INFORMATION

TOURIST INFORMATION
• San Marco 71/f ☎ 041 529 8711
• Aeroporto Marco Polo ☎ 041 541 5887
• Stazione Santa Lucia ☎ 041 529 8727
• Viale Santa Maria Elisabetta, Lido di Venezia (summer only) ☎ 041 526 5721

URBAN TRANSPORTATION
If you arrive by car, you must leave the vehicle in one of the parking lots on the outskirts. Venice's public transportation system is operated by ACTV (☎ 041 522 2633) and uses two types of boats, *vaporetti* (bigger and slower) and *motoscafi* (smaller and faster). All boats are numbered and follow set routes, which frequently change so check they are still valid. *Vaporetti* leave from docks that are clearly marked with the service numbers. As the same numbers sometimes go in two directions, check that you are heading the right way before you board. Tickets can be bought at the dock or at shops showing the ACTV sticker. You can save money by buying a 12-, 24- or 72-hour pass. All tickets must be validated at the machine on the dock before boarding. ACTV publishes two booklets, one showing routes, the other timetables. Water taxis are fast and expensive; they can be hailed on various canals, or it is easier to telephone ☎ 041 723 112; 041 522 9750; 041 966 170; 041 522 8538. Gondolas are a fun way to travel but they are very expensive. The seven *traghetti* (ferries) crossing the Grand Canal at various points are also useful. Pay as you board.

AIRPORT INFORMATION
Venice's Marco Polo Airport (☎ 041 260 9260), on the northern edge of the lagoon, handles domestic and international flights. For city connections take a bus or taxi from outside the terminal to the Piazzale Roma at the edge of the city, where the road ends, and then connect with your hotel by *vaporetto* (water bus). The transfer takes around 20 minutes. Purchase tickets from the office inside the terminal before boarding. Alilaguna runs a boat service from the airport to the city center. It leaves from outside the terminal and calls at Murano, the Lido, Arsenale, San Marco and the Záttere. The fastest way to the city is by water taxi; these leave from outside the terminal and take around 20 minutes to the center.

CLIMATE – Average highs and lows

	JAN.	FEB.	MAR.	APR.	MAY	JUN.	JUL.	AUG.	SEP.	OCT.	NOV.	DEC.
	5°C	8°C	12°C	17°C	21°C	24°C	27°C	26°C	23°C	18°C	12°C	8°C
	41°F	46°F	54°F	63°F	70°F	75°F	81°F	79°F	73°F	64°F	54°F	46°F
	0°C	2°C	5°C	9°C	13°C	17°C	19°C	18°C	16°C	12°C	7°C	3°C
	32°F	36°F	41°F	48°F	55°F	63°F	66°F	64°F	61°F	54°F	45°F	37°F

VENICE SIGHTS

Key to symbols

🔲 map coordinates refer to the Venice map on page 62; sights below are highlighted in yellow on the map 🖂 address or location ☎ telephone number ⊘ opening times 🍴 restaurant on site or nearby 🚢 nearest boat or ferry stop 💷 admission charge: $$$ more than L5,000, $$ L3,000 to L5,000, $ less than L3,000 🔖 information

BASILICA DI SAN MARCO

Venice's cathedral, the Basilica di San Marco (St. Mark's Basilica), was built in 1094 on the site of the ninth-century basilica housing the body of St. Mark, Venice's patron saint. Its profusion of domes and sculptures, mosaics and marbles, and a superb fusion of Byzantine, Islamic and Western art and architecture, make it one of Europe's most exotic cathedrals. Allow time to study the thousands of mosaics high above the undulating marble pavements, and to admire the Romanesque carvings around the main door. Don't miss the great gold altar panel, the Pala d'Oro, encrusted with jewels and precious enamels, or the four gilded bronze horses possibly dating from as early as the fourth century BC and stolen by the Venetians from Constantinople in 1204.

🔲 D2 🖂 Piazza San Marco ☎ 041 522 5697 ⊘ Basilica: daily 9:30–4:30; Pala d'Oro: Mon.–Sat. 2–4 🚢 1, 52 (San Marco)

CA' D'ORO

The beautiful 15th-century Venetian-Gothic Ca' d'Oro, the Golden House, got its name from the gilding that once covered its elaborate facade. Behind the facade it houses a fascinating small art gallery set around the palazzo's central *portego*, or inner courtyard. Its showpieces include Andrea Mantegna's impressive *Saint Sebastian* and a Vivarini's polyptych of *The Passion*. There are also lesser works by Titian, Giorgione and Tintoretto, and some lovely sculptural fragments, bronzes and tapestries.

🔲 C3 🖂 Calle di Ca' d'Oro, off Strada Nova ☎ 041 523 87 90 ⊘ Daily 9–2 🚢 1 (Ca' d'Oro) 💷 $$

Many of Venice's sights can be appreciated by taking a boat trip on the Grand Canal

CAMPANILE

Venice's original campanile was reputedly built in 902; this graceful edifice collapsed in 1902, killing no one and leaving St. Mark's untouched. The Venetians vowed, *"Dov'era e com'era"* – "Where it was and like it was," and 10 years later a perfect replica was complete. It's worth the elevator ride to the top for the superb views of the city and as far as the Alps. Take a look at the weather instruments that record temperature, tides, wind, moon phases and much more.

🔲 D2 🖂 Piazza San Marco ☎ 041 522 4064 ⊘ Daily 9:30–4:30 🚢 1, 52 (San Marco) 💷 $$$

CANAL GRANDE

The Canal Grande (Grand Canal), an enchanting stretch of water crossed by three bridges and lined with a magical parade of palaces, divides Venice. By day it's traversed by *vaporetti*, tugboats and gondolas and photographed by millions of visitors. The pearly morning light imbues it with magic, while darkness adds its own enchantment. For a trip of a lifetime, take a number 1 boat from the train station, sit back and enjoy.

🔲 B2, C1, C2, C3, D2, D3 🚢 1

The Scala d'Oro (Golden Staircase) leads to the sumptuous upper floor of the Palazzo Ducale

COLLEZIONE PEGGY GUGGENHEIM

An 18th-century palace on the Grand Canal is home to the modern art collection amassed by the American millionaire, Peggy Guggenheim. There are exciting works by Magritte and Picasso, while Jackson Pollock and Joseph Cornell represent the United States. The lovely garden is the perfect backdrop for Marino Marini's disturbing *Angel of the Citadel* and some striking sculpture by Henry Moore.

✚ C1 ✉ Palazzo Venier dei Leoni, Calle San Cristoforo, San Gregorio 701 ☎ 041 520 6288 ⓖ Wed.–Mon. 11–6 ⛴ 1 (Salute) 💰 $$$

GALLERIE DELL'ACCADEMIA

The Gallerie dell'Accademia (Academy Gallery) is Venice's greatest art gallery, a true must-see. Arranged chronologically, the gallery's 24 rooms will introduce you to Bellini's luminescent *Virgins*, Giorgione's enigmatic *Tempest* and the dizzying perspective of Tintoretto's *Translation of the Body of St. Mark*. Don't miss Veronese's sumptuous *Feast in the House of Levi* or the two lively and colorful narrative painting cycles by Carpaccio and other artists, the *Miracle of the True Cross* and the *Life of St. Ursula*. Don't waste time looking for works by Canaletto; there's only one in the whole gallery.

✚ B1 ✉ Campo della Carità ☎ 041 522 2247 ⓖ Tue.–Sat. 9–7; Sun. 9–8, Mon. 9–2 ⛴ 1 (Accademia) 💰 $$$ ℹ An audio-guide of the gallery's highlights is available in English from the front desk

MUSEO CIVICO CORRER

The Museo Civico Correr (Correr Museum) is the best place for a fascinating overview of the history of the republic of Venice, the Serenissima. A bit of background reading will enhance your enjoyment, but the museum is packed with documents, maps, pictures, regalia, coins and miscellania relating to the city. It's housed in the Procuratie Nuove, which runs the whole way along the south side of St. Mark's Square. At the end, overlooking the piazzetta, you can visit the Libreria Sansoviniana, a 16th-century architectural gem designed by Sansovina to house the state library.

✚ C2 ✉ Piazza San Marco, Ala Napoleonica ☎ 041 522 5625 ⓖ Daily 9–5 (last admission 3:30) ⛴ 1, 52, 82 (San Marco) 💰 $$$ You can buy a combination ticket to the Palazzo Ducale, Museo Civico Correr, Museo Archeologico, Biblioteca Marciana, Glass Museum on Murano, Lace Museum on Burano, Plazzo Mocenigo and Ca' Rezzonico

PALAZZO DUCALE

Tackle the huge Gothic complex of the Palazzo Ducale (Ducal Palace) when you're fresh, for this is triumphalism on the grandest scale. Each reception and council room outdoes the one before in size, scale and splendor. The palace was the seat of Venetian government, where the Doge lived and held state, the council met, ambassadors were received and prisoners incarcerated. The present building dates largely from the 15th century, with alterations made after two 16th-century fires. Follow the marked route through the building. It leads through overwhelmingly lavish rooms culminating in the sumptuous Sala del Maggior Consiglio (Great Council

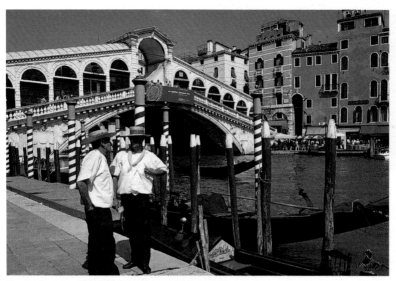

Revel in the sights and sounds as you cross the Rialto bridge

Chamber), dominated by Tintoretto's *Paradiso*, the world's largest painting. Don't miss the prison building, reached by crossing over the famous Bridge of Sighs, which span a canal to the right of the Palazzo's waterfront facade.

➕ D2 ✉ Piazzetta San Marco ☎ 041 522 4951 🕐 Daily 9–7 (last admission 5:30), Apr.–Oct.; 9–5 (last admission 3:30), rest of year. Guided tours morning only 🚢 1, 52, 82 (San Marco) 💰 $$$ ℹ️ An audio-guide in English is available from the front desk

PIAZZA SAN MARCO

Napoleon called the Piazza San Marco (St. Mark's Square) "Europe's largest drawing room," and this wonderful open space is crowded around the clock with chattering crowds. It's Venice's only piazza – the others are all officially *campi* – and is lined with a harmonious melange of fine buildings and arcades. The 15th-century Torre dell'Orologia (Clock Tower), with its zodiac clock, leads into the Merceria, an elegant shopping street that connects to the Rialto. Near the water, on the piazzetta, you'll see two columns topped by St. Mark's lion and St. Theodore's crocodile, both ancient symbols of the city.

➕ D2 ✉ Piazza San Marco 🚢 1, 52, 82 (San Marco)

RIALTO

During the Middle Ages, the Rialto was Europe's financial and banking center, a sort of medieval Wall Street, where fortunes were made and lost. The Grand Canal is spanned here by a shop-lined bridge, which you should cross to wander in Venice's main market, one of the city's best sights. Stalls are bright with fruit and vegetables or glistening with fish and shellfish, while the surrounding streets are hemmed with enticing food stores and lined with cheerful souvenir stalls.

➕ C2 ✉ Rialto 🍴 Trattoria alla Madonna, see page 203 🚢 1 (Rialto)

SAN GIÓRGIO MAGGIORE

Palladio bequeathed two great churches to Venice, the Redentore and San Giórgio Maggiore (St. George the Great). The harmonious structure of San Giórgio adds the finishing touch to the view of St. Mark's Basin; take a boat to get there. The church's clean and graceful lines perfectly embody the architect's strict neoclassical tenets, while the view from the campanile has to be one of Venice's best.

➕ D1 ✉ Campo San Giórgio, Isola San Giórgio ☎ 041 522 7827 🕐 Daily 10–12:30 and 2:15–5:30 (times vary in winter) 🚢 82 (San Giórgio)

The Northeast

Housed in the Scuola Grande di San Rocco, Tintoretto's *Crucifixion* is one of Venice's most powerful paintings

SANTA MARIA DELLA SALUTE

The great domed church of Santa Maria della Salute (Our Lady of Health and Salvation) dominates the entrance to the Grand Canal. It was constructed in 1630 in thanksgiving for Venice's deliverance from the plague in which 45,000 people died. Every November on the feast of *La Salute*, Venetians cross a temporary bridge to give thanks for their deliverance more than 350 years ago. Not only is it one of the city's outstanding landmark buildings, the church's impressive interior contains fine paintings and sculpture.

C1 ⊠ Campo della Salute ☎ 041 522 5558 ◉ Daily 9–noon; 3–5:30 ⛴ 1 (Salute)

SANTA MARIA GLORIOSA DEI FRARI

Both Titian and the composer Monteverdi are interred in the lofty Franciscan Gothic church of the *frari* (brothers). Built as a preaching church around 1250, Santa Maria Gloriosa dei Frari (Glorious Virgin Mary of the Brothers) contains two superb Titians, the great *Assumption*, prominently hung over the high altar, and his *Madonna of Ca' Pesaro*. Best of all, though, is Giovanni Bellini's luminous *Madonna and Child with Saints*. Considered one of the world's greatest pictures, you'll find it tucked away in the right transept.

B2 ⊠ Campo dei Frari ☎ 041 522 2637 ◉ Mon.–Sat. 9–6, Sun. 1–6 ⛴ 1 (San Tomà) ▥ $ (free on Sun.)

SANTI GIOVANNI E PÁOLO

Venice's largest church is dedicated to St. John and St. Paul and was built by the Dominicans in the 14th century. It's a massive and imposing Gothic structure that is the resting place of more than 25 Doges. The monuments on their tombs represent the best of Venetian medieval sculpture. Inside, don't miss Giovanni Bellini's polyptych of *St. Vincent Ferrer*; outside, the great equestrian statue of the mercenary Colleoni by Verocchio is among the city's sculptural treasures.

D3 ⊠ Campo SS Giovanni e Páolo ☎ 041 523 5913 ◉ Daily 7:30–12:30 and 3–7:30; closed Sun. morning ⛴ 41, 42, 51, 52 (Ospedale); 12, 13 (Fondamente Nove)

SCUOLA DI SAN GIÓRGIO DEGLI SCHIAVONI

From 1502 to 1508, Carpaccio painted the modest headquarters of Venice's Slavic (Schiavoni) community with one of the most beguiling picture cycles you're ever likely to see. Here are scenes from the lives of Dalmatia's patron saints, St. George, St. Tryphon and St. Jerome. The highlights are *St. George Slaying the Dragon* and *St. Augustine in His Study*.

E2 ⊠ Ponte dei Greci ☎ 041 522 8828 ◉ Tue.–Sat. 10–12:30 and 3–6, Sun. 10–12:30 ⊪ Corte Sconta. see page 203 ⛴ 1, 52 (San Zaccaria) ▥ $$

SCUOLA GRANDE DI SAN ROCCO

In 1564 Tintoretto won a competition to decorate the walls of the headquarters of the wealthy confraternity of St. Roche. He spent the next 23 years working on the stupendous cycle of wall-paintings and ceiling panels, more than 50 in all, which illustrate Old and New Testament scenes. Start your tour upstairs in the Sala dell'Albergo with its stupendous and revolutionary *Crucifixion*, then move into the upper hall, before you view the 1587 ground-floor paintings.

B2 ⊠ Campo San Rocco ☎ 041 523 4864 ◉ Daily 10–4 ⛴ 1 San Tomà ▥ $$ ⓘ An audio-guide in English is available from the front desk

WALK: QUIET STREETS AND SMALL CANALS

Refer to route marked on city map on page 62.

Venice is a city without traffic, a city where the only sounds on the streets are those of human feet and human voices. You'll walk a lot during a Venetian stay and some of your most serendipitous discoveries will be made en route. This walk runs through the *sestiere* city areas of Dorsoduro and San Polo, and will take about an hour.

The *squero*, one of the last traditional working gondola boatyards

Start on the Fondamenta delle Záttere facing the water. Head right and turn right before the first bridge and walk along the Rio di San Trováso. Cross the first bridge, then turn left and pass the church of San Trováso.

As you walk along Rio di San Trováso, be sure to look for the gondola yard, *squero,* on the other side of the canal. Established in the 17th century, there are always gondolas under construction to be seen. The church of San Trováso was built 1584 to 1657. Inside it's cool and spacious and there are two fine paintings by Tintoretto, the *Temptation of St. Anthony* and the *Last Supper.*

Keep walking bearing right until you come to another canal; this is the Rio Ognissanti. Walk beside it, crossing one canal and passing a total of five bridges on your left. Cross another canal, then walk straight ahead down Calle Chiesa until you meet a wider canal. Turn right. Keep the canal on your left and pass two bridges. When you come to another canal in front of you, turn right, keeping the water on your left once more. Continue straight ahead along the Fondamenta del Soccorso until you come to the Campo dei Cármini.

The Scuola Grand dei Cármini stands on one side of the square. Once the Venetian base of the Carmelite order, this 17th-century building's upstairs hall has an exuberant ceiling painted by Giambattista Tiepolo. All azure skies and spiraling perspectives, the panels show a crucial scene from the order's history, *Simon Stock Receiving the Scapular.*

The church itself is a mixture of styles from Gothic to baroque.

Veer left through the square and walk into Campo Santa Margherita.

One of the most appealing of all Venetian squares, Campo Santa Margherita has a genuine neighborhood feel. There are always fruit and vegetable stalls set up, local stores and bars predominate. It's a good place to pause for a drink or an ice cream at Causin, a long-established *gelateria.*

Go straight ahead through the long square and down the narrow street at the far end, Calle della Chiesa. Cross the bridge over the wide Rio di Ca' Foscari into Campo San Pantalòn. Bear right across the square, past the church, and turn left down the Calle San Pantalòn.

San Pantalòn, otherwise San Pantaleone, was a healer. The church ceiling is wildly decorated with 60 panels depicting his life. The artist Fumiani never saw his work completed, falling off a scaffold at the end of his labors. Of more artistic merit is the fine *San Pantaleone Healing a Boy,* the last work Veronese painted.

Cross the next street, turn right and then immediately left down another narrow calle ending at a bridge over a canal, and you come to the Rio della Frescada. Turn left, then directly right past the front of the Scuola Grande di San Rocco (see page 68). After visiting the Scuola, exit and turn left then right down the Salizzada San Rocco and skirt around the church of Santa Maria Gloriosa dei Frari (see page 68) into the Campo dei Frari. From here, you can pick up the yellow signs that will lead you back to the Rialto.

The Northeast

ISLANDS IN THE LAGOON

There's more to the Venetian lagoon than just the city. This fragile, land-locked sea is scattered with islands, some thriving and historic communities, others as remote and peaceful as if they were a hundred miles from the noise and glitter of St. Marks. Try to explore a few; they fall handily into groups, and you could spend a marvelous day away from the crowds.

Graves and Glass

San Michele and Murano are very different. San Michele is the site of the city's main cemetery. Murano is home to Europe's oldest glass-making industry. It might seem odd to visit a cemetery, but alight for half-an-hour on your way to Murano at this unique burial ground, surrounded by high walls and studded with cypresses. Among the well-tended graves and monuments bright with flowers are the last homes of Ezra Pound, Sergei Diaghilev and Igor Stravinsky.

The 15th-century Barovier Wedding Cup

Bustling Murano makes a good contrast. Glass has been made here since 1291, when the furnaces were moved away from the city as a fire precaution. Venetian craftsmen were Europe's most skillful glass-blowers, producing intricate and delicate work under secretive conditions. Today, the skills are very much in place, and there are large numbers of workshops where you can see glass being blown. Sadly, most of the design is horrendous, though there are treasures. The fascinating Museo Vetrario (Glass Museum) has a huge collection; don't miss the Barovier wedding cup, an enamel-worked 15th-century piece. Murano's main church is Santa Maria e Donato, a superb 12th-century structure with a wonderful colonnade and equally fine mosaics and marble pavements within.

Four Islands to the North

You'll need a whole day to do justice to the four islands lying across the lagoon to the north of the city – Burano, Mazzorbo, Torcello and San Francesco del Deserto. Burano, all brightly painted houses, drunkenly leaning campaniles, narrow canals and sun-splashed piazzas, is still a fishing community with a salty atmosphere and robust inhabitants. It's historically noted for the exquisite lace made by the island women; the industry has practically died out, but you can admire local work in the the Museo dei Merletti (Lace-making Museum).

A bridge links Burano to pastoral Mazzorbo with its clutch of canalside houses, vegetable plots and grass. It's a lovely place to pass a short time and you'll feel a sense of history here. This sense of Venice's age is at its strongest in timeless Torcello, just across the water. This dreamy island with its overgrown canals and green fields is one of the most evocative and magical places in Italy. Once the most important island in the lagoon, Torcello was pushed off history's map and left to gentle decay by 12th-century silt and malaria. Today, only the great basilica of Santa Maria Assunta and the neighboring church of Santa Fosca remind us of its heyday. Santa Maria was first built in the seventh century; the pulpit dates from this time, but the rest of the church is 11th century. Its chief glories are two 12th-century mosaics completely covering the apse and the opposite wall. High above the altar, the apse mosaic shows a lovely Byzantine *Madonna and Child*, their poignant beauty highlighted by the simple gold background, while the graphic *Last Judgment* scenes at the west end make a dramatic contrast. Leave time to see smaller and more intimate Santa Fosca; its arcaded porch is full of wheeling swifts.

If time permits, ask a boatman to row you across to San Francesco del Deserto from Burano. This Franciscan monastery, with its serene old church and beautiful gardens, is one of the lagoon's least-known and loveliest corners.

The Northeast

San Lazzaro degli Armeni and San Servolo

The islands of San Lazzaro degli Armeni and San Servolo are each fascinating in their own way. Since the 18th century, San Lazzaro has been an Armenian monastery, a center of learning for this ancient branch of Christianity. Young Armenians still come here to study their culture and religion. One of the multi-lingual monks will show you the church and museum; look for the room where the poet Byron spent the winter of 1816 struggling with the intricacies of the Armenian language. The monastery has run a polyglot printing press for more than 200 years and you can buy the items it produces.

San Servolo was also once a monastery island and Benedictine foundation that later became a hospital and asylum. Today, it's a training center for a range of craft and conservation techniques needed for architectural restoration. Students from Italy and many other countries study here.

Murano 🚤 12, 13, 41, 42

Basilica dei Santi Maria e Donato ✉ Fondamenta Giustinian ☎ 041 739 056 🕔 Daily 8–noon and 4–6:30

Museo Vetrario ✉ Fondamenta Giustinain 8 ☎ 041 739 586 🕔 Thu.–Tue. 10–4 ✋ \$\$

San Michele 🚤 41, 42

Burano 🚤 12

Scuolo di Merletti ✉ Piazza Galuppi ☎ 041 730 034

Top: Burano's colorful houses reflected in its canals
Bottom: Lace of all types is sold in Burano

🕔 Tue.–Sun. 10:30–12:30 and 2–4 ✋ \$

Mazzorbo 🚤 12

Torcello 🚤 12

Basilica di Santa Maria della Assunta ☎ 041 730 084 🕔 Daily 10–5 ✋ \$\$

Museo dell'Estuaria ☎ 041 730 761
🕔 Tue.–Sun.10:30–12:30 and 2–4 ✋ \$

San Francesco del Deserto 🚤 12

Convento di San Francesco del Deserto ☎ 041 528 6863 🕔 Daily 9–11 and 3–5 🚤 Access by *sándolo* (rowing boat) from Burano. Negotiate price with boatman on the dock near the church on Burano

San Lazzaro degli Armeni 🚤 20

Monastero Mekhitarista ☎ 041 526 0104 🕔 Daily 3:20–5

San Servolo 🚤 10, 20

Fondazione Europea pro Venetia Viva
☎ 041 526 8546 🕔 By appointment only

The Northeast

REGIONAL SIGHTS

Key to symbols

⊞ map coordinates refer to the region map on page 58; sights below are highlighted in yellow on the map
⊠ address or location ☎ telephone number
⊙ opening times ⅋ restaurant on site or nearby
▮ admission charge: $$$ more than L5,000, $$ L3,000 to L5,000, $ less than L3,000 ⅰ information

AQUILÉIA

The pancake-flat plains south of Udine, which feature acres of dull cornfields and characterless villages, leave you unprepared for the treasure of Aquiléia. The colony was established in 181 BC and by the fourth century had become a patriarchate, a region ruled by a prince-bishop or patriarch. The first patriarch was Theodore, who built a great basilica. Sacked by Attila and the Lombards, this early church was rebuilt several times, and today is a superb blend of Romanesque and Gothic elements. Its chief glory is its jewel-like mosaic pavement, undulating along the nave like a multi-colored carpet. Its Christian and pagan scenes are as fresh as when they were assembled around AD 320 during Theodore's patriarchate. Look for the mosaic bestiary around the base of the 11th-century campanile and the evocative 12th-century Byzantine frescoes in the shadowy crypt.

Sleepy Aquiléia also has two museums that will help put its one-time importance into perspective – the Archeological Museum has everything from fine Roman sculpture to a reconstructed galley and a stroll along the River Natissa will take you to the Museo Paleocristiano (Paleochristian Museum), a pithy collection of more local Roman finds.

⊞ C2
Tourist information ⊠ Piazza Capitolo ⊙ Fri.–Tue. 8:30–1 and 5–7, May–Oct.; 8:30–1 and 4–6, rest of year
Basilica ⊠ Piazza del Capitolo ☎ 0431 910 1067 ⊙ Daily 8:30–7, Apr.–Oct.; 8:30 12:30 and 2:30–5:30, rest of year
Museo Archeologico ⊠ Via Roma 1 ☎ 0431 910 1035 ⊙ Tue.–Sun. 9–7, Mon. 9–2 ▮ $$
Museo Paleocristiano ⊠ Piazza Pirano, Monastero delle Benedettine ☎ 0431 91 131 ⊙ Sun.–Wed. 9–2, Thu.–Sat. 9–7

ÁSOLO

Ásolo's charms gave the Italian language a new verb – *asolare*, meaning to pass the time in pleasant aimlessness. This medieval walled town, sprinkled with enchanting piazzas and pretty churches and set in the Dolomite foothills, is perhaps the loveliest in the Veneto. Its surrounding villa-studded countryside is stunning.

Famous figures have loved Ásolo, among them 15th-century Catarina Cornaro, one of the few women to have played an important part in Venetian history. Scion of a powerful family, she became, through marriage, queen of Cyprus, but was duped out of the island by the Venetian state, which gave her Ásolo as a consolation prize. The actress Eleanor Druse was born here in 1859. Famous as much for her love-life as her acting, Druse often retreated home to escape gossip and scandal, and although she died in far-off Pittsburgh, she is buried here. There's plenty of information on her life in the Museo Civico, which also devotes space to the English poet Robert Browning, who lived here for some time.

⊞ B2
Tourist information ⊠ Via Santa Caterina 258 ☎ 0423 529 046 ⊙ Mon.–Sat. 10–noon and 4–7
Museo Civico ⊠ Loggia del Capitano ☎ 0423 952 313 ▮ $

Roman remains at Aquiléia

The jagged peaks of the Dolomites contrast with fertile upland pastures

The Northeast

DRIVE: THE GREAT DOLOMITES

Duration: 3 to 4 hours

This drive follows the route known as La Grande Strada delle Dolomiti (the Great Dolomites Road), which was constructed in 1909 to link Bolzano and Cortina d'Ampezzo. It runs 110 kilometers (70 miles) through Europe's most breathtaking mountain scenery and offers frequent opportunities to take a scenic side road or a cable car up the mountain slope. The road is well-maintained, but inevitably twisting in places, so bear this in mind if you suffer from vertigo or travel sickness.

From Bolzano (see page 76), take the SS241 along the Val d'Ega to the Lago di Carezza.

East of Bolzano, you leave the road over the Brenner Pass, one of the historic trans-Alpine routes, and head along the gorge of the Val d'Ega. This narrow corridor, edged with waterfalls, offers the first taste of the superb views along this route, with the Catinaccio and Latemar massifs rising on either side of the road. Make your first stop at the Lago di Carezza, a picture-postcard lake whose deep blue waters reflect mountain ridges sprinkled with dark fir trees and punctuated with white gravel slides. The road climbs from the lake to the Passo di Costalunga (5,750 feet), the first of the high passes along this route, which marks the boundary between the Alto Adige and Trentino regions.

Continue on the SS241 through the Passo di Costalunga to Vigo di Fassa.

Once over the pass, the road descends through the Val di Fassa, running beside the River Avisio to Vigo di Fassa, a mountain resort town with a pretty 15th-century Gothic church. Vigo makes a good starting point for

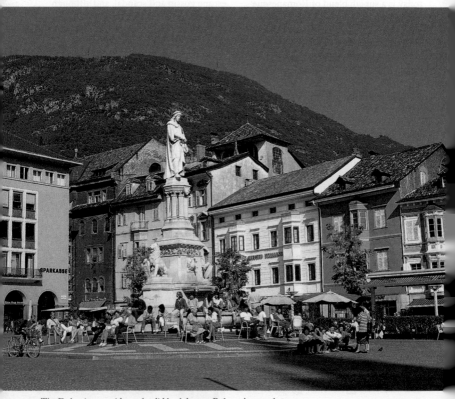

The Dolomites provide a splendid backdrop to Bolzano's central square

hikers wanting to explore the Catinaccio range. There are trails catering to all levels of fitness and experience, and a cable car takes away the worst of the initial hike. You can also hike south back to the Lago di Carezza.

About 1.5 kilometers (1 mile) outside Vigo, turn left onto the SS48 to Canazei. The road becomes increasingly dramatic, with views of wild countryside, soaring mountains and constantly changing vistas as it hairpins its way to Canazei. This is another mountain resort town, with good hotels and a range of restaurants catering to the winter skiers, summer climbers and walkers who make it their base. There's a choice of cable-car rides into the surrounding mountains.

Stay on the SS48, climbing steeply to the Passo Pordoi and on to Arabba. Twenty-seven hairpin turns over 12 kilometers (7 miles) of road mark the next section of driving, leading inexorably to the Passo Pordoi (7,400 feet), one of the highest passes on the route. Enjoy the superlative scenery until you arrive at the little village of Arabba, a cluster of family-run hotels set in peaceful mountain pastureland. The huge massif to the south is the Marmolada; you can take a cable car up to the Porto Vescovo for a closer look at its icy slopes.

If you want to make this drive a round trip, turn left onto the SS243 for the Passo di Gardena. At Plan de Gralba, turn right onto the SS242. Stay on this road through Ortisei (where it becomes the SS242d) and after 3.5 kilometers (6 miles) branch left to Ponte Gardena where you can join the SS12 south to return to Bolzano. To continue to Cortina, stay on the SS48 through Arabba and Pocòl to Cortina d'Ampezzo.

Donatello's statue of the mercenary Gattamelata outside Pádova's Basilica di San Antonio

You'll cross another pass on the way to Pocòl. This is the Passo di Falzarego (8,200 feet). Look for the relatively rare stone pines that dot the slopes of the high meadows around here. The descent to Cortina runs along the slopes of the Tofane massif to emerge into the stunning mountain bowl that encircles this chic resort.

Bolzano tourist information (see page 76)
Cortina d'Ampezzo tourist information ✉ Piazzetta San Francesco 8 ☎ 0436 3231 🕐 Mon.–Fri. 9–12:30 and 4–7, Sat. 10–12:30 and 4–7, Sun. 10–12:30

Tourists and locals enjoying a moment's pause in the sun in central Bolzano

BOLZANO

Capital of the German-speaking Alto Adige region, mountain-hemmed Bolzano (Bozen) makes a good base for exploring the scenic splendors of the Dolomites (see page 74). This area ultimately became part of Italy at the end of World War I and retains a distinctly Teutonic flavor, which is manifested in its cuisine, language and efficiency. Head first for the café-fringed Piazza Walther, the central square, to visit the Gothic Duomo (Cathedral) with its eye-catching carved spire and yellow-and-green tiled roof. Its lovely Porta del Vino (Wine Door) is a riot of carvings of peasants working the vineyards, and was erected in 1387 when the church was granted a license to sell wine.

Nearby, the Chiesa dei Domenicani contains Bolzano's best frescoes; you'll find a 14th-century cycle in Cappella di San Giovanni (St. John's Chapel) and 15th-century scenes of life in the cloisters. North from here lies the Piazza dell'Erbe, scene of the colorful daily market, while across the Talvera river is the grandiose Piazza della Vittoria, with its monumental Fascist architecture and a triumphal arch built by Mussolini in 1928. To taste the glorious mountains,

you could take a cable car to Soprabolzano, from where a tiny tramway runs to the hamlet of Collalbo.

🞤 A3

Tourist information ✉ Piazza Walther 8 ☎ 0471 970 6660 🕓 Mon.–Fri. 9–12:30 and 2:30–6, Sat. 9–12:30 ℹ For information on the Dolomites, visit the regional tourist office at Piazza Parrochia 11/12 ☎ 0471 993 808 🕓 Mon.–Fri. 9–12:30 and 3–5:30 **Duomo** ✉ Piazza Walther 🕓 Daily 8–12:30 and 3–6 **Chiesa dei Domenicani** ✉ Via Cappuccini 🕓 Daily 8–12:30 and 3–6

CIVIDALE DEL FRIULI

Tucked up near the border with Slovenia, the lovely old town of Cividale is a beguiling tangle of medieval streets and interesting buildings. It lies on the Natisone river and is one of the few places in Italy with tangible reminders of the Lombards. This Teutonic warrior race invaded Italy in the sixth century, establishing three dukedoms and leaving a sparse legacy of superb carvings and sculpture. The finest example here is the Tempietto Longobardo (Lombard Temple), whose eighth-century stucco arch features smiling saints, a peerless example of Lombard art. There's more to be seen in the Museo Cristiano (Christian Museum) in the precincts of

the 15th-century Duomo (Cathedral).
Here you can admire the stunning Altar
of Ratchis, a hauntingly lovely eighth-
century masterpiece, and the octagonal
Baptistery of Callisto, made from fifth-
century stone and marble fragments. The
cathedral's main draw is the silver *pala*
(altar piece), a heavily embossed 12th-
century work showing the Blessed Virgin,
angels and saints.

➕ C2

Tourist information ✉ Corso Paolino d'Aquileia 10
☎ 0432 731 461 🕐 Mon.–Fri. 9–1 and 3–5

Tempietto Longobardo ✉ Piazza del Duomo
☎ 0432 700 867 🕐 Daily 10–1 and 3:30–5:30,
Apr.–Oct. ♿ $

Duomo ✉ Pazza del Duomo 🕐 Daily 9:30–12:15
and 3–6

MERANO

Staid and placid Merano (Meran), with
its mild climate and thermal springs,
provides a splendid contrast to the
dramatic mountain scenery that surrounds
it. The town attracted wealthy Central
Europeans at the beginning of the 20th
century. They came here to "take the
cure," and stroll in its parks and along its
promenades. The most famous is the
Passeggiata d'Inverno e d'Estate (Winter
and Summer Path), which runs along the
banks of the Passirio river. Higher up, you
can enjoy the winding Passeggiata
Tappeiner, which runs through vineyards
and gardens overlooking the town.

The Via dei Portici marks Meran's
historic center. The streets are a charming
mix of local architecture, good shops, and
fin-de-siécle elegance. The cathedral and
castle are worth a visit. But for the true
Meran experience, take a dip in the
thermal baths. You can also use the town
as a base from which to explore the
Texelgruppe mountains, less than 10
kilometers (6 miles) away, or the far more
dramatic Ortles range, an incredible area
of rocks and glaciers.

➕ A3

Tourist information ✉ Corso Libertà 45 ☎ 0473 235
223 🕐 Mon.–Sat. 9–6:30, Sun. 9:30–12:30, Apr.–Oct.;
Mon.–Fri. 9–12:30 and 2:30–6:30, Sat. 9–12:30, rest of
year 🎌 Third week in Oct.: Grape Fest with
processions, concerts and wine and food tastings

Statues around Pádova's largest square, Prato della
Valle, commemorate notable native citizens

PÁDOVA

The Veneto's most important economic
center and a major university city, Pádova
(Padua) was heavily bombed during World
War II. The subsequent rebuilding made
first impressions less than immediately
alluring. But there are some real gems
here, chief among them the frescoes by
Giotto in the Scrovegni Chapel. Painted
in the early 1300s, the scenes of the life of
Christ and his Blessed Mother are one of
the turning points of Western art
development, with a wholly innovative
naturalism and fluency.

Also visit the Civic Museum next door
before heading through the town center to
visit the Basilica di San Antonio, a many-
domed church dedicated to Padua's own
St. Anthony. Outside stands the fine
equestrian statue of the mercenary
Gattamelata (Honey Cat), sculpted by
Donatello in 1453.

Down Via del Santo from the basilica,
you'll find Padua's two main squares, the
Piazza delle Frutta and the Piazza delle
Erbe. The morning's the best time to stroll
here; the daily fruit and vegetable markets
are in full swing. The extraordinary
building between the two squares is the
Salone, a vast 13th-century structure once

Hills rise behind the stately port city of Trieste

used as the city council's assembly hall. It contains a huge wooden model of a horse, made for a joust in 1466. Other buildings include the university and the wonderful Café Pedrocchi, once the meeting point for the city's intellectuals.

🕂 B1

Tourist information ✉ Stazione Ferroviaria ☎ 049 875 2077 🕐 Mon.–Sat. 9–7:30, Sun. 8:30–12:30, Apr.–Oct.; Mon.–Sat. 9:20–5:45, Sun. 9–noon, rest of year ℹ You can take a cruise along the Brenta river from Padua to Venice and back again from Mar. to early Nov. It gives a chance to visit some of the magnificent villas en route. Details from Siamic Express ✉ Via Trieste 42 ☎ 049 660 944

Cappella degli Scrovegni and Musei Civici ✉ Piazza Eremitani 8 ☎ 049 820 4550 🕐 Tue.–Sun. 9–7, Feb.–Oct.; 9–6, rest of year 💷 $$

Basilica di San Antonio ✉ Piazza del Santo ☎ 049 663 944 🕐 Daily 6:30 a.m.–7:45 p.m., Apr.–Oct.; 6:30 a.m.–7 p.m., rest of year

Salone ✉ Piazza delle Erbe ☎ 049 820 5006 🕐 Daily 9–7, Feb.–Oct.; 9–6, rest of year 💷 $

TREVISO

Home to the Benetton company, Treviso is an alluring and prosperous provincial town enclosed by 16th-century walls, with canals, long porticoes and frescoed facades. The main street is the Calmaggiore. This leads right through the center, beautifully rebuilt and restored after heavy bombing in both world wars.

Treviso's cathedral is the Duomo San Pietro, where you'll find a wonderfully atmospheric crypt with a positive thicket of 12th-century columns. Treviso is noted for the production of *radicchio*, the red-leaf salad vegetable. The winter variety, eaten grilled over charcoal, is a culinary treat. Wine lovers can use Treviso as the gateway to some of the Veneto's best wine areas; two wine trails head out from the town of Conegliano to the north.

🕂 B2

Tourist information ✉ Palazzo Scotti, Via Toniolo 41 ☎ 0422 547 632 🕐 Mon.–Fri. 8:30–12:30 and 3–6, Sat. 8:30–noon

Duomo San Pietro ✉ Calmaggiore 🕐 Daily 7–noon and 3–7

TRIESTE

With its superb Piazza Unità opening to embrace the sea, Trieste rates as one of Italy's finest port cities. Founded in Roman times, Trieste's ownership over the centuries has swung between the different powers whose interests lay in this corner of the Adriatic. Thus, Italian, Austro-Hungarian and Slavic influences have all shaped today's city, which finally became part of Italy in 1954.

Beautifully set on the slopes of a limestone plateau overlooking the sea, Trieste's appearance owes much to the Empress Maria Teresa, who constructed the monumental 18th-century city center as a fitting background for its role as the main Hapsburg southern port. This central area has good shops and wide streets, well worth a visit before you climb through the remnants of Roman and medieval Trieste to the hilltop Castello (Castle) and Cattedrale di San Giusto (St. Just's Cathedral). The main museums in town are the Revoltella, the Museo di Storia e dell'Arte (History and Art Museum) and the Museo Morpurgo. Or you could follow the footsteps of James Joyce, the Irish author of *Ulysses*, who lived here for many years.

By far the nicest attraction is the idiosyncratic Castello di Miramare just outside town. It's a wonderfully situated castle overlooking the sea and standing in delightful gardens. It was built for the Archduke Ferdinand Maximilian in the 1860s; assassinated in 1867, Ferdinand was never able to enjoy his creation.

➕ C2

Tourist information ✉ Via San Nicolò 20 ☎ 040 679 611 🕐 Mon.–Fri. 9–1 and 4–7, Sat. 9–1

Castello ✉ Piazza della Cattedrale 3 ☎ 040 309 362 🕐 Tue.–Sun. 9–7, Apr.–Sep.; Tue.–Sun. 9–5, rest of year 🎫 $

Cattedrale di San Giusto ✉ Piazza della Cattedrale 🕐 Daily 8–noon and 3–7

Revoltella ✉ Via Diaz 27 ☎ 040 300 398 🕐 Wed.–Mon. 9–7 🍴 Terrace bar open Jul.–Sep. 🎫 $$

Museo di Storia e dell'Arte ✉ Via della Cattedrale 15 ☎ 040 310 500 🕐 Tue. and Thu.–Sun. 9–1, Wed. 9–7 🎫 $$

Museo Morpurgo ✉ Via Imbriani 5 ☎ 040 636 969 🕐 Tue. and Thu.–Sun. 9–1, Wed. 9–7 🎫 $$

Castello di Miramare ✉ Viale di Miramare ☎ 040 224 4143 🕐 Castle: daily 9–6, Apr.–Sep.; 9–5, Mar. and Oct.; 9–4, rest of year; gardens: daily 8–7, Apr.–Sep.; 9–6, Mar. and Oct.; 9–5, rest of year 🎫 $$

VERONA

One of the north's most captivating cities, overflowing with artistic delights and hedonistic pleasures, beautiful Verona lies on the banks of the Adige river. Start your tour in the sweeping Piazza Brà, the largest square. It's dominated by the first-century Arena, one of the world's largest surviving Roman amphitheaters and scene of Verona's famous summer opera festival. You can climb its tiers of seats to enjoy great views of the city. The pedestrian Via Mazzini, lined with swanky shops and cafés, leads to the heart of the city, centered around the intimate Piazza dell'Erbe, the venue since medieval times for the market, and lined with loggias, townhouses and Renaissance palaces. From here, head down Via Cappello for a glimpse of the Casa di Giulietta (Juliet's House), complete with balcony. Shakespeare based his tragedy on true families, the Cappelli and Montecchi, though Romeo and Juliet are fictional. This hasn't deterred thousands of modern lovers from leaving their initials on every available surface of the house's walls.

Behind the Piazza dell'Erbe lies the stunning ensemble of the Piazza dei Signori; its 12th-century buildings were once the focus of public life, and there are wide views from the top of the Torre dei Lamberti (Lamberti Tower). Don't miss the Arche Scaligeri (Scaligeri Monuments), the superb Gothic funerary monuments to Verona's medieval ruling family. The main figure is Cangrande (Big Dog), protector of Dante and a great artistic patron.

North from here lies the Duomo (Cathedral) and Santa Anastasia, Verona's largest church, built from 1290 to 1481. Nearby, you can see the Ponte Pietra (Stone Bridge), a first-century Roman bridge; the present one is a careful reconstruction of the original, which was bombed in World War II. Across the river you'll spy the remains of the Roman theater. Head parallel with the river to the Castelvecchio, the medieval fortress seat of the Scaligeri. It houses the town's Museo Civico d'Arte (Civic Art Museum), but is fascinating as a building – a maze of passages, walkways and stairs around a serene courtyard. Another short walk will bring you to the church of San Zeno, a superb Romanesque basilica that's considered the finest in northern Italy and was built on an earlier church in 1117.

The Northeast

Its lovely bronze doors are enclosed by marble bas-reliefs and topped by a "Wheel of Fortune" rose window. Inside, don't miss Mantegna's hauntingly lovely *Madonna and Saints* over the high altar.

➕ A1

Tourist information ✉ Piazza Chiesa 34 and Stazione Porta Nuova ☎ 045 806 8680 🕐 Daily 9–7 ℹ The VeronaCard is valid for three days and covers admission to museums, churches, monuments and entrance to Gardaland (see page 45) $$

Arena ✉ Piazza Brà ☎ 045 800 3204; box office 045 800 5151 🕐 Daily 9–6, except during opera season (Jul.–Aug.) 9–3:30; box office Mon.–Fri. 9–noon and 3:15 to 4:45, Jul.–Aug.; on performance days 10–9, non-performance days 10–5:45 💷 $$ ℹ Book well in advance for opera

Casa di Giulietta ✉ Via Cappello 23 ☎ 045 803 4303 🕐 Tue.–Sun. 9–6:30 💷 $$

Torre dei Lamberti ✉ Piazza dei Signori, Cortile Mercato Vecchio ☎ 045 803 2726 🕐 Tue.–Sun. 9–6 💷 $$

Duomo ✉ Piazza del Duomo 🕐 Mon.–Sat. 1:30–4, but open for prayer all day 💷 $

Santa Anastasia ✉ Corso Santa Anastasia 🕐 Daily 10–1 and 3–6 💷 $

Castelvecchio and Museo Civico d'Arte ✉ Corso Castelvecchio 2 ☎ 045 594 734 🕐 Daily 9–6:30 💷 $$

San Zeno ✉ Piazza San Zeno 🕐 Daily 10–1 and 3–6 💷 $

VICENZA

Vicenza grew rich in the second half of the 20th century on textiles, electronics and printing. Prosperity has given the city a gloss and polish without detracting from its historic charm. The center is a splendid amalgam of Gothic architecture from the days when Vicenza was a Venetian possession, and the classical buildings of the great 16th-century architect Andrea Palladio. Vicenza's main street, Corso Andrea Palladio, commemorates him and is lined with examples of his work. Here, one of his palaces now houses the Museo Civico, a fairly pedestrian collection enlivened by some masterpieces by Tiepolo and Tintoretto.

The church of Santa Corona, a mid-13th-century Dominican building, houses two superb paintings, Giovanni Bellini's serene *Baptism of Christ* and the

contrasting *Adoration of the Magi* by Paolo Veronese. Nearby is the Gallerie di Palazzo Montanari (Montanari Palace Gallery), where a splendid baroque palace houses two collections, a range of intimate domestic pictures by Longhi, Guardi and other Venetian artists, and a huge collection of richly colored Russian icons. Across Piazza Matteotti you'll find Palladio's Teatro Olimpico (Olympic Theater), Europe's oldest indoor theater, which opened in 1585. Palladio died before it was completed and the astonishing backdrop of a classical city behind the stage was added by Scamozzi. Head south from here to the Piazza dei Signori, the heart of the *centro storico* (historic center), to visit the basilica, Palladio's first major project and the one that made his reputation. The harmonious structure solved a long-standing problem of how to buttress the 15th-century city hall. The building facing the basilica is the Loggia del Capitaniato, a late and unfinished Palladian structure built for the Venetian military commander.

Behind here, the Piazza dell'Erbe sells fruits and vegetables as it has since medieval times – a good place to shop or enjoy a drink at one of the cafés. Leave time to take in one of Palladio's famous villas. The Villa Capra or La Rotonda was built as a pleasure pavilion – its balanced classical lines providing the inspiration for many public buildings in the United States.

➕ B2

Tourist information ✉ Piazza Matteotti 12 ☎ 0444 320 854 🕐 Mon.–Sat. 9–12:30 and 3–6

Museo Civico ✉ Piazza Matteotti ☎ 0444 321 348 🕐 Mon.–Sat. 9–12:30 and 3–6, Sun. 9–12:30 and 2–7, Apr.–Oct.; Tue.–Sat. 9–12:30 and 3–5, Sun. 9–12:30, rest of year 💷 $

Santa Corona ✉ Contra'Santa Corona 🕐 Daily 8:30–noon and 2:30–6

Galleria di Palazzo Montanari ✉ Contra'Santa Corona 25 ☎ 800 578 875 🕐 Daily 10–6 💷 $$

Teatro Olimpico ✉ Piazza Matteotti 1 ☎ 0444 320 854 🕐 Tue.–Sat. 9–12:30 and 2:25–5, Sun. 9–12:30 (also Sun. 2–7, Apr.–Oct.) 💷 $$

Basilica ✉ Corso San Felice Fortunato 219 ☎ 0444 547 246 🕐 Mon.–Sat. 9–noon and 3:30–6:30

La Rotonda, Villa Capra ✉ Via Rotonda 29 ☎ 0444 321 793 🕐 Daily 10–noon and 3–6, Apr.–Oct.; Wed. only 10–noon and 3–6, rest of year 💷 $$

Skiers enjoy great views, snow and brilliant sunshine in the Dolomites

WINTER SPORTS

Italy's mountains offer a vast range of skiing, with good facilities and a relaxed atmosphere. Many northern Italians, with the Alps right on their doorstep, are keen skiers and head for the slopes most weekends during the season. The Valle d'Aosta area in the northwest gives access to Mont Blanc and the splendid Gran Paradiso, but Italy's favorite winter play area is the Dolomites in the northeast.

Where To Go
From Christmas through March, the Dolomites offer some of Europe's best skiing in fantastically beautiful mountain scenery. Although Italians are generally much more relaxed about skiing than the Swiss or French, their resorts are excellently run with well-tended *pistes* (slopes) and plenty of access in the shape of cable cars, chairlifts and drags. The main resorts are Cortina d'Ampezzo, east of Bolzano (see page 76), and Madonna di Campiglio on the fringe of the Dolomiti di Brenta. Both towns are among Europe's most stylish international winter sports centers, with superb facilities and prices to match. If you're looking for good value for your money, head for the Val Gardena or the Val Badia; both are noted for good snow and good value. Wherever you go, you'll find the full range of ski runs, schools, classes and personal guides, plus snowboarding, which is incredibly popular in Italy.

Cross-country skiers are catered to also, with miles of well-groomed tracks; two of the best centers are Ortisei and Dobbiaco in the Val Pusteria. Non-skiers will find lovely Alpine walks through silent woods, sleigh-rides, bars and restaurants where you can enjoy lunch or a drink, and resort activities such as swimming, ice-skating and some of the most tempting window-shopping in Europe. Après ski offerings range from a quiet dinner in a wood-paneled restaurant to throbbing discos and smoky piano bars.

Accommodations
The best way to experience Italian winter sports is to book a package during the *settimane bianche* (white weeks). These generally fall during the quiet weeks of January and February and are superb value. Contact the regional tourist boards for details.

Valle d'Aosta tourist information ✉ Piazza E Chanoux 8 ☎ 0165 236 627

Trentino-Alto Adige tourist information ✉ Corso III Novembre 131, Trento ☎ 0461 895 111

TUSCANY, UMBRIA AND THE MARCHE

"ITALY'S Renaissance heartland is where modern prosperity and historic towns combine with some of Italy's most beautiful landscape."

Ancient olive groves are an integral part of the Tuscan landscape

Tuscany, Umbria and the Marche

TUSCANY, UMBRIA AND THE MARCHE

The political regions of Tuscany (Toscana), Umbria and the Marche cut right across northern central Italy. This is the Renaissance heartland, where the great 14th-century upsurge of culture and the arts truly began. Its timeless landscape epitomizes the visitor's dream of Italy. Prosperous cities, a sound infrastructure, an abundance of history, art, culture and good food and wine make this area one of the most-visited in the whole peninsula. Bear this in mind when planning your trip; art-lovers will do best out of season when museums and galleries are less crowded, while the countryside looks its dazzling best in May and June.

Tuscan Towns and Villages

Florence is Tuscany's major city, the capital of this thriving region, with high-technology industry, a university and a rich agricultural community. It's also among Italy's most popular tourist spots. Visitors seem to outnumber the locals in many parts of the city, but Florence has a life of its own that few visitors experience. Local life is more accessible in the region's lesser cities, many of which deserve a day's visit.

Medieval Siena is the perfect contrast to Florence, while Pisa contains one of Europe's most perfect

Portoferraio on Elba, one of Italy's holiday islands

architectural ensembles. Lucca, Cortona and Volterra have much to offer and are all set in contrasting and beautiful landscape. You may also appreciate San Gimignano, the best known hill town, and Montalcino, Montepulciano and the city of Pienza in the south.

Traveling in Tuscany

To enjoy the beauty of Tuscany at its best, you may want to rent a car for the freedom to explore off-the-beaten-track roads and villages. Tourists are important to the Tuscan economy, and

facilities are excellent, with a wide range of accommodations and restaurants throughout the region. English is widely spoken, particularly in the main tourist centers, and levels of courtesy and service are high. You'll find Tuscans a reserved and rational people, not given to the dramatic outbursts found in other parts of Italy. Accustomed to an annual influx of international visitors, they are professional and reliable, though not over-friendly. In Tuscany, as everywhere in Italy, a few words of Italian will work wonders.

Tuscany, Umbria and the Marche

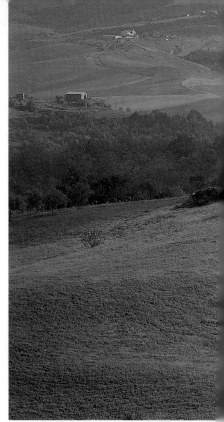

Rural Tuscany

For many people, Tuscany encapsulates Italian landscape. Rolling hills, vineyards, olive groves and glowing wheatfields punctuated by pencil-thin cypress trees are quintessentially Italian, and all can be found in Tuscany. There's more; head north to explore the Alpi Apuane where you'll find dramatic mountains, their flanks glistening white with marble quarries. Or discover the scenic splendors of the Garfagnana, Tuscany's "Little Switzerland." South of Siena lie the rolling wheatlands and bare clay slopes of the *crete,* a strange almost lunar landscape, while along the coast stretch the melancholy plains and low hills of the Maremma. Eastern Tuscany has more wooded hills, punctuated by river valleys planted with corn and tobacco, an area still largely unexplored by visitors.

The Green Heart of Italy

The last 10 years have seen Umbria emerge from Tuscany's shadow as a fascinating and beautiful area well worth

An elderly Tuscan enjoying the tranquility

visiting in its own right. Many visitors prefer its less crowded cities. It's a varied, tranquil and lovely region and is well-deserving of its title, *il cuore verde d'Italia* (the green heart of Italy). Historically poor and undeveloped, the region's infrastructure and economy have seen huge strides during the last 30 years. The growing prosperity blends with the traditional to attract growing numbers of visitors.

Part of Umbria'a charm is its largely untouched countryside, scattered with historic hill towns, each increasingly able to cater to visitors' needs. The landscape includes gentle hills, vineyards, woodland and the dramatic peaks of the Monti Sibillini to the east. The whole region is permeated by a hazy blue light distinctively Umbrian. The light is quite appropriate to this mystical region that's the birthplace of St. Francis and St. Benedict.

A *casa colonica*, traditional Tuscan farmhouse, in the lovely area between Volterra and San Gimignano

Umbrian People and Places

Courteous and friendly, the Umbrese are welcoming and kind. Outside the main towns, few people speak more than a few words of English, but they do have time and patience with visitors. Many of the remote areas are inhabited by people whose way of life has seen little change for decades. But accommodations are easy to find, restaurants are excellent, and roads, towns and villages are still relatively quiet. The main attractions are Perúgia, the capital, Assisi with its Franciscan associations, and Orvieto with its superb cathedral. Leave time for historic Spoleto and Gubbio, and don't neglect the smaller towns of Spello, Todi and hilltop Trevi. Country-lovers will find some of Italy's most unspoiled scenery at its best in the wild uplands above Nórcia.

A Place Apart – the Marche

Daunted by the barrier of the Apennines, relatively few visitors penetrate the Marche, a wonderfully varied region with mountains, jumbled hills and valleys, fertile plains and a long coastline. The northern Marche has most to offer. Incomparable Urbino is one of Italy's most perfect Renaissance towns. San Leo is dramatically situated and San Marino is now popular, while Pesaro, with its two miles of beach, draws sun-seekers from all over Europe.

South lies lovely Ascoli Piceno in the Tronto valley, possibly the most logical route to the Marche from Umbria. Hotels and restaurants, particularly on the coast, are more than adequate, but the road system away from the coast still lags behind those of many other Italian regions.

Tuscany, Umbria and the Marche

FLORENCE

Florence is the capital of Tuscany and one of the world's great artistic shrines. But with a resident population of fewer than 400,000 and more than 5 million annual visitors, Florence (Firenze) can be overwhelming for the wrong reasons: the heat, crowds and traffic mar many people's enjoyment. At first sight the city can seem architecturally dour, with narrow streets and overpowering buildings. Open and relaxed spaces are few and far between. It's the contents of the buildings that tourists come to see, so be prepared to spend much of your time inside and plan ahead. The churches, musems and galleries contain a plethora of treasures within a surprisingly small area.

Background
The Roman city of Florentia re-emerged as an independent city-state, its prosperity based on wool, banking and commerce, in the 12th century.

The Medici Balls
On buildings and statues all over Florence you'll notice the Medici emblem, a cluster of red balls *(palle)* on a black background. This is the coat-of-arms of the city's ruling family, with which they adorned every building owned by, or connected to, them. The number of balls varied throughout the centuries, so you'll notice any number between five and 12. Their original meaning is obscure, but most historians agree they derive from either medicinal pills (family members were once apothecaries) or coins, a reference to the Medici interests in banking and money-lending.

Between the 13th and mid-15th centuries, the Medici were the pre-eminent family; they ruled Florence and later Tuscany until the 18th century. During World War II, Florence was occupied by the Germans; because of its artistic importance, they declared it an open city. Huge damage was caused to the city and its treasures by the floods of 1966 when the Arno river burst its banks.

Plan Ahead
Choose the time of your visit carefully, bearing in mind that the city is less crowded in the winter months, though there is no longer any time of year when Florence is empty. Winter temperatures are better for sightseeing, as few museums and public buildings in Florence are air-conditioned. Above all, don't do too much. See what you want to see, not what you feel you should see. Be prepared to walk a fair amount; many of the major attractions are in the city center.

Venture off the tourist circuit and explore the quieter back streets and hidden piazzas, where you'll find neighborhood stores, artisans' workshops and atmospheric corners. To avoid the worst crowds, arrive at opening time or late in the day at the big museums. Enjoy a relaxing lunch or you'll be wilting by mid-afternoon.

The City
Florence's highlights lie close together on the north bank of the Arno river. You should see the Piazza della Signoria, which contains the Palazzo Vecchio, the Piazza del Duomo with the cathedral and baptistery, and the two great galleries of the Uffizi and the Bargello. Many superb works of art are found in the city's churches; Santa Maria della Carmine for Masaccio, Santa Croce for Giotto, San Marco for

Fra Angelico and San Lorenzo for Michelangelo are top of the list. Be sure to take in the Ponte Vecchio, the elegant stores on and around the Via dei Tornabuoni and the markets.

Friendly Eating

Florence is overflowing with restaurants of every type. Many are specifically aimed at tourists, with prominently displayed fixed-price menus. It's a good idea to check how many Italians are eating in a restaurant. As a general rule, you'll find the cheaper restaurants near the railroad station, chic places in the city center, and small and friendly eating houses on the south side of the Arno river.

Lunch is served any time after 12:30 and dinner from around 7:30. For a simple lunch, try a slice of freshly baked pizza-to-go or a quick snack in a bar or traditional wine shop, a *fiaschetteria*.

The graceful curve of the dome of Florence's cathedral, with the city beyond

The food markets are particularly tempting, and you could put together a

Tuscany, Umbria and the Marche

picnic. Tuscan food is simple and excellent, with plenty of soups, superb pork products, grilled meats dishes and vegetables. Bean dishes are especially popular – other Italians nickname Tuscans *mangiafagioli*, bean-eaters. The most famous wine is Chianti, but look for Brunello di Montalcino and Vino Nobile, superb wines that come from Montepulciano.

Shopping

Florence is home to some of Italy's most serious shops and intriguing boutiques. Leather goods such as shoes, bags and accessories are famous, as are fine china, exquisite bed and table linen, and gold jewelry. Designer-label fans can visit Pucci and Gucci on their home ground, and brilliantly glazed majolica pottery, marbled paper, prints and antiques make tempting souvenirs.

Via Tornabuoni and the surrounding streets house the most elegant stores; less expensive fashion can be found around Piazza della Repubblica and via Calzaiuoli, while jewelers line the Ponte Vecchio. There are many factory leather outlets near Santa Croce. The main street market is the huge Mercato San Lorenzo, which has the added bonus of its proximity to the Mercato Centrale, Florence's central food market. Most stores will ship direct to the United States.

Entertainment

Many tourists are content to round off the day with a leisurely dinner and evening stroll, but Florence also offers a good range of theaters, concerts, opera, ballet, cinemas, clubs and discos. Summer visitors can catch one of the two big cultural festivals, the *Estate Fiesolana* or the *Maggio Musicale Fiorentino*. Concerts, opera and ballet are often performed outdoors in a historic setting. Look out for the free monthly tourist magazine *Chiavi d'Oro Toscana* (Concierge Tourist Information); it has full listings and lots of other helpful information.

CLIMATE – Average highs and lows

JAN.	FEB.	MAR.	APR.	MAY	JUN.	JUL.	AUG.	SEP.	OCT.	NOV.	DEC.
4°C	8°C	13°C	18°C	23°C	26°C	28°C	27°C	23°C	17°C	10°C	6°C
39°F	46°F	55°F	64°F	73°F	79°F	82°F	81°F	73°F	63°F	50°F	43°F
0°C	2°C	5°C	9°C	13°C	17°C	20°C	19°C	16°C	11°C	5°C	2°C
32°F	36°F	41°F	48°F	55°F	63°F	68°F	66°F	61°F	52°F	41°F	36°F

FLORENCE SIGHTS

Key to symbols

✚ map coordinates refer to the Florence map on page 89; sights below are highlighted in yellow on the map

✉ address or location ☎ telephone number
🕐 opening times 🍴 restaurant on site or nearby
🚌 nearest bus or tram route
🎟 admission charge: $$$ more than L5,000, $$ L3,000 to L5,000, $ less than L3,000 ℹ information

CAPPELLA BRANCACCI

Comprehensively and sensitively restored in the 1980s, the Cappella Branacci frescoes represent a pivotal point in art development. Commissioned in 1424 by Felice Brancacci, a wealthy merchant, the cycle illustrates the life of St. Peter. It was painted by Masolino, his dazzling pupil Masaccio, and Filippino Lippi, who completed the work 60 years later. Masaccio's radiant work, with its superb handling of light and space, drama and realism, was an inspiration for many other Renaissance artists. Highlights are the *Tribute Money*, with its weighty figures, the heart-rending *Expulsion from Paradise* and *St. Peter Healing the Sick*.

✚ A1 ✉ Santa Maria del Carmine, Piazza del Carmine (enter through cloisters) ☎ 055 238 2195 🕐 Mon. and Wed.–Sat. 10–5, Sun. 1–5 🚌 B 🎟 $$

CAPPELLE MEDICEE

Set behind San Lorenzo is Brunelleschi's serene 1419 structure that served as the Medici parish church. The Cappelle Medicee (Medici Chapels) were built as the mausoleum for Florence's most powerful family. Family members were interred in the crypt, the Sagrestia Nuova, (New Sacristy) and Buontalenti's grandiose domed *Chapel of the Princes*. The Sagrestia Nuova was built by Michelangelo between 1520 and 1534 and contains some of his most powerful sculpture. Reclining figures representing *Night*, *Day*, *Dawn* and *Dusk* decorate the tombs of Lorenzo the Magnificent and his son Giuliano. The fluid lines of the artwork are a perfect foil for the measured austerity of the architecture. The chapel

The baptistery rises serenely over the city's crowds

also contains the artist's lovely *Madonna and Child*, as well as charcoal drawings and graffitti thought to be by the master.

✚ C4 ✉ Piazza Madonna degli Aldobrandini ☎ 055 238 8602 🕐 Daily 8:30–1:50 (except alternating Sun. and Mon., when it's closed) 🚌 In pedestrian zone 🎟 $$$

DUOMO, BATTISTERO AND CAMPANILE DI GIOTTO

The richly marbled Gothic Duomo (Cathedral) of Santa Maria del Fiore, the first domed structure erected in Europe since Roman times, was built between 1296 and 1436 on the site of a seventh-century church. Pass through the cathedral's austere interior, with its fine Uccello fresco, to climb the 463 steps to the top of Brunelleschi's dome, its herringbone brickwork copied from the Pantheon in Rome. The chief draw of the marble Battistero (Baptistery), built between the fifth and seventh centuries and marble-covered in the 11th and 13th centuries, is the three sets of bronze doors with their Old Testament scenes. Pisano cast the south pair in 1326, and they inspired Ghiberti to design those at the north and east in the 1400s; the originals are in the Museo dell'Opera del Duomo. The graceful campanile was designed by

Giotto and built by Pisano and Talenti between 1334 and 1359. Its pink, green and white marble walls are decorated with copies of the original superb relief sculptures, now also in the Museo dell'Opera.

➕ C3 ✉ Piazza San Giovanni ☎ 055 271 071 🕐 Mon.–Sat. 1:30–6:30, Sun. 9–1 🚌 1, 6, 7, 11, 14 💷 $$

GALLERIA DEGLI UFFIZI

Arguably the world's greatest collection of Renaissance paintings, the Galleria degli Uffizi (Office Gallery) is an elegant arcaded building designed by Vasari as administrative offices. Here, in chronological order, are pictures representative of the greatest names in art from the 13th through 18th centuries. You can trace the technical development of painting through masterpieces of perspective such as Uccello's *Battle of San Romano* (1456), while Renaissance neo-Platonic philosophy is expressed in the iconography underlying Botticelli's beautiful *Birth of Venus* and *Primavera*. Don't miss Piero della Francesca's austere double portrait of Federigo di Montefeltro and his wife, Battista Sforza, Leonardo da Vinci's sublime *Adoration of the Magi* and Titian's *Venus of Urbino*. It is recommended to come early or late to avoid the lines; it is possible to book your visit in advance.

➕ C2 ✉ Loggiato degli Uffizi 6 ☎ 055 238 8651 🕐 Tue.–Sat. 8:30–6; Sun. 8:30–1 🚌 In pedestrian zone 💷 $$$

GALLERIA DELL'ACCADEMIA

Founded as an art school in 1784, the Academy Gallery today houses the world's most important collection of Michelangelo sculptures. The main attraction is his *David*, possibly the most famous in the history of sculpture. Other sculptures by the artist include the four *Prisoners*, the figures struggling to escape the stone. The gallery also contains paintings and sculptures by other Renaissance artists.

➕ D4 ✉ Via Riccasoli 60 ☎ 055 238 8609 🕐 Tue.–Sat. 9–6:30, Sun. 9–1 🚌 San Marco 💷 $$$

GIARDINO DI BOBOLI

Florence's green lung is a revelation of geometric garden design. First laid out for the Medici in 1550 and open to the public since 1766, the Giardino di Boboli (Boboli Gardens) are truly Renaissance in spirit, an amalgam of nature and artifice. Fountains, dusty grass, crumbling statues, aromatic bosky shrubs, trees and murky pools combine to create a garden very different from the Anglo-Saxon ideal. Highlights include the offbeat statue of Bacchus astride a tortoise, and the 1785 *Limonaia*, where citrus trees were once stored to protect them from winter frosts.

➕ C1 ✉ Piazza Pitti ☎ 055 236 8616 🕐 Tue.–Sun. 9–7:30, Apr.–Oct.; 9–6:30, Mar.; 9–4:30, rest of year 🍴 Refreshment kiosk in gardens 🚌 B, C, 11, 36 💷 $

MUSEO NAZIONALE DEL BARGELLO

The Bargello was built in 1255 as the first seat of Florence's government, and it once housed the law courts. In 1574 it passed to the police department and served as a prison until 1859. Renovated and restored, it opened as a museum in 1865. Today it houses Italy's finest collection of Renaissance sculpture. Airy rooms surround a spacious courtyard and you'll find works by Michelangelo, Cellini and the flamboyant Giambologna. The vaulted first-floor hall, once the main courtroom, contains the museum's masterpieces. Here are Donatello's jaunty bronze *David*, the first free-standing nude to be modeled since Roman times, his fine *St. George*, and the competition baptistery door reliefs by Ghiberti and Brunelleschi. Upstairs there are bright enameled terracottas by the della Robbia family.

➕ D2 ✉ Via del Proconsolo 4 ☎ 055 238 86 06 🕐 Daily 8:30–1:50 🍴 Dino, see page 204 🚌 19 💷 $$

PALAZZO MEDICI–RICCARDI

Many visitors bypass the Palazzo Medici, designed by Michelangelo in 1444. The solid exterior with its heavy rusticated stonework is by the graceful courtyard

It's good luck to drop a coin in the snout of Il Porcellino, the bronze boar in Mercato Nuovo

WALK: THE HEART OF FLORENCE

Refer to route marked on city map on page 89.

This walk (about 2 hours long) takes you through the heart of historic Florence and is useful for getting your bearings and choosing sights.

Start in the Piazza della Signoria

This square is the historic center of Florentine power, as is evident from the looming Palazzo Vecchio, the elegant Logge dei Lanzi and the numerous sculptures.

Head toward the Arno river through the Piazzale degli Uffizi, with the Galleria degli Uffizi on your left. Turn right onto the Lungarno Archibuiser to the Ponte Vecchio, Florence's oldest bridge.

Cross the bridge and walk along the Via de' Guicciardini to the monumental Palazzo Pitti, housing another of Florence's major art collections. Cross the Piazza dei Pitti to the Piazza San Felice, then cut right down the Via Mazzetta to Piazza Santo Spirito, with its lively atmosphere and great Brunelleschi church. Walk down Via de Presto di San Martino to the church's right and across Piazza Frescobaldi to re-cross the river on the beautiful Ponte Santa Trinita. Continue along Via de' Tornabuoni, where you'll find stores such as Versace and Gucci. Then take a right along Via Porta Rossa to the Mercato Nuova, with its famous brass boar, the Porcellino. This is a great place for souvenir shopping.

A left turn here onto Via Calimala leads through the grandiose 19th-century Piazza della Repubblica, scattered with tempting pavement cafés, to Via Roma. This street opens up onto the Piazza di San Giovanni, where you turn right to visit the religious heart of the city, the Piazza del Duomo, with the cathedral, baptistery and campanile.

An option for keen walkers is a detour north from the cathedral to San Lorenzo, the great Medici church, and up Via dell' Ariento to Florence's wonderful Mercato Centrale, the city's major produce market, housed in a superb 19th-century cast-iron structure. Return to the cathedral.

For a shorter route from the cathedral, turn left onto the Via dei Calzaiuoli. A few blocks down on the right is the church of Orsanmichele, Florence's medieval guild church, with its Renaissance sculptures and Bernardo Daddi fresco. Via dei Calzaiuolo leads back to the Piazza della Signoria.

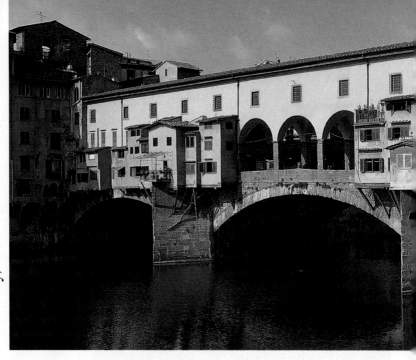

with its *sgrafitto* decoration. Many other Florentine palazzi, such as the Strozzi and Pitti were influenced by this structure. The interior contains the *Cappella dei Magi*, a tiny chapel totally covered with one of the city's most charming fresco cycles. Executed by Gozzoli from 1459 to 1463, it shows the Magi, gorgeously dressed in contemporary high fashion, walking through an idealized Tuscan landscape rich with flowers and birds.

✚ C4 ⊠ Via Cavour 1 ☎ 055 276 0340 Ⓒ Mon. and Tue. 9–1 and 3–6, Sun. 9–1 🚌 1, 6, 7 💰 $$

PALAZZO PITTI

Built for the Pittis, this opulent palace was the Medici residence from 1550 until their fall in 1743, when they bequeathed their collections to the city. It now houses four museums, the most important being the Galleria Palatina and the Museo degli Argenti. The former is primarily a picture gallery, with haphazardly hung masterpieces as important as those in the Uffizi (see page 92); here you'll find Raphael's sweet-featured *Madonna of the Chair*, a sexy Mary Magdalene by Titian, and some fine portraits. The *objets d'art* in the Museo degli Argenti mostly represent a triumph of expensive bad taste, though

the Roman glass and cameo collection are worth tracking down. The Pitti also houses the Appartamenti Monumentali (State Rooms), the Galleria del Costume (Costume Museum) and the Galleria d'Arte Moderna (Modern Art Gallery).

✚ B1 ⊠ Piazza Pitti ☎ Galleria Palatina 055 238 8611; Museo degli Argenti 055 238 8709 Ⓒ Galleria Palatina: daily 8:30–6:45; Museo degli Argenti: 8:30–2 🚌 B, C, 11, 36, 37 💰 $$$

PIAZZA DELLA SIGNORIA

The logical place to begin or end your sightseeing, the Piazza della Signoria was the physical center of Medici and Florentine power. The council met in the Palazzo Vecchio, which overlooks the square where executions took place, riotous crowds assembled and religious fanatics preached. The square itself and the graceful Loggia dei Lanzi display an impressive range of sculptures. The mounted horseman, a statue by Giambologna dated 1595, is Duke Cosimo I, the Medici who brought all Tuscany under military rule. Don't miss Cellini's sinuous *Perseus*, who holds aloft Medusa's head.

✚ C2 ⊠ Piazza della Signoria 🍴 Bars and restaurants nearby 🚶 In pedestrian zone

Jewelers' shops line the Ponte Vecchio, one of the world's most famous bridges

PONTE VECCHIO

Perhaps not the most beautiful Florentine bridge, but certainly the most photographed and crowded, the Ponte Vecchio (Old Bridge) was built in 1345 to replace an earlier one. It is lined with shops, exclusively goldsmiths and jewelers since 1593. Above these runs a corridor used by the Medici to travel from the Pitti to the Uffizi. The only bridge not destroyed by the Germans in World War II, it also survived the floods in 1966.

✚ C1 ✉ Ponte Vecchio 🍴 La Sangrestia, see page 204 🚌 In pedestrian zone

SAN MARCO

Rebuilt in 1437 and decorated by Fra Angelico, the convent of San Marco is one of Florence's loveliest treasures. It's a peaceful religious house where each of the 44 cells is adorned with a tiny fresco to aid prayer. Designed by Michelozzo in 1437, it was funded by Cosimo il Vecchio, the first truly prominent Medici, who used to spend time in the monastery. The pilgrim's hall contains many paintings by Angelico and his school, and more are found in the cloisters and on the stairs, notably the radiant *Annunciation*. The great Dominican reformer Savanarola was prior here at the end of the 15th century.

✚ D4 ✉ Piazza San Marco ☎ 055 238 8608 🕐 Daily 8:30–2; closed alternate Sun. and Mon. 🚌 1, 6, 7, 10, 11, 17, 20, 25, 31, 32, 33 💷 $$

SANTA CROCE

This huge plain Franciscan preaching church, terribly damaged by the 1966 floods, was built in 1294, though the colorful marble facade dates from 1863 when it was funded by a Florence-loving Englishman, Sir Francis Sloane. The interior contains superb early Gaddi frescoes that tell the story of the Santa Croce (Holy Cross). Seek out the Bardi and Peruzzi chapels with their beautiful frescoes by Giotto. Michelangelo is buried here, as are Machiavelli, Galileo Galilei and the composer Rossini. In the serene cloisters stands the Cappella dei Pazzi (Pazzi Chapel), designed by Brunelleschi in the 1430s and among the most beautiful of Renaissance buildings.

✚ E1 ✉ Piazza Santa Croce ☎ 055 244 619 🕐 Daily 8–12:30 and 3–6:30 🍴 Enoteca Pinchiorri, see page 204 🚌 23, 13, B 💷 $

Tuscany, Umbria and the Marche

THE FLOOD OF 1966

As you walk the streets of Florence, keep an eye open above head height for the small stone plaques on many buildings; these plaques mark the height to which the floodwaters of the Arno river rose on the night of November 4, 1966. It was an event that proved a catastrophe for the city and its art.

October 1966 was a very wet month throughout Italy, while the first two days of November saw 18 inches of rain fall in the Florence area. Water pressure rose dangerously in an upstream reservoir, and the authorities, fearing its dam might break, opened the sluices. They failed to warn anyone in the city of Florence; only the jewelers whose shops lined the Ponte Vecchio were alerted by their own night watchman who noticed that the bridge was shaking as the waters rose. As the traders cleared their stock, they asked watching police if the alarm had been officially raised, only to be told that no orders had been received. Shortly after, the banks of the Arno could no longer contain the unprecedented tons of water. They broke, releasing a flash flood of more than 500,000 tons of water and mud that poured with startling speed through the city.

Thirty-five Florentine citizens were drowned in the first onrush, many trapped in the underpass of Santa Maria Novella railroad station. The muddy floodwaters mixed with heating oil stored in cellars and basements, and it was this ghastly cocktail that did the damage.

Damage to homes, shops and businesses was huge, with many families losing all their possessions. The world's attention, though, was focused on the damage to works of art, particularly in the Santa Croce area, one of the lowest parts of Florence. More than 3,000 paintings were damaged, some irretrievably.

Antiquities were destroyed, and thousands of priceless books and manuscripts lost. Within days, voluntary workers, many of them art students, were arriving to begin the rescue operation.

Above: Cars re-emerging in the city center as water levels start to fall
Right: The devastated shops on the Ponte Vecchio

They worked nonstop in appalling conditions heaving art works to safety and starting the drying-out process on books and manuscripts.

Money poured in from all over the world, and by the following summer Florence was itself again – at least superficially. Behind the scenes, however, the task of art restoration was immense, and more than 35 years later work still continues on paintings, sculpture, books and manuscripts. One of the biggest spin-offs was the tremendous strides made in the development of restoration techniques developed to cope with the aftermath of the flood. Frescoes had to be stabilized, oil paintings painstakingly reassembled from fragments, and priceless books dried and cleaned. Later projects throughout Italy, such as the restoration of such major works as Michelangelo's fresoes in the Sistine Chapel in Rome and Piero della Francesca's frescoes in Arezzo, owe much to the techniques developed in the aftermath of the flood. International co-operation between restorers all over the world forged ahead and galleries and museums worldwide have profited by the new approach to restoration problems.

REGIONAL SIGHTS

Key to symbols

➕ map coordinates refer to the region map on page 84; sights below are highlighted in yellow on the map
✉ address or location ☎ telephone number
🕐 opening times 🍴 restaurant on site or nearby
⛴ ferry 💶 admission charge: $$$ more than L5,000, $$ L3,000 to L5,000, $ less than L3,000 ℹ information

AREZZO

Prosperous Arezzo, its modern wealth based on its position as the world's largest gold manufacturing center, spreads down a hill above the Arno valley in eastern Tuscany. A major Etruscan city, it thrived under the Romans and was a prosperous medieval republic until 1384, when it was annexed by Florence. Today, its chief glory is the superb fresco cycle, *The Legend of the True Cross*, by the enigmatic Renaissance artist Piero della Francesca, in the church of San Francesco. Newly emerged from a lengthy restoration, these luminous paintings, executed between 1452 and 1466, tell the story of the cross used to crucify Christ.

Near the San Francesco, you'll find the Pieve di Santa Maria, an earlier Romanesque church with an exuberant facade and Pietro Lorenzetti's glowing high altar polyptych showing the *Madonna and Child with Saints*. The church is backed by the Piazza Grande, a sloping medieval square with a loggia on its north side, scene of Arezzo's major festival, the *Giostra del Saraceno*, a splendid jousting display preceded by costumed processions.

The Duomo (Cathedral) stands at Arezzo's highest point; this harmonious building was constructed over more than four centuries, its facade finally finished in the 20th century. Inside, there are glowing stained-glass windows, Guido Tarlati's lovely tomb said to have been designed by Giotto, and the tiny fresco *Magdalene*, another work by Piero della Francesca.

Elsewhere, Arezzo's shops offer plenty of temptations; the town is a noted antiques center, with many classy showrooms and a monthly antiques fair, the *Fiera Antiquaria*.

The distinctive medieval towers of San Gimignano

➕ C3
Tourist information ✉ Piazza della Stazione ☎ 0575 377 678 🕐 Mon.–Sat. 9–1 and 3–7, Sun. 9–1, Apr.–Sep.; Mon.–Sat. 9–1 and 3–6, first Sun. of month 9–1, rest of year
San Francesco ✉ Via Cavour 🕐 Daily 8:30–noon and 2–6:30; fresco cycle by guided tour only (sometimes in English, check for details). Tickets available in advance from office at San Francesco 💶 $$
Pieve di Santa Maria ✉ Corso Italia 🕐 Daily 8–1 and 3–6:30
Duomo ✉ Piazza del Duomo 🕐 Daily 8:30–12:30 and 3–6:30 ℹ *Giostra del Saraceno* is held on the first Sun. in Sep. Smaller-scale versions are staged for tourists throughout the summer. For details contact the tourist office

ASCOLI PICENO

One of the Marche's hidden gems, Ascoli Piceno stands in a steep hollow 25 kilometers (15 miles) from the Adriatic coast. Today's street-plan still follows that of the Roman colony established here after the defeat of the Picini, an early tribe. The heart of the town is the lovely Piazza del Popolo, a serene ensemble of medieval and Renaissance buildings, all glowing with the warm travertine stone of which Ascoli is constructed.

On its north side stands the lovely Gothic San Francesco church, with its graceful five-arched loggia and slender bell-towers. Other delights include the Duomo (Cathedral) with its monumental square, an art gallery and archeological museum, and a tangle of beguiling and picturesque streets at the top of the Via del Trivio above the Tronto river.

➕ E2
Tourist information ✉ Piazza del Popolo 1 ☎ 0736 253 045 🕐 Mon.–Fri. 8:30–1 and 3–7, Sat. 8:30–12:30 and 3–7, Sun. 9–1
San Francesco ✉ Piazza del Popolo 🕐 Daily 8–12:30 and 3–7
Duomo ✉ Piazza Arringo 🕐 Daily 8–12:30 and 3–7
Pinacoteca Civica ✉ Piazza Arringo 🕐 Mon.–Fri. 9–1 and 3–7:30, Sat. 9–1, Sun. 4:30–7:30, Jun.–Sep.; Mon.–Sat. 9–1, Sun. 9–12:30, rest of year 💶 $
Museo Archeologico ✉ Piazza Arringo 🕐 Tue.–Fri. and Sun. 9:30–1:30, Sat. 3:30–5:30 💶 $ ℹ *Quintana* is held on the first Sun. in Aug.; medieval-costume parades and jousting spectacular

Medieval civil engineering at its best – the Basilica di San Francesco in Assisi

ASSISI

Assisi is inextricably linked with St. Francis (1182–1226), the founder of the Franciscan order. The town is his shrine and is visited by pilgrims from all over the world. In late 1997, Assisi was terribly damaged by a series of earthquakes. The wonderful Basilica di San Francesco bore the brunt, with some of its treasures lost forever. The lower church, built around 1228, has reopened, while the upper church, once covered with the 28 panels of Giotto's *Life of St. Francis*, remains closed. The most powerful of the lower church frescoes are Simone Martini's *Life of St. Martin* and Lorenzetti's heart-rending *Deposition* and *Crucifixion*, fitting companions to the tomb of St. Francis.

At the opposite end of town you'll find Santa Chiara, the burial place of St. Clare, the companion of St. Francis and the founder of the Poor Clares, the Franciscan nuns. The huge square outside this harmonious pink-and-white striped Gothic building gives lovely views over the valley. Above here stands the Duomo (Cathedral), built from 1140 to 1253. The beautiful Romanesque facade fronts a simple building where you can see the font used to baptize St. Francis and St. Clare.

Back toward the basilica is the Piazza del Comune, a lovely medieval square on the probable site of Assisi's Roman forum. The focal point is the superb first-century Tempio di Minerva, a perfectly preserved Roman temple facade with six Corinthian columns and a graceful pediment, while the Pinacoteca Comunale (Art Gallery) occupies the old Palazzo Comunale.

The evocative San Damiano is a country church and convent with strong Franciscan associations; it was here the saint composed the *Canticle to the Sun*. Equally lovely is the Eremo delle Carceri, a monastery standing in oak woods and a place of retreat for St. Francis. You can see his oratory, as well as a venerable oak tree, said to be the one where the birds gathered to hear him preach.

✚ D2

Tourist information ✉ Piazza del Comune 9 ☎ 075 812 450 🕐 Mon.–Sat. 8:30–1 and 3:30–6:30, Sun. 9–1
Basilica di San Francesco ✉ Piazza Inferiore di San Francesco 🕐 Daily 7–6
Basilica di Santa Chiara ✉ Piazza Santa Chiara 🕐 Daily 7–noon and 2–dusk
Duomo ✉ Piazza San Rufino 🕐 Daily 7–noon and 2:30–dusk
Pinacoteca Comunale ✉ Piazza del Comune 🕐 Daily 10–1 and 3–7, Mar.–Sep.; 10–1 and 2–5, rest of year 🎫 $$
San Damiano 🕐 Daily 10–6
Eremo delle Carceri 🕐 Daily dawn–dusk

CHIANTI

Between Florence and Siena lies Chianti, an area of wooded hills and vineyards, dotted with intriguing villages and threaded by winding backroads. Its most famous product is wine, and its trademark Gallo Nero (Black Cockerel) is known all over the world.

Chianti's good climate and fascinating surroundings have been attracting northern Europeans since the 1960s, and international visitors have bought and converted many of the lovely old houses, while once unspoiled hill towns such as Radda in Chianti and neighboring Gaiole are packed with visitors from around the world. The best way to enjoy this still-lovely region is to leave the main roads. Explore the woods and smaller villages and sample the wines at any of several hundred vineyards as you go. Wine-lovers will enjoy Greve in Chianti; in September it's the scene of the area's biggest wine fair. Greve has a lively Saturday market in its main piazza, where you'll also find a statue of Giovanni da Verazzano, the discoverer of New York Harbor. He was born in the neighboring village of the same name.

Greve in Chianti ✚ C3
Tourist information ✉ Via Verrazzano ☎ 055 854 6287 ◉ Mon.–Sat. 10–1 and 2–4 ❚ Greve Wine Fair is held in Sep., further details from the tourist office

GÚBBIO

Few tourists venture as far as Gúbbio, tucked beneath rolling mountains near Umbria's eastern border. This charming town, once the most important *comune* between Rome and Ravenna, is rich in quaint streets, superb old palaces, churches and paintings. Start a tour at the bottom of the old town, where you'll find the church of San Francesco, with an engaging fresco (1410) by Ottaviano Nelli, and the 14th-century Loggia dei Tiratori, Italy's best-preserved example of a weaver's shed where wool was spread to dry away from direct sunlight.

Up the hill stands the solid bulk of the 14th-century Palazzo dei Consoli,

Gúbbio's civic masterpiece, fronted by the sweeping Piazza Grande. It now houses the town's museum and art gallery. Nearby stands the cathedral and the Palazzo Ducale, built by Federigo di Montefeltro from neighboring Urbino (see page 115) in 1470. From here, you can climb Monte Ingino behind the town to visit the Basilica di Sant' Ubaldo, the town's patron saint. The gigantic wooden *ceri* (candles), used in Gubbio's famous and exuberant festival, the *Corsa dei Ceri*, are stored here.
✚ D2
Tourist information ✉ Piazza Odersi 3–5 ☎ 075 922 0790 ◉ Mon.–Sat. 8:30–1:30 and 3–6, Sun. 9:30–12:30
Museo Civico ✉ Pazza Grande ☎ 075 927 42 98 ◉ Tue.–Sun. 10–1 and 3–5 🖐 $ ❚ *Corsa dei Ceri* is held May 15

LAGO TRASIMENO

Italy's fourth largest lake, a shallow expanse of warm water fringed with beaches and laid-back little towns, Lago Trasimeno (Lake Trasimeno) makes an excellent stopping point for a couple of days of relaxation. Castiglione del Lago on the western shore has a fine fortified 16th-century castle jutting into the lake and nice swimming beaches. Passignano, on the opposite shore, is a friendly town with a lakeside promenade and good bars and restaurants. In the hills behind Passignano, you'll find Castel Rigone, a pretty village with fantastic views. Tuoro is another hill village above the lake; between here and Passignano is the site of Hannibal's great defeat of the Romans in 217 BC. Village names like Sanguineto (Place of Blood) and Ossaia (Place of Bones) are permanent reminders of the great Carthaginian general.
✚ C2
Castiglione del Lago tourist information ✉ Piazza Mazzini ☎ 075 965 2484 ◉ Mon.–Sat. 8:30–1:30 and 3–7:30, Sun. 8–1, Jun.–Sep.; Mon.–Fri. 8:30–1:30 and 3–7, Sat. 8–1:30, rest of year
Passignano tourist information ✉ Via Roma 36 ☎ 075 827 635 ◉ Mon.–Sat. 9–noon and 4–7, Jun.–Sep.; Mon.–Fri. 9–noon and 3–6, Sat. 9–noon, rest of year 🚢 Boats run daily to Isola Maggiore, Trasimeno's largest island, from Passignano. Contact SPNT (☎ 075 827 157) for further information

Tuscany, Umbria and the Marche

Vines bearing Sagrantino grapes clothe the slopes below pretty Montefalco

DRIVE: EASTERN UMBRIA TO THE VALE OF SPOLETO

Duration: 3½ to 4 hours

This drive starts in remote Gúbbio (see page 101), a stone-built, fortress-like town in the hills of northeast Umbria.

From Gúbbio, take the SS298 southwest through the hills toward Perúgia.
This scenic road takes you past tiny villages and farms to join the *superstrada* SS3bis in the lovely upper valley of the Tiber river. It's only a short way into its journey to Rome and the sea at Ostia.

Turn left onto the SS3bis and continue for 10 kilometers (6 miles) before joining the SS147 south marked Assisi, Foligno and Spoleto. At the Assisi exit, follow the signs up the hill toward the town.
The huge domed church in the lower modern part of Assisi is Santa Maria degli Angeli, first built in 1569, though the present building dates from 1832. The basilica is constructed around the *Porzuincola*, the tiny chapel where St. Francis lived in the earliest days of the Franciscan movement, while beneath the main altar is the site of his death. In the garden outside, you can see thornless rose bushes, said to be the descendants of those into which the saint threw himself while grappling with temptation; as he fell they lost their spines, while their leaves became stained with drops of blood.

Tuscany, Umbria and the Marche

window in the 18th century; look for the quirky gargoyles over the doorway.

From Bevagna, continue 6.5 kilometers (about 5 miles) southeast to Montefalco. Montefalco is a superbly located town packed with artistic delights and noted for its fine wines. Made with the Sagrantino grape, found nowhere else in Europe, the pick of these full-flavored reds is perhaps Sagrantino Passito, a stunning sweet red dessert wine. Montefalco's chief attraction is the colorful and charming fresco by Benozzo Gozzoli in the church of San Francesco, now a museum. Painted in 1452, the cycle depicts scenes from the life of St. Francis with a wealth of charming detail. Other treasures here include Perugino's 1503 *Nativity*, complete with a fine view of Lake Trasimeno (see page 101) in the background. The nearby church of San Agostino contains mummies of local holy people, while the church of Santa Chiara has the preserved body of St. Chiara of Montefalco.

From Montefalco, head east across the plain through San Luca to Trevi (see page 115). Pick up the SS3, which will take you south to Spoleto (see page 114).

Montefalco
San Francesco ⊙ Tue.–Sat. 10–1 and 4–7, Jun.–Aug.; Tue.–Sat. 10–1 and 2–5, rest of year 🖐 $$

Do not drive into Assisi unless you have hotel reservations; the streets are very narrow and steep, and there is no municipal parking. Leave your car in one of the pay parking lots outside and walk into Assisi (see page 100). From Assisi you can take the unclassified, part-dirt road over Monte Subásio to Spello (see page 111), and then join the SS75 to Foligno.

This beautiful route leads through upland meadows, carpeted in spring and early summer with spreads of wild narcissi, gentians, cistus and myriad orchids. The road gives wide views over the plain. It's the perfect spot for a picnic. Above the treeline, you can see for miles and wander on the grassy slopes and little tracks on the mountain's heights.

Alternatively, head straight for Foligno on the SS75. Turn right here across the plain and continue for 7.5 kilometers (about 5 miles) to Bevagna.

The main square of this sleepy and undiscovered town contains two of Umbria's finest Romanesque churches, San Silvestro and San Michele. They were both built at the end of the 12th century. The facade of San Silvestro, now deconsecrated, was constructed using old fragments of Roman buildings; its shadowy interior has a marvelous sunken crypt. Opposite, San Michele's facade was embellished with a rose

An old Umbrian farmhouse set in vineyards

The riotously embellished facade of the church of San Michele in Foro, Lucca

LUCCA

Set in northern Tuscany at the foot of the Alpi Apuane, Lucca, with its tree-lined encircling walls, magnificent churches and solid provincial prosperity, is instantly appealing. There are three outstanding churches, all built and decorated in the ornate 13th-century style known as Pisan Romanesque.

San Michele in Foro dominates the main piazza. Its exuberant facade is a riot of intricate columns, grotesques and carvings. Nearby, the Duomo (Cathedral) is fronted by a superb portal carved by Pisano. The interior houses the Tempietto, a shrine containing the venerated icon known as the Volto Santo (Holy Face), and the wondrous Renaissance tomb of Ilario del Carretto by Jacopo della Quercia. North is San Frediano, its facade glittering with 13th-century mosaics, its interior boasting a 12th-century font. Near here, just off Via Fillungo, Lucca's main shopping street, you'll find the Piazza Anfiteatro, a glorious oval built around the original Roman amphitheater. Lucca's best museum is the Museo Nazionale Guinigi, a wide-ranging collection of paintings, sculpture and furniture.

Be sure to leave time to walk the 16th-century walls and look for the Torre Guinigi, a 15th-century tower with a holm oak growing from the top.

Near Lucca there's a clutch of elegant country villas, the summer homes of the wealthy citizens of the 15th through 18th centuries. Many have superb gardens that are open to the public.

🚺 B3

Tourist information ✉ Piazzale Verdi, Porta S Donato Vecchia ☎ 0583 419 689 🕐 Daily 9–7
🚹 An English-language audio guide to Lucca is available from the tourist office

San Michele in Foro ✉ Piazza San Michele
🕐 Daily 7:30–12:30 and 3–6

Duomo di San Martino ✉ Piazza San Martino
🕐 Daily 7–7, May–Sep.; 7–5, rest of year

San Frediano ✉ Piazza San Frediano 🕐 Mon.–Sat. 7:30–noon and 3–8, Sun., 9–1 and 3–6

Museo Nazionale Guinigi ✉ Via della Quarquonia
☎ 0583 496 033 🕐 Tue.–Sat. 9–7, Sun. 9–2 🎫 $$

Casa Natale di Puccini ✉ Corte San Lorenzo 9
☎ 0583 584 028 🕐 Tue.–Sun. 10–6, Jul.–Aug.;
Tue.–Sun. 10–1 and 3–6, Mar.–Jun. and Oct.–Dec.;
Mon.–Fri. 10–1, Sat.–Sun. 10–1 and 3–6, rest of year
🎫 $

Torre Guinigi ✉ Palazzo Guinigi, Via Sant'Andrea
☎ 0583 48 524 🕐 Daily 9–7:30, Mar.–Sep.; 10–6,
Oct.; 10–4:30, rest of year 🎫 $

Villa Reale ✉ Marlia ☎ 0583 30 108 🕐 Tue.–Sun. tours at 10, 11, 3, 4, 5, Mar.–Nov. 🎫 $$$

Villa Grabau ✉ San Pancrazio ☎ 0583 406 098
🕐 Tue.–Sun. 10–1 and 3–7, Easter–Oct. 🎫 $$$

MONTALCINO

Hilltop Montalcino, encircled by walls and dominated by its *rocca* (fortress), was independent until 1260 when it became part of Siena. It heroically held out until 1555 as the last bastion of Sienese independence against the Florentines. Its role is still commemorated during Siena's Palio (see page 117). Centuries of stagnation followed, until the 1960s saw the revival of its famous wine, Brunello di Montalcino, and the growth of tourism.

First explore the 14th-century fortress, and be sure to climb the walls for superb views over the idyllic southern Tuscan landscape. The fortress also contains the *enoteca*, a wine-cellar where you can sample a range of the superlative red wines. Montalcino's Museo Civico houses high-quality Sienese paintings and sculpture; among the finest is Sano di Pietro's *Madonna dell'Umiltà*, a rare portrayal of a kneeling Mary, the Blessed Mother.

For a real architectural treat, take the road south to the Abbazia di Sant'Antimo, a 12th-century Benedictine abbey that stands alone amid olives and cypresses on the Francigena, one of Europe's ancient pilgrim routes. This glorious Romanesque building is noted for the carving on its pillars (don't miss Daniel in the lion's den) and its luminous interior. Much of the stone is alabaster, which helps suffuse the whole church with light.

✚ C2

Tourist information ✉ Costa del Municipio 8 ☎ 0577 849 331 🕐 Tue.–Sun. 10–1 and 3:30–7, May–Sep.; Tue.–Sun. 10–1 and 3–5, rest of year 🎪 *Torneo della Apertura della Caccia* (second Sun. in Aug.) and *Sagra del Tordo* (last Sun. in Oct.) feature costumed processions, archery tournaments and street banquets

Rocca ✉ Piazzale Fortezza 🕐 Daily 9–1 and 2:30–8, mid-Jul. to mid-Sep.; Tue.–Sun. 9–1 and 2:30–8, May to mid-Jul.; Tue.–Sun. 9–1 and 2–6, rest of year 💷 $

Abbazia di Sant'Antimo ✉ Castelnuovo dell'Abate 🕐 Daily 10:30–12:30 and 3–6, Apr.–Sep.; 11–12:30 and 3–5, rest of year

MONTEPULCIANO

The highest of southern Tuscany's hilltop towns, Montepulciano sprawls down a narrow ridge, its picturesque side streets opening to gracious squares where you'll find a fascinating mixture of medieval, Renaissance and baroque architecture in churches and palaces. Following the town's alliance with Florence in 1511, money poured into the town, resulting in superb civic and private buildings designed by the architects Sangallo and Vignola. The focus is the Piazza Grande, where you'll find the Palazzo Comunale with wonderful views from its tower, and the brick-faced cathedral, whose serene Renaissance interior contains some great works of art, notably the glowing *Assumption* painted by Taddeo di Bartolo in 1401.

You can see more art in the Museo Civico before heading outside the walls to San Biagio (St. Blaise), a glowing honey-colored pilgrimage church designed by Sangallo in 1518. Leave time to taste the town's red wine, the Vino Nobile, which you'll find in wine shops all over town.

✚ C2

Tourist information ✉ Via Ricci 9 ☎ 0578 758 787 🕐 Tue.–Sun. 10–noon and 4–6 🎪 *Cantiere Internazionale d'Arte* is held Jul.–Aug.; contemporay music festival; *Bravío delle Botti* is held the last Sun. in Aug.; costumed processions, barrel race and street banquets

Palazzo Comunale ✉ Piazza Grande 🕐 Mon.–Sat. 10–noon and 4–6

Museo Civico ✉ Palazzo Neri-Orselli, Via Ricci 🕐 Tue.–Sun. 10:30–12:30 and 4:30–7, Apr.–Sep. 💷 $$

San Biagio ✉ Via di san Biagio 🕐 Daily 9–noon and 3–6

NÓRCIA

For lovers of low-key, friendly towns, Nórcia should be high on the list. Tucked away in eastern Umbria at the foot of some of the region's most dramatic mountains, this solid little walled town is famed as the birthplace of St. Benedict, founder of the Benedictine order and patron saint of Europe.

The church of San Benedetto lies on Nórcia's harmonious main piazza; its lovely Gothic facade dates from 1389. The interior has the remains of a Roman building, reputedly the birthplace of the saint and his sister, St. Scholastica. Across the square looms the Castellina, a massive fortress designed by Vignola in 1563. It now houses the town's museum.

Nórcia is famous for food – prosciutto, salami, sausages, pungent mountain cheeses and, above all, truffles, the black gold of Umbrian cuisine. You could fuel your appetite by hiking on the Piano Grande to the east; this unique upland plain, surrounded by grassy flower-covered mountains, is one of Umbria's least-known and most beautiful areas.

✚ D1

Tourist information ✉ Piazza Garibaldi 1, Cascia ☎ 0743 71 147 🕐 Daily 9–12:30 and 4–6:30, Apr.–Oct.

Tuscany, Umbria and the Marche

There are plenty of shopping temptations in Orvieto's quiet back streets

ORVIETO

A crag formed by an ancient volcano first attracted the Etruscans to the site of modern Orvieto, where they built their town, Volsinii. You can still view Etruscan tombs here, but most visitors are lured to the town by what is arguably Italy's finest Gothic Duomo (Cathedral).

Construction started in the 13th century to celebrate the Miracle of Bolsena. During Mass, the communion host dripped blood on the altar cloth; this was the origin of the feast of the Body of Christ, which continued for centuries. The facade alone, glittering with mosaics and liberally endowed with sculpture, took more than 300 years to complete. The best-known interior work is Luca Signorelli's fresco *Last Judgment* (1504), a taut and technically stunning masterpiece that was recently superbly restored.

Orvieto's other highlights include the Etruscan collection in the Museo Faina and the Pozzo di San Patrizio (St. Patrick's Well), an engineering tour de force with an impressive double ramp leading 62 feet into the living rock. Orvieto is noted for its colorful *maiolica* and other ceramics; you'll find a wealth of tempting stores in the streets around the Piazza de Duomo.

� C1

Tourist information 🖂 Piazza del Duomo 24 ☎ 0763 341 772 🕐 Daily 9–1 and 3–7

Duomo 🖂 Piazza del Duomo 🕐 Daily 7–1 and 2:30–7, Apr.; 7:30–1 and 2:30–8, May–Jun.; 7–1 and 2:30–7:30, Jul.–Sep.; 7–1 and 2:30–6:30, Mar. and Oct.; 7–1 and 2:30–5:30, rest of year 🔖 Cathedral free; Cappella Nuova (Signorelli's *Last Judgment*) $$

Museo Claudio Faina 🖂 Piazza del Duomo ☎ 0763 341 511 🕐 Tue.–Sun. 9–1 and 3–6:30, Mar.–Oct. 🔖 $$

Pozzo di San Patrizio 🖂 Piazza Cahen ☎ 0763 343 768 🕐 Daily 10–7, Apr.–Sep.; 10–6, rest of year 🔖 $$

PERÚGIA

Umbria's capital, Perúgia, is surrounded by ugly modern suburbs, but it's worth negotiating these to explore the unspoiled – and traffic-free – historic center. Parking is difficult, so leave the car in the lower town and use the escalators (*scala mobile*) to rise painlessly up to the hilltop core. Most of the main sights lie on or near Corso Vanucci, a wide and gracious street running to Piazza IV Novembre, where you'll find the Duomo (Cathedral) and the exquisite 13th-century Fontana Maggiore. This recently restored two-basin fountain was sculpted by Nicola and Giovanni Pisano and is surrounded by statues and carvings; those showing the months of the year are particularly charming. The Palazzo dei Priori, the town hall, also houses the Galleria Nazionale dell'Umbria, one of central Italy's most important art collections, stunningly presented in light and airy galleries. Here you can trace the development of Umbrian painting, with some superb Sienese and Florentine works as an added bonus. Highlights include Duccio's lovely *Madonna and Child*, Fra' Angelico's heavenly blue triptych *Madonna with Angels and Saints*, and the radiant symmetry of Piero della Francesca's great polyptych *Madonna and Child with Saints* – note the use of perspective in the Annunciation panel.

Umbria's great duo, Perugino and Pinturicchio, are represented by numerous paintings, suffused with light and color and perfectly encapsulating the distinct Umbrian style. Perugino is also the star of the Collegio del Cambio just down the street. He was commissioned in 1496 to decorate Perúgia's money changers' guild home, and he covered the walls and ceiling with figures, landscapes and decoration in a fusion of classical and Christian themes. His pupil, Raphael, was also involved.

Close by, you can visit the Collegio della Mercanzia, the Merchants' Guild, to admire some superlative 15th-century wood paneling. Perúgia's other treasures include the graceful Renaissance Oratorio di San Bernardino, the grand and opulent church of San Pietro, and San Domenico, whose cloisters house the Galleria Nazionale Archeologico dell'Umbria.

Perúgia has a wide choice of shops, bars and cafés along the Corso Vanucci, where you can buy Perúgini chocolates on their home ground. Look for Baci (Kisses); each luscious foil-wrapped mouthful comes with its own romantic message.

➕ D2

Tourist information ✉ Piazza IV Novembre 3 ☎ 075 572 5341 🕐 Mon.–Sat. 8:30–1:30 and 3:30–6:30, Sun. 9–1

Duomo ✉ Piazza IV Novembre 🕐 Daily 8–noon and 3:30–6

Galleria Nazionale dell'Umbria ✉ Palazzo dei Priori, Corso Vanucci ☎ 075 574 1247 🕐 Mon.–Sat. 9–1:30 and 3–7; Sun. 9–1 🎫 $$$

Collegio del Cambio ✉ Corso Vanucci 25 ☎ 075 572 8599 🕐 Daily 9–12:30 and 2:30–5:30, Mar.–Oct.; Mon.–Sat. 8–2, Sun. 9–12:30, rest of year 🎫 $$

Collegio della Mercanzia ✉ Corso Vanucci 15 ☎ 075 573 0366 🕐 Daily 9–12:30 and 3–6, Mar.–Oct.; Mon.–Sat. 8–2, Sun. 9–12:30, rest of year 🎫 $$

Oratorio di San Bernardino ✉ Piazza San Francesco 🕐 Daily 8–noon and 3–6

San Pietro ✉ Corso Cavour 🕐 Daily 8–noon and 3–6, but often closed, so check times

San Domenico and Museo Archeologico Nazionale dell'Umbria ✉ Corso Cavour ☎ 075 572 7141 🕐 Mon.–Sat. 9–1:30 and 2:30–7, Sun. 9–1 🎫 $$

PIENZA

The pocket-size Renaissance city of Pienza stands in the fertile rolling landscape of southern Tuscany, with the shapely peak of Monte Amiata to the south. Once known as Corsignano, it was the birthplace of the redoubtable Pope Pius II, Aeneas Sylvius Piccolomini, born in 1405. Elected to the papacy in 1458, Pius embarked on a scheme to transform his native village into an "ideal city." He commissioned the architect Rossellino to design a cathedral, papal palace and town hall. This core of the existing town is harmoniously grouped around a charming square and named after the Pope. You can walk through the entire place in about 10 minutes, but Pienza merits more time

Tuscany, Umbria and the Marche

Hilltop Perúgia is the gateway to Umbria's high mountain ranges

Tuscany, Umbria and the Marche

The unmistakable silhouette of the Leaning Tower of Pisa

than this. Start at the Duomo (Cathedral), with its lovely facade and interior inspired by the northern churches Pius had seen on his travels. The side chapels have some outstanding altar pieces by contemporary artists. Pius' residence, the Palazzo Piccolomini, stands next door; you can visit the papal apartments and admire the views from the triple-tiered loggia.

➕ C2

Duomo ✉ Piazza Pio II ⏱ Daily 9–noon and 3–6
Palazzo Piccolomini ✉ Piazza Pio II ☎ 0578 48 503
⏱ Tue.–Sat. 10–12:30 and 4–7, Apr.–Oct.; Tue.–Sat. 10–12:30 and 3–6, rest of year

PISA

Pisa's famous structure, the Leaning Tower, is just one of a quartet of beautiful buildings that make up the Campo dei Miracoli (Field of Miracles). The Duomo (Cathedral), Battistero (Baptistery), Campo Santo and the tower itself date from Pisa's Golden Age. In the 11th through 13th centuries, the city was still a port and one of the leading Mediterranean maritime powers.

Today Pisa is a busy industrial and university city, surprisingly unspoiled in many areas. The earliest building of the cathedral complex is the black-and-white

striped cathedral itself, begun in 1064 in the unmistakable Pisan Romanesque style. The interior is mainly Renaissance, but the magnificent pulpit by Giovanni Pisano dates from 1302 and shows scenes from the life of Christ; look for the apse mosaic by Cimabue. Construction started on the Torre Pendente (Leaning Tower) in 1173; the spongy sub-soil caused it to lean before it was even half completed. By 1989 it was more than 16 feet from the upright and nearing its limits. It was stabilized in the 1990s, but there has been interminable wrangling over what to do next and the situation is far from resolved. The baptistery, with its dome and Romanesque arcades, was built between the 12th and 13th centuries and is the largest in Italy. Along the north edge of the Campo dei Miracoli runs the perimeter wall of the cemetery, or Campo Santo, once lavishly decorated with frescoes but sadly destroyed during World War II bombing. It's worth venturing south from here toward the Arno river and there are attractive streets and squares, a great daily food market. The river bank is lined with gracious ranks of fine palaces.

➕ A3

Tourist information ✉ Via Benedetto Croce 24/26
☎ 050 40 096 ⏱ Mon.–Fri. 9–12:30 and 3–6, Sat. 9–noon; ✉ Piazza Stazione ☎ 050 42 291 ⏱ Daily 9–7; ✉ Via Cammeo 2 ☎ 050 560 464 ⏱ Daily 9–7
Duomo ✉ Piazza del Duomo ☎ 050 560 547
⏱ Tue.–Sat. 10–7:40, Sun. 1–7:40, Apr.–Oct.; Tue.–Sat. 10–12:45, Sun. 3–4:45
Torre Pendente (Leaning Tower) ✉ Piazza del Duomo ⏱ Closed
Battistero and Campo Santo ✉ Piazza del Duomo ☎ 050 560 547 ⏱ Daily 8–7:40, May–Sep.; 9–5:40, Mar.–Apr. and Oct.–Nov.; 9–4:40, rest of year

PISTÓIA

Encircling walls enclose historic Pistóia, one of Tuscany's least-visited cities. The town displays a 12th-century zebra-striped Duomo (Cathedral), a Gothic baptistery and some impressive palaces. Inside the Pisan Romanesque cathedral, you'll find sculpture by masters such as Verrochio and Rossellino, though the most astounding artwork is the Dossale di

Colorful 16th-century reliefs by the della Robbia workshop over the door of the cathedral in Pistóia

San Jacopo (St. James' Altarpiece). This solid-silver altar weighs almost a ton and is covered with 628 sculpted figures; started in 1287, it took almost 200 years to complete. The Piazza del Duomo also contains a 14th-century baptistery and a much-older belltower, once a Lombard watchtower. Other churches include San Giovanni Fuoricivitas, a wonderful green-and-white 12th- to 14th-century structure, and Sant'Andrea, which contains a 1297 pulpit by Giovanni Pisano. July sees the town's famous *Giostro dell'Orso*, a medieval jousting tournament, preceded by spectacular processions.

➕ B3

Tourist information ✉ Piazza del Duomo 4 ☎ 0573 21 622 🕐 Mon.–Sat. 9–1 and 3:15–6:30 (also Sun. 9–1, Jul.–Aug.)

Duomo ✉ Piazza del Duomo 🕐 Daily 9–noon and 4–7; Cappella di San Jacopo: Mon.–Sat. 10–noon and 4–6, Sun. 11–noon and 4–6 🖐 $ Cappella di San Jacopo

SAN GIMIGNANO

Even without the famous towers, hilltop San Gimignano, "Medieval Manhattan," would be a town worth visiting. Crowded all year, your best option may be to stay a day or two. Once the day-trippers have gone, the town takes on a completely different atmosphere.

San Gimignano once boasted 72 towers, which were built by rival nobles in the 12th and 13th centuries. The survival of 15 is due to San Gimignano's subjugation to Florence in about 1350, after which it quickly became a rural community. You can climb one of the towers, the Torre Grossa, for astounding views. San Gimignano's picturesque streets, tempting shops, cafés and houses are enough for many visitors, but the town is rich in art and history, so leave enough time to enjoy some of it.

Sights cluster around the two main squares, the Piazza della Cisterna and the Piazza del Duomo. Here you'll find the 13th-century Collegiata, one of the most comprehensively frescoed churches in Tuscany, with scarcely an inch of wall left undecorated. Themes include the Creation and the Old and New Testaments, while the tiny Chapel of St. Fina shows the life of San Gimignano's own saint. Other town highlights include the Museo Civico, packed with lovely Gothic and Renaissance paintings, and the church of Sant'Agostino on the far side of town. It has luminous 15th-century Benozzo Gozzoli frescoes showing the life of St. Augustine, and the bonus of having few visitors.

✚ B3

Tourist information ✉ Piazza del Duomo ☎ 0577 940 008 🕐 Daily 9–1 and 3–7, Mar.–Oct.; 9–1 and 2:30–6:30, rest of year

Torre Grossa and Museo Civico ✉ Piazza del Duomo ☎ 0577 940 340 🕐 Daily 9:30–7:30, Apr.–Sep.; 9:30–6, Mar.–Oct.; 9:30–1:30, rest of year 💷 $$

Collegiata ✉ Piazza del Duomo 🕐 Daily 9:30–12:30 and 3–6, Apr.–Sep.; 9:30–12:30 and 2:30–5:30, rest of year

Sant' Agostino ✉ Piazza Sant Agostino 🕐 Daily 7:30–noon and 3–7, Apr.–Sep.; 7:30–noon and 3–6, rest of year

SIENA

The warm colors of Siena's stones and brickwork and the exuberant black-and-white stripes of its Duomo (Cathedral) make it instantly more appealing to many visitors than its larger neighbor, Florence. Large and prosperous in the 13th and 14th centuries, the city's population was decimated by the 1348 Black Death; the city never recovered, thereby leaving a legacy of one of Europe's most perfectly preserved cities. The sloping square known as the Campo is the heart of Siena. Its south side is dominated by the magnificent 14th-century Palazzo Pubblico and the 320-foot belltower, the Torre del Mangia. Once the seat of civic government and still the city's town hall, the palace is also home to the Museo Civico with many frescoed rooms. The chief draws are Simone Martini's 1315 *Maestà*, the charming equestrian portrait of *Guidoriccio da Fogliano* and Lorenzetti's great 1338 frescoes *Allegories of Good and Bad Government*.

It's worth lingering in the Campo to enjoy an overpriced drink, while you visualize Siena's ebullient medieval horserace, the Palio, which takes place in July and August. From here, head to the cathedral, a wonderful mix of Romanesque and Gothic, its splendid facade a riot of statuary. Inside, you'll find masterpieces by Donatello, Pisano and the young Michelangelo. The cathedral's floor is entirely covered with a sumptuous marble pavement showing biblical and allegorical scenes. These were completed from 1349 to 1547 by just about every leading contemporary artist. Don't miss the Libreria Piccolomini painted by Pinturicchio in 1502 with scenes of the life of Pope Pius II, the Piccolomini Pope. Near the cathedral you'll find the baptistery and the Museo dell'Opera, which contains works from the cathedral,

Siena's zebra-striped cathedral presides over a medieval huddle of rosy-red rooftops

including Duccio's supreme *Maestà*. Opposite stands Siena's medieval hospital, Santa Maria della Scala, which closed in the late 1990s. It's now a museum where you can admire lively frescoes showing everyday medieval hospital life. Nearby there are more paintings in the Pinacoteca Nazionale, whose collection traces the whole development of Sienese painting.

✚ B2

Tourist information ✉ Piazza il Campo 56 ☎ 0577 280 551 ⏰ Mon.–Sat. 8:30–7:30, Apr.–Sep.; Mon.–Fri. 8:30–1 and 3:30–6:30, Sat. 8:30–1, rest of year

Duomo ✉ Piazza del Duomo ⏰ Daily 7:30–7:30, mid-Mar. to Oct.; 7:30–1:30 and 2:30–5, rest of year 🎫 $$

Museo dell'Opera ✉ Piazza del Duomo 8 ⏰ Daily 9–7:30, mid-Mar. to Sep.; 10–1 and 2:30–5, Nov. to mid-Mar. 🎫 $$

Ospedale di Santa Maria della Scala ✉ Piazza del Duomo ☎ 0577 586 410 ⏰ Daily 10–6, May–Jun.; 10–6:30, Jul.–Aug.; 10:30–5:30, Sep. and Apr.; 10:30–4:30, Mar and Oct.; 10:30–1:30, Jan.–Feb. and Nov.–Dec. 🎫 $$

Museo Civico ✉ Piazza il Campo ⏰ Mon.–Sat. 9:30–7:45, Sun. 9:30–1:45, mid-Mar. to mid-Nov; Mon.–Sat. 9–1:45, rest of year 🎫 $$$

Pinacoteca Nazionale ✉ Palazzo Buonsignori, Via San Pietro 29 ☎ 0577 281 161 ⏰ Tue.–Sat. 8:30–7, Sun.–Mon. 8:30–2, Jul.–Sep.; daily 8:30–2, rest of year 🎫 $$$

Torre del Mangia ✉ Piazza il Campo ⏰ Daily 10–7:30, Jul.–Aug.; 10–6, May–Jun. and Sep.; 10–5, Apr. and Oct.; 10–4, Mar.; 10–1, rest of year 🎫 $$

SOVANA

Tiny Sovana rests in the far southeast of Tuscany in the sparsely inhabited and undeveloped area called the Maremma. Thriving in Etruscan, Roman and early medieval times, the Maremma's prosperity was later eroded by malaria. Sovana is perhaps the best of these, though neighboring Pitigliano, built on a spectacular tufa crag, is also worth a visit.

Less than 130 people live in Sovana, their houses lining the broad brick expanse of the Via di Mezzo, which widens to form the tiny piazza. Here, you'll find Santa Maria, a tranquil 13th-century church, which houses a unique ninth-century pre-Romanesque

stone canopy over the altar. Opposite the church is a small museum, while a flower-edged lane leads to the huge Duomo (Cathedral), which was built during the eighth to 12th centuries From here you can explore the labyrinth of sunken Etruscan roads carved out of the tufa, which lead to Etruscan tombs. These date from the seventh century BC and range from *colombari*, niches for funerary urns, to elaborately carved structures such as the famous Tomba Ildebranda.

✚ C1

Santa Maria ✉ Piazza del Pretorio ⏰ Daily 9–1 and 3–6

Museo del Palazzo Pretorio ✉ Piazza del Pretorio ⏰ Tue.–Sat. 10–12:30 and 3–6 🎫 $

Duomo ⏰ Daily 9–1 and 3–6

Tomba Ildebranda ⏰ Tue.–Sat. 10–12:30 and 3–6 🎫 $

SPELLO

The enchanting medieval town of Spello rambles down the lower slopes of Monte Subasio in the Vale of Spoleto, the perfect place to catch a taste of unspoiled Umbria. Narrow streets lined with flower-hung houses, some classy food shops and good bars and restaurants all combine to make the town a tempting stopping point.

Five Roman gates give access; head through Porta Consolare to Via Cavour, the main street, where you'll find the church of Santa Maria Maggiore. Inside, three walls of the Cappella Baglioni are decorated with Pinturicchio's glowing frescoes (1501) with scenes of the life of Mary. Next door is the Pinacoteca Civica with more paintings, including Mary, the mother of Jesus, with St. Felix who's holding a portrait of Spello, little changed over the centuries. Farther uphill is Sant'Andrea, with another Pinturicchio, and the town streets climb still farther, giving access to Monte Subasio.

✚ D2

Tourist information ✉ Piazza Matteotti 3 ☎ 0742 301 009 ⏰ Mon.–Sat. 9:30–1 and 3–6

Santa Maria Maggiore ✉ Via Cavour ⏰ Daily 9–1 and 3–6

Pinacoteca Civica ✉ Piazza Matteotti 10 ☎ 0742 301 497 ⏰ Mon.–Sat. 10–1 and 3:30–6 🎫 $$

Sant'Andrea ✉ Via Cavour ⏰ Daily 9–1 and 3–6

Tuscany, Umbria and the Marche

The Benedictine abbey of Monte Oliveto Maggiore set amid cypresses, south of Siena

DRIVE: RENAISSANCE TUSCANY

Duration: 2½ to 3 hours

Start this drive in Monteriggioni, a walled town lying just off the Siena – Florence raccordo (link road).

You can walk from one end of Monteriggioni to the other in five minutes, as the town consists of little more than a spacious square with a tranquil old church, two dozen houses, two excellent restaurants and a hotel, all encircled by impressive walls punctuated by towers. Beneath the walls, vegetable gardens flourish and the tiny streets are decorated with flowers. Built by the Sienese in 1213 as a border outpost againt Florence, Monteriggioni was immortalized by Dante in *The Inferno*, where he refers to its towers as giants in an abyss; the verse is inscribed over the town's main gateway. Monteriggioni is best visited in early morning or late afternoon.

From Monteriggioni, take either the SS2 or the Siena to Florence raccordo (link road) to Siena (see page 110). If you are not visiting Siena, take the tangenziale (bypass) to bypass the city; look for the exit back to the SS2, signposted Roma.

The SS2 follows the route of the Cassia, one of the great Roman consular roads that

fanned out all over the Roman Empire and is still known by this name.

About 28 kilometers (17 miles) south, the Cassia skirts Buonconvento, well worth a stop.

Buonconvento was another of Siena's key outposts; today, it's a bustling small town with some lovely old buildings and a tiny and exquisite museum displaying lovely Sienese paintings with grave-eyed Madonnas.

Turn left into the hills at Buonconvento, following the signs through woods and past cypresses to the Abbazia di Monte Oliveto Maggiore.

The great abbey of Monte Oliveto is set in the *crete*, the strange landscape of clay landslips and escarpments, which characterizes this part of Tuscany. The abbey was founded in the early 1300s by a branch of the Benedictines and soon became one of Italy's most powerful foundations, falling from influence in the 19th century. Monks still live here, restoring books and producing wine and olive oil.

The main artistic attraction is the Chiostro Grande (Great Cloister), which has scenes of the life of St. Benedict. The scheme was started by Luca Signorelli, who completed nine panels before handing it over to Il Sodoma, who painted the other 27. The frescoes are full of life – look for the birds and animals. The monastery also has a lofty

Hot thermal springs feed the central pool in the tiny hamlet of Bagno Vignoni

church with some wonderful inlaid choir stalls and a fine Renaissance library.

Return to Buonconvento and head south to follow the SS2 for 2 kilometers (about a mile) before branching right to Montalcino (see page 104).

As this road climbs to approach the town, you'll pass wineries advertising the famous Brunello wine.

Leave Montalcino by the main road back to the SS2, a lovely stretch through vineyards, olive groves and wide views over southern Tuscany. Turn right on the S2 and continue for 6 kilometers (4 miles) before turning left at San Quírico d'Órcia onto the SS146 for Pienza (see page 107) and Montepulciano (see page 105).

You could stay on the SS2 south for 5 kilometers (3 miles) to make a detour to Bagno Vignoni, one of Tuscany's most memorable hamlets. It's built around a hot spring, which was well known to the Romans and Renaissance Popes and rulers. The central square is a huge Renaissance *piscina*, or bath, overlooked by a charming loggia. It's best seen in cool weather, when whisps of steam rise from the gently bubbling waters.

Buonconvento
Museo d'Arte Sacra ✉ Via Soccini 17 🕐 Daily 10–noon (also Tue.–Sat. 4–6, Apr.–Sep. and 3–5, rest of year) 🏛 $ ❗ Opening times may change ☎ 0577 806 788/0577 806 606
Abbazia di Monte Oliveto Maggiore ✉ Monte Oliveto Maggiore 🕐 Daily 9:15–12:30 and 3:15–6, Apr.–Sep.; 9:15–12:30 and 3:15–5, rest of year

[Map shows region of Tuscany with locations including Firenze, Monteriggioni, Siena, Monteroni d'Arbia, Abbazia di Monte Oliveto Maggiore, Ponte d'Arbia, Buonconvento, San Quírico d'Orcia, Montepulciano, Montalcino, Pienza, Bagno Vignoni, Grosseto, Viterbo, Roma; roads SS2, SS69, SS11, SS326, SS146, SS223, A1; scale 20 km / 10 miles; Chianti region labeled]

Tuscany, Umbria and the Marche

Todi's winding streets tumble down the hillside high above the Tiber valley

SPOLETO

Still relatively undiscovered, Spoleto has plenty to offer, with the bonus of excellent shopping and fine dining. The old town spreads down the hill from the hilltop fortress to the charming Piazza del Mercato on the site of the Roman forum, with the still-intact Roman Arco di Druso nearby.

Spoleto's 12th-century Duomo (Cathedral) is one of central Italy's loveliest; the entire apse features the blues and golds of Filippo Lippi's frescoes. Other churches are earlier still, Sant' Eufemia is a superb Romanesque building, while San Sansano features sixth-century frescoes. You can walk outside town to San Pietro, with its Lombard-Romanesque carvings on the facade; your route will take you across a wooded gorge spanned by the magnificent 250-foot arches of the Ponte dell Torri, a monumental bridge and aqueduct rebuilt by Gattapone in the 14th century. June and July see the Festival of the Two Worlds, Italy's most prestigious international arts festival. Founded in 1958, it's an Italian-American joint venture with a sister festival in Charleston, West Virginia.

✚ D1

Tourist information ✉ Piazza della Libertà 7 ☎ 0743 220 311 🕐 Daily 9–1 and 3–7:30, Apr.–Sep.;

10–1 and 3–7:30, rest of year

Duomo ✉ Piazza del Duomo 🕐 Daily 8–1 and 3–6:30, Mar.–Oct.; 8–1 and 3–5:30, rest of year

Sant' Eufemia ✉ Via Fontesecca 🕐 Daily 10–12:30 and 3:30–7, Apr.–Sep.; 10–12:30 and 2:30–6, rest of year 🖐 $

San Sansano ✉ Piazza Fontana 🕐 Daily 7:30–noon and 3–6:30, Apr.–Sep.; 7:30–noon and 3–5:30, rest of year

San Pietro ✉ On east side of N3 outside town 🕐 Daily 10–12:30 and 3:30–7, Apr.–Sep.; 10–12:30 and 2:30–6, rest of year. Times change, so check with tourist office

TODI

Once an important Etruscan outpost ("Tuder" means border), ancient Todi is stunningly situated on a great bluff above the Tiber river, its mellow roofscape and towers inviting exploration. It reached its heyday in the 13th century and saw the construction of the superb ensemble of buildings around the main square, the Piazza del Popolo. Here you'll find the lovely Romanesque-Gothic Duomo (Cathedral), approached by a broad flight of 18th-century steps. The interior has a lovely carved choir, but it's the pink facade with its great rose window that draws the eye. The square has some fine medieval palaces, particularly the Palazzo dei Priori and the Palazzo del Capitano, which houses Todi's museum, now under restoration. Each palace has a sweeping flight of external stairs.

San Fortunato, a huge 13th-century church lies nearby; from here you could walk through the public gardens to reach Santa Maria della Consolazione, which many experts consider one of the best Renaissance churches in Italy.

🚹 D1

Tourist information ✉ Piazza del Popolo 38 ☎ 075 894 3395 🕐 Daily 9–1 and 4–7, Apr.–Sep.; Mon.–Sat. 9–1 and 4–7, Sun. 9–1, rest of year

Duomo
✉ Piazza del Popolo 🕐 Daily 8:30–12:30 and 3–7, Apr.–Sep.; 8:30–12:30 and 2–5:30, rest of year

San Fortunato ✉ Piazza San Fortunato 🕐 Daily 9:30–12:30 and 3–5

Santa Maria della Consolazione ✉ Viale della Consolazione 🕐 Daily 9–1 and 3–7

TREVI

All travelers heading through the Vale of Spoleto notice Trevi, a perfect town perched on a cone-shaped hill, but few bother to make the detour to visit it. Wend your way up through the olive groves (which produce some of Umbria's best oil) and spend a couple of hours wandering around an unspoiled hill town. You'll find narrow streets giving access to tiny alleys, intricately paved with patterned cobblestones, and an unhurried small-town atmosphere. Like many Umbrian towns, there are some treasures, notably two paintings by Perugino in the churches of San Martino and the Madonna delle Lacrime.

🚹 D2

URBINO

Nowhere outside Tuscany did the Renaissance flower as vividly as in beautiful Urbino, the Marche's most stately and distinguished small city. The birthplace of Raphael and the great architect Bramante, Urbino flourished in the 15th century under the rule of Duke Federigo di Montefeltro to become one of Europe's most sophisticated and enlightened courts.

The hill town of Trevi is distinguished by its honey-colored houses

Today, this university city is dominated by Federigo's 1465 Palazzo Ducale, still among central Italy's most sublime buildings. Designed by Luciano Laurana, it houses the Museo Nazionale delle Marche in the elegant rooms around the central courtyard. Its two outstanding treasures are Piero della Francesco's *Madonna di Senigallia* and his tiny *Flagellation*, one of the most enigmatic paintings in the world. You'll find these in the Duke's private apartments, where you can also admire the stunning wood inlay in the study. His portrait hangs nearby (he always painted in profile, having lost his right eye in battle), while Laurana's *View of an Ideal City* perfectly encapsulates the Renaissance ideal.

There's a fine six-panel Uccello, Titian's *Resurrection* and Raphael's *La Muta*, but most visitors will remember the harmonious beauty of the building itself. Away from the palazzo, Urbino has a large 18th-century Duomo (Cathedral), while Raphael devotees can visit the artist's birthplace. Climb up to the Fortezza Albornoz gardens for views over the city, then pause for a drink in the Piazza della Repubblica, where the only sound you'll hear in the blissfully traffic-free center is the sound of human voices.

✚ D3

Tourist information ✉ Piazza Rinascimento 1
☎ 0722 24 401 🕐 Mon.–Sat. 9–6, Apr.–Sep.;
Mon.–Sat. 9–2, rest of year

Palazzo Ducale, Galleria Nazionale delle Marche
✉ Piazza Rinascimento ☎ 0722 2760/2220 🕐 Daily
9–7, Apr.–Sep.; 9–2, rest of year 🎟 $$$

Duomo ✉ Piazza Rinascimento 🕐 Daily 9–1 and 3–6

Casa Natale di Raffaello ✉ Via Raffaello ☎ 0722
320 105 🕐 Daily 9–2, Apr.–Sep.; 9–1, rest of year 🎟 $

THE VALNERINA

Many Italians claim that the Valnerina –
the little valley of the Nera river – is the
loveliest in Italy. If you're looking for wild,
mountainous country, steep gorges and
rushing rivers, this is the place. It has the
bonus of a handful of delectable villages
and imposing artistic sights thrown in.
Bustling Terni marks the start of the
Valnerina, and from here, the scenic
SS209 follows the valley floor.

Your first stop should be the Cascate
delle Marmore, a 545-foot waterfall
created by the Romans in 271 BC. The
falls now feed a hydroelectric plant and
are sometimes diverted, but at full power

Roman remains are a vivid reminder of Volterra's
long history

are truly dramatic. Farther up the valley
stands the evocative abbey of San Pietro in
Valle; its hillside situation is breathtaking,
while its church contains some of Umbria's
most important 12th-century frescoes.
Pause again at the medieval village of
Scheggino, with its trout-filled canals and
warren of alleyways, before pushing up the
valley. The hills on either side become
steeper and the valley narrows, with tiny
hamlets clinging to the slopes.

✚ D1

Abbazia di San Pietro in Valle ✉ San Pietro in Valle
🕐 Daily 10–noon and 2–5, Apr.–Sep.

VOLTERRA

Imposing and isolated, Volterra stands on
a plateau surrounded by *balze* (cliffs),
which have steadily eroded since Etruscan
times. This ancient settlement has signs of
Etruscan and Roman occupation in the
shape of walls, gates and a theater. It also
has one of the most comprehensive
Etruscan museums, the Museo
Guarnacci, in central Italy. Most of this
town is medieval. Its heart is the Piazza
dei Priori, with its battlement town hall
built in the first half of the 13th century.
The piazza has other impressive medieval
palaces, and behind the square stands the
black-and-white striped 12th-century
Duomo (Cathedral), its dim interior lit
through alabaster windows.

The Pinacoteca Comunale has a
pleasing collection of Sienese and
Florentine paintings, Ghirlandhaio's and
Signorelli's serene Madonnas making a
sublime contrast to the angular forms and
acidic colors of Fiorentino's superlative
Deposition. This part of eastern Tuscany
has always been mining country, and
you'll see translucent alabaster carvings
for sale in many of the local workshops.

✚ B3

Tourist information ✉ Via Turazza 2 ☎ 0588 86 150
🕐 Daily 9–1 and 3–6, Apr.–Sep.; 9–1, rest of year

Museo Guarnacci ✉ Via Don Minzoni ☎ 0588 86
347 🕐 Daily 9:30–1 and 3–6:30, Apr.–Oct.; 9–2, rest of
year 🎟 $$

Duomo ✉ Piazza San Giovanni 🕐 Daily 9–1 and 3–6

Pinacoteca Comunale ✉ Via dei Sarti 1 ☎ 0588 86
290 🕐 Daily 9:30–1 and 3–6:30, Apr.–Oct.; 9:30–1:30,
rest of year 🎟 $$

SIENA'S PALIO

The Siena Palio is no mere tourist attraction; this spectacular bareback horserace, dating from medieval times, is a truly Sienese festival.

The Palio is named after the victory *pallium*, a banner embroidered with the image of the Blessed Virgin. The contest is between the city's wards, the *contrade*, and the race runs on July 2 and August 16, each occasion preceded by weeks of preparation, build-up, bets and pageantry. The 17 wards have their own church, museum and social center. Allegiance to your native *contrade* is absolute; children are baptized in the *contrade* fountain, and each neighborhood holds an annual parade. Ten neighborhoods take part in the Palio; they are chosen by lot, as are the horses. The jockeys are heavily protected before the race for fear of bribes or worse. Each group has its traditional enemies and allies and the pre-race weeks are filled with intrigue as alliances are forged and broken.

The days before the race are filled with processions and trial races. On race-day the horses are blessed in the church. It's the best of luck if the horse defecates during the service. In the late afternoon, a stunning procession, the *corteo storico*, takes place in the *campo*, with drummers, flag-throwers and costumed captains and grooms. Huge bets are placed and once the race starts anything goes. Ninety seconds of incredible excitement follow as the horses gallop three times round the square, which has a temporary surface of sand, and mattresses to protect the most dangerous corners. The winning horse, with or without the jockey, is handed the Palio and mobbed by its jubilant supporters. Parties and parades go on all night and into the following weeks; the *contrade* hold street banquets as they relive every moment of the day.

You can watch the procession and race from the *campo*, which means standing for at least two hours prior to the race, and up to six hours if you want to be near the rails, with no exit once the barriers are closed. There are seats in the windows of the houses overlooking the *campo*; these are sold out for months before the race and should be booked a year ahead. (Contact Palio Viaggi at Gramsci 7 ☎ 0577 280 828.)

Tuscany, Umbria and the Marche

A historical procession heralds the start of the frenetic excitement of the Palio

CENTRAL ITALY

Central Italy

" **L** *AZIO is a thriving area rich in history, while the neighboring regions of Abruzzo and Molise offer scenic beauty and undiscovered attractions.* *"*

The Emperor Constantine, under whose rule the Roman Empire adopted Christianity

Central Italy

CENTRAL ITALY

Three regions bridge the gap between the north and south of Italy – Lazio, the Abruzzo and Molise. Rome and its attractions tend to overshadow the rest of the Lazio region, with its gentle landscape and quiet towns. Across the Apennines lies the Abruzzo, one of the least known areas of Italy, with wild mountainous landscape and villages where international visitors are still a novelty. Its neighbor, Molise, offers more remote rolling hill country and economically has much more in common with the south than with central Italy. All three regions have long coastlines, relatively undiscovered by international visitors.

Lazio

Until the 1860s, Lazio was part of the Papal States, the territory held by the Vatican. During the process of Italian unification, Rome with its historical connotations of centralized power became the symbol of the new united Italy and the obvious choice as the country's new capital. In fact, Rome had to wait until 1870 to join the united Italy, the last but symbolically most important part of the Italian peninsula to do so.

Like other areas that were once part of the Papal States, Lazio was traditionally poor and had little sense of identity and few historic towns, though its economy has made major strides in recent years.

Its landscape varies from the gentle rolling hills of the north to steep mountains to the south and east of Rome. Lake Bolsena in the north attracts many visitors, as does Lazio's coastline, at its best south of Rome.

A classically inspired summer house in the gardens of Rome's Villa Borghese

Central Italy

Abruzzo and Molise

Abruzzo and Molise were one region until 1963; since then, the Abruzzo has forged ahead at the expense of Molise – the contrast between the two on every level is startling. They are both sparsely populated, mountainous areas prone to earthquakes, with a tradition of standing outside the mainstream of Italian affairs. Over the last 40 years, Abruzzo has pulled itself out of poverty, developing the tourist potential of its national park's mountain wilderness and expanding a string of lucrative resorts along its sandy coastline.

Despite this, huge areas are still remote and unspoiled, and you'll find a true sense of regional identity manifested in a genuine pride in local festivals, crafts and costumes. The landscape, a wilderness of upland plains, remote valleys and high peaks, is superb.

Molise is poor, disorganized and undeveloped, with more than 40 percent of its terrain covered by mountains and industrial cities. If you're heading south to Apulia (Puglia), you'll pass through Térmoli, a fishing port and attractive resort.

Central Italy

A Sense of the South

If you're traveling into Central Italy
from the north or from Rome itself,
you'll at once sense an almost
indefinable difference and grasp why
this central area is viewed as "southern"
by Italians from the north. Towns are
not as stylish or prosperous, villages are
not so spick-and-span. There's more
remote countryside, less cultivated land.
The pace seems slower, the people more
laid-back, noisy and ebullient. In some
parts of the mountainous areas, the
high-tech world seems to have barely
impinged and foreigners still cause
comment. The tourist infrastructure is
not as good as that, say, in Tuscany and
Umbria, with fewer hotels of
international standards. The area is
well-served by *autostrade* (freeways); the
A24/25, which cuts through the
Apennines east of Rome to penetrate
the Abruzzo, is one of Italy's finest and
most scenic. Good roads run down
both the west and east coasts, and the
whole of Lazio is easy to explore. In
Abruzzo and Molise, the roads in
remoter areas are often steep, winding
and narrow.

Highlights

Rome is going to be your number one
stop in this part of Italy, and you should
set aside four or five days to explore the
city and what it has to offer. It might
make sense to do most of your
exploring into Lazio from a Roman
base; Tivoli, the Castelli Romani, Óstia
Antica and Tarquínia are all potential
day trips from Rome via public
transportation. If you're heading further
afield, a rental car may be better. The
Abruzzo National Park and the Gran
Sasso are good choices. If you're
looking for a few days of relaxation,
there are charming tranquil resorts
south of Rome and all along the coast
of the Abruzzo.

Capodimonte stands on the shores of
Lake Bolsena

When To Go

If you're planning to spend most of your
time in central Italy in Rome, there's
much to be said for a winter trip when
the city is less crowded and the stifling
heat won't be a problem. Late
November and December can be wet,
but January and February are generally
crisp and dry, with surprisingly warm
midday sun. Spring comes early to

Central Italy

Rome, making April and May lovely months to enjoy the city. Crowds and heat build in summer, which is the best time to visit the Abruzzo mountains if you're interested in fresh air and exercise. Avoid Rome in July and August when the city is crammed with tourists, but Romans themselves are on vacation, leaving many stores and restaurants closed. Fall, with its soft light and golden colors, can be a magical time to visit the region.

The People

The inhabitants of this central area are notably different from Northerners. Romans have a reputation for surliness and impatience with visitors. It pays to go out of your way to charm by using those few Italian phrases. If you're exploring remoter areas, few people speak English. This all adds to the delight, and there are few places in Italy where you'll get a better sense of traditional attitudes.

ROME

The capital of Italy provides magic and
frustration in almost equal measure.
Packed with art, steeped in history,
humming with life, this most beautiful
of cities will ensnare you with its
charms, even if its traffic, noise and

confusion make you wonder why you
came. A heady mixture of classical,
medieval, Renaissance and baroque
sights fill its streets and squares.
Golden light filters through pine trees
to ancient stones; fountains splash
quietly in sun-dappled piazzas. But
traffic also roars up polluted streets,
crowds push and shove, noise and heat

Central Italy

levels can be intense. Accept this mixture and put aside your preconceptions. Rome (Roma) is a living city, not a museum, and therein lies its enchantment.

Getting Your Bearings
It shouldn't take you long to realize that Rome, laid out and built long before

the automobile age, is not a huge city in international terms. It lies on either side of the Tiber (Tevere) river and sprawls across seven hills. The Vatican, St. Peter's and the Trastevere quarter with its excellent restaurants lie on the west bank of the river; everything else you'll want to see is to the east.

This eastern part is roughly dissected by the Via del Corso, which runs from Piazza del Popolo to Piazza Venezia and is dominated by the vast "wedding cake" of the Victor Emmanuel Monument. South is the Forum, the Colosseum and the heart of classical Rome. Between the Corso and the Tiber river lies the *centro storico* (historical center), a wonderful mix of medieval streets, Renaissance palaces and beguiling squares. East of the Corso there are more fine buildings and palaces, Rome's most elegant shopping streets, verdant parks, splendid viewpoints and the elegant Via Vittorio Veneto, home to the American Embassy and the smartest hotels.

Sightseeing
There are hotels scattered all over the city, but bear in mind that nowhere is going to be quiet. The *centro storico* is perhaps the best for its proximity to just about everything, and there's a good selection of hotels here. The only area to avoid is around the Stazione Termini train station.

To start your visit, spend a couple of hours on an organized tour. Several companies offer "get on and off" options, with tickets valid all day. Once oriented, it's important to prioritize. There's no way you're going to be able to see everything, so decide what's important to you and see it properly. Big sights such as the Vatican and the Forum are best tackled early in the day while you're fresh, and be sure to rest for a couple of hours during the midday

The great dome of St. Peter's reflected at sunset in the Tiber river

heat. Most people directly involved with tourism speak English and are generally helpful, but ordinary Romans will not be particularly willing to go out of their way to help – so be tolerant.

You shouldn't miss St. Peter's Basilica, the Vatican Museums or classical sights such as the Roman Forum and Colosseum. Add to these a couple of other major museums and churches and you'll be busy for at least three days. In addition, there's a wealth of delights ranging from ancient churches and idiosyncratic museums to lovely parks, elegant shops and jolly markets. As a capital city, Rome hosts splendid temporary exhibitions and shows; pick up a copy of the monthly *l'Evento* from a tourist office to find what's happening.

Culinary Pleasures

Like all Italians, Romans eat out regularly, so choose a restaurant patronized by locals to enjoy some specialties. There's an excellent choice in Trastevere and the old streets around Piazza Navona and the Pantheon, while more obviously upscale choices can be found nearer the Via Veneto. Roman cooking often features offal, tripe and brains, but there are other dishes, such as the delicious *saltimbocca alla Romana* – veal cooked with prosciutto and sage – which are typical.

Do sample the mixed vegetable *antipasti*, often found in family-run restaurants, and pasta dishes such as spicy *rigatoni all'amatriciana* and the delicious and familiar *spaghetti alla carbonara* with bacon and egg.

Central Italy

Mosaics

Rome's oldest churches are rich in mosaics. They serve as reminders of the early Christian church and the last days of the Roman Empire, when faith went hand in hand with Byzantine skill. Mosaics are composed of tiny pieces of polychrome stone, marble and gilding, shaped so that they will lock together on a vault or curved roof. They are built to create pictures and images of Christ and the saints and are usually set against a gold background and filled with charming details of plants, birds and animals. To see them at their best, visit the churches of Santa Prassede, Santa Costanza, San Clemente (see page 131), Santa Maria in Trastevere (see page 132) and Santa Pudenzia, where the mosaics were created between the fourth and ninth centuries.

Artichokes, often eaten deep-fried or raw, are a great Roman specialty, and you should certainly try these. Food-to-go includes fabulous pizza by the slice, an ideal quick lunch. As everywhere in Italy, ice cream is wonderful, with a great range of flavors. Local wines come from the Castelli Romani, the hills outside Rome, but you'll find wines and liqueurs from all over Italy as well as international brands.

Retail Therapy

Shop till you drop in hedonistic Rome, where elegant women devote most of their lives to the art. The smartest stores cluster around the Via Condotti and the Via Frattina near the Piazza di Spagna, where you'll find the top names in fashion, lingerie, leather and jewelry, as well as luxury housewares. Prices are

lower, but the style is still good along the Via del Corso and the Via Nazionale, while department-store fans should try La Rinascente, Coin, Upim and Standa. Souvenir shops abound all over the city, though if you're looking for religious mementos, buy them in the shops in the vicinity of St. Peter's. Be sure to take in a food market; the daily one in the Campo dei Fiori is the tops for color and atmosphere.

Peace and Quiet

Rome has its parks and gardens, and you'll occasionally stumble across a grassy square complete with benches to rest your weary feet. To escape the traffic's roar, head for the Villa Borghese (see page 130), the Botanical Gardens in Trastevere or the Colle Oppio near the Colosseum. Best of all,

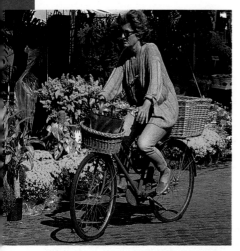

Campo dei Fiori, Rome's most attractive market

take a picnic to the Forum, and eat it among the grassy ruins and wildflowers on the Palatine Hill.

Entertainment

Dinner and a quiet stroll may be all you're after, but there's plenty of entertainment available – *l'Evento* will fill you in. Opera is a superb option in summer, when performances are held outdoors in the Villa Borghese, and concerts and recitals take place all over the city. Several theaters show films in their original language, and there's also live rock and jazz and nightclubs for dancing.

ESSENTIAL INFORMATION

 TOURIST INFORMATION
•Largo Goldoni ☎ 06 6813 6061
•Lungotevere Castel Sant' Angelo
☎ 06 6880 9707
•Piazza Cinque Luna ☎ 06 6880 9240
•Piazza del Tempio della Pace ☎ 06 6992 4307
•Piazza S Giovanni in Laterano ☎ 06 7720 3535
•Piazza Sonnino (Trastevere) ☎ 06 5833 3457
•Stazione Termini, Galleria Gommata
☎ 06 4890 6300
•Via dell'Omata, Santa Maria Maggiore
☎ 06 4788 0294
•Via Nazionale ☎ 06 4782 4525
•Tour companies: Ciao Roma ☎ 06 474 3795
ATAC's 110 City Tour ☎ 06 4695 2252

 URBAN TRANSPORTATION
Public transportation – orange buses and trams and a two-line subway system – can be slow. Bus tickets must be purchased before boarding; you'll find them at automatic machines or shops and newsstands displaying an ATAC sticker. They are valid for any number of bus journeys plus one subway journey within a 75-minute period and must be validated on boarding at the rear of the vehicle. The *biglietto integrato* is valid for a day's unlimited travel on buses, trams, subway and the suburban rail service. A weekly

pass, the *carta integrata settimanale*, is valid for buses and the subway only. Taxis are yellow or white and can be picked up from one of the stands indicated by a blue-and-white sign; they do not stop on the street. You can call a taxi from Autoradio Taxi (☎ 06 3570), Capitale Taxi (☎ 06 4994) or Cosmos Radio Taxi (☎ 06 88 177); the meter will start running immediately after your call. Do not trust anyone offering a private taxi service and be sure the meter is at zero if you pick up a taxi at a stand.

AIRPORT INFORMATION
Rome has two airports, Leonardo da Vinci at Fiumicino to the west of the city, and Ciampino, south of Rome. You are most likely to arrive at Leonardo da Vinci. The easiest way to get to and from Leonardo da Vinci is by train from Stazione Termini; there are departures every 30 to 60 minutes between 7 a.m. and 9:30 p.m. Trains also run from the airport to Ostiense and Trastevere railroad suburban stations; if you use these you will have to get an onward connection. There is a nightly bus service between the airport and Stazione Termini. To reach Rome from Ciampino, take the subway line A to Anagnina and connect with the COTRAL bus service, which runs 6:50 a.m.–11:40 p.m.

CLIMATE – Average highs and lows

JAN.	FEB.	MAR.	APR.	MAY	JUN.	JUL.	AUG.	SEP.	OCT.	NOV.	DEC.
13°C	13°C	15°C	17°C	21°C	25°C	28°C	28°C	26°C	21°C	17°C	14°C
55°F	55°F	59°C	63°F	70°F	77°F	82°F	82°F	79°F	70°F	63°F	57°F
4°C	4°C	5°C	8°C	12°C	16°C	19°C	19°C	17°C	13°C	8°C	5°C
39°F	39°F	41°F	46°F	54°F	61°F	66°F	66°F	63°F	55°F	46°F	41°F

ROME SIGHTS

Key to symbols

✚ map coordinates refer to the Rome map on page 124; sights below are highlighted in yellow on the map

✉ address or location ☎ telephone number

⏰ opening times 🍴 restaurant on site or nearby

Ⓜ nearest subway station

🚌 nearest bus or tram route

💶 admission charge: $$$ more than L5,000, $$ L3,000 to L5,000, $ less than L3,000 ℹ information

BASILICA DI SAN PIETRO

The present Basilica di San Pietro (St. Peter's Basilica), the heart of the church for Catholics worldwide, stands on the site of the saint's burial place. It was built from 1506 to 1626. The principal architects were Bramante and Bernini, working to Michelangelo's concepts; the soaring dome is his creation. The sweeping colonnades, fountains and triumphant facade are a fitting prelude to the vast and opulent interior, dominated by Bernini's great high altar *baldicchino*, with its spiraling columns. Don't miss Michelangelo's sublime *Pietà*, the bronze statue of St. Peter with his right foot worn away by caresses, and the crypt where numerous Popes are buried around the tomb of St. Peter.

✚ A3 ✉ Piazza San Pietro, Città di Vaticano website www.vatican.va ☎ 06 6988 3712 ⏰ Basilica: daily 7–6, Dome and roof: daily 8–4:45. Closed during religious services Ⓜ Ottaviano-San Pietro 🚌 23, 46, 62, 81 ℹ Dress code: no shorts, short skirts or bare shoulders

CAMPIDOGLIO

The architectural ensemble of the Campidoglio, approached up a graceful ramp, is one of Rome's most elegant squares. Designed in the 1550s by Michelangelo, its side buildings house the Capitoline Museum, which is undergoing restoration. The grandiose Palazzo Senatorio at the far end is occupied by Rome's city hall. The fine bronze equestrian statue of Marcus Aurelius in the center is a copy of the Roman original.

✚ C2 ✉ Piazza del Campidoglio 🚌 44, 62, 80, 160

Throw a coin into the Fontana di Trevi and you're sure to return to Rome

COLOSSEO

Every modern public stadium's design ultimately copies that of the Colosseo (Colosseum), a massive structure dating from AD 72. Its tiers of seats held 55,000 people, while the sophisticated "backstage" facilities allowed the arena to be flooded. Shows here featured gladiators, slaves and animals often fighting to the death; few Christians were martyred here. The Colosseum served as a source of building material during the Middle Ages, hence the missing sections.

✚ D2 ✉ Piazza del Colosseo ☎ 06 700 4261 ⏰ Daily 9–6, Apr.–Sep.; 9–3, rest of year (ground floor closed Sun. and Mon. afternoon Ⓜ Colosseo 🚌 75, 85, 117 💶 $$; ground floor free

FONTANA DI TREVI

You'll hear the Fontana di Trevi (Trevi Fountain), the best known of all Rome's fountains, before you see it. Tucked into a tiny piazza amid a warren of narrow streets, it's a riot of figures, tritons and horses set against an architectural backdrop. The latest in a series of fountains here since Roman times, Trevi dates from 1732 and gets its name from the three streets – *tre vie* – which converge here. It's traditional to throw a coin in the fountain before you leave Rome to ensure your return.

✚ C3 ✉ Piazza Fontana di Trevi ⏹ Al Moro, see page 207 🚇 Spagna or Barbarini 🚌 52, 53, 71, 95

FORO ROMANO

The Foro Romano (Roman Forum), today a romantic jumble of fallen columns and tumbling walls, was the heart of the Roman Empire and contained all the most important political, religious and municipal buildings. Time and imagination are needed to puzzle it out, but be sure to track down the House of the Vestal Virgins, home to the guardians of the sacred flame, and the second-century Temple of Antoninus and Faustinus (AD 141). Other highlights include the fine Arch of Septimius Severus, and the whole of the Palatine Hill. Once covered with palaces (and giving us the word "palace" itself), today its ruins lie among oleanders and cypresses, an evocative reminder of the transience of glory.

✚ C2 ✉ Largo Romolo e Remo 1 ☎ 06 699 0110 🕐 Daily 9–6, Apr.–Sep.; 9–3, rest of year; closed Sun. and Mon. afternoon 🚇 Colosseo 🚌 60, 75, 81, 117 🎫 Palatine $$$; Forum free ℹ English audio-guide

GALLERIA E MUSEO BORGHESE

Built in 1613 by Cardinal Scipione Borghese as a summer retreat, the Villa Borghese is now a museum housing the cardinal's superb art collections. The cardinal's favorite sculptor was Bernini, whose works dominate; the *David* is said to be a self-portrait, and there's an *Apollo and Daphne*, full of flight and panic. Don't miss Canova's *Pauline Borghese*, Napoleon's sister. The statue perfectly captures her seductive looks – she was renowned for her jewels, clothes and lovers. The pictures, too, are spectacular, with treasures by Raphael, Titian's sensuous *Sacred and Profane Love* and Caravaggio's famous *Boy with a Fruit Basket*.

✚ D4 ✉ Villa Borghese, Piazzale Scipione Borghese 5 ☎ 06 548 577 🕐 Tue.–Sun. 9–7 🚇 Spagna 🚌 52, 53, 116 🎫 $$$

MUSEI VATICANI

Allow plenty of time to enjoy the 1,400 rooms that make up the Musei Vaticani (Vatican Museums), the world's largest. You can follow one of the color-coded routes to the museum's highlights, the Cappella Sistina (Sistine Chapel) and the Stanze di Raffaello (Raphael Rooms). The walls and ceiling of the lofty Sistine Chapel are entirely frescoed, most notably by Michelangelo. His extraordinary creation scenes from the Old Testament cover the vault and were painted from 1508 to 1512; they show more than 300 figures and include his extraordinarily powerful *Last Judgment*. Raphael's Rooms, all symmetry and harmony, provide a balance to the huge energy of the Sistine. Elsewhere you'll find classical sculpture, paintings and much more (there's even a piece of moon rock presented by the U.S. government), while the richness of the building itself is an added bonus.

✚ A3 ✉ Musei Vaticani, Viale Vaticano ☎ 06 6988 3333 🕐 Mon.–Fri. and last Sun. of month 8:45–15:30, Sat. 8:45–12:30 🚌 23, 46, 64, 81 🎫 $$$; free last Sun. of month ℹ English audio-guide available

PALAZZO ALTEMPS

A beautifully restored 15th- through 16th-century palazzo houses Cardinal Ludovisi's classical sculpture collection, augmented by those of other private collectors. The building is a joy in itself; charming rooms with vaulted ceilings surround a frescoed loggia above an inner courtyard. Don't miss the famous sculpture *Dying Gaul* and the tender Greek *Aphrodite Rising from the Waves*, dating from the fifth century BC. The museum is best visited as darkness falls, when the statues are lit by spotlights.

✚ B3 ✉ Piazza Sant'Apollinare 8 ☎ 06 683 3759 🕐 Tue.–Sat. 9–10, Sun. 9– 8 🚌 70, 81, 116, 186 🎫 $$ ℹ English audio-guide available

PALAZZO MASSIMO

The Museo Nazionale Romano (National Roman Museum), housed in the 19th-century Palazzo Massimo, is the showcase

Central Italy

for a breathtaking collection of sculptures, bronzes, mosaics and frescoes dating from Roman times. Beautifully displayed with excellent information in English, the artifacts are displayed to trace different themes running through Roman history from the Republican era up to the fifth century. Here you'll find superlative busts and bronze figures, alongside fine Roman copies of the best of ancient Greek sculpture. Highlights include the *Discus Thrower*, a sensuous *Sleeping Hermaphrodite* and a wonderfully languid *Apollo*. The third floor is devoted to wall frescoes and mosaics; the beautiful first-century BC garden paintings from the dining room of Livia's villa could grace any modern house.

🞢 D3 ⊠ Piazza dei Cinquecento 67 ☎ 06 4890 3500 🕙 Tue.–Sat. 9–7, Sun. 9–2 🍴 Café in museum 🚇 Termini 🚌 16, 38, 90, 92, 105 💷 $$ 🛈 English audio-guide available

PANTHEON

The greatest surviving complete Roman building, the Pantheon was erected from AD 119 to 128. This superbly engineered building gives a vivid impression of the grandeur of ancient Rome. Built as a temple, it survived the fall of Rome due to its early conversion in AD 609 to a Christian church. The stately portico leads to a huge dome; here you'll find the tombs of Raphael and two Italian kings.

🞢 C3 ⊠ Piazza della Rotunda ☎ 06 6830 0230

🕙 Mon.–Sat. 9–5:30, Sun. 9–1 🚇 Spagna 🚌 46, 64, 119, 175

PIAZZA NAVONA

The elongated shape of the Piazza Navona follows the lines of the Roman racetrack that once occupied this site. Today's piazza was rebuilt in 1644 by Pope Innocent X, who commissioned its lovely fountains from Bernini in 1651. The central one, known as the Fountain of the Four Rivers, shows the Nile, Ganges, Danube and the Plate. The Nile's head is veiled, as the source had yet to be discovered. Borromini's baroque church of Sant'Agnese stands on the west side.

🞢 B3 ⊠ Piazza Navona 🚌 70, 81, 116, 186

SAN CLEMENTE

No other church gives a better sense of Rome's layers of history than the ancient and evocative church of San Clemente. This shadowy 12th-century basilica has columns, a marble choir and fine pulpit, with Byzantine mosaics glittering in the apse above. Beneath this, you'll find a fourth-century church with ghostly eighth-century frescoes, while lower still the remains of Roman streets and a Mithraic temple have been excavated.

🞢 D2 ⊠ Via di Giovanni in Laterano ☎ 06 7045 1018 🕙 Daily 9–12:30 and 3:30–6 🚇 Colosseo 🚌 85, 117, 186 💷 $

Surrounded by splendor in the Piazza Navona, these elderly Romans enjoy a chat

Central Italy

SANTA MARIA IN ARACOELI

The 124 steep steps leading up to the church of Santa Maria in Aracoeli (Our Lady of the Altar of Heaven) were built in 1348 as a thanksgiving at the end of a plague. Medieval pilgrims climbed them on their knees to the church, which was built in 1260 and whose plain facade hides a sumptuous interior. The huge columns in the nave were taken from Roman buildings; against their solidity, the gilded 16th-century ceiling provides a contrasting note of grandeur.

🔶 C2 ⊠ Piazza d'Aracoeli ☎ 06 679 8155
🕐 Daily 7–noon (also 4–6:30, Jun.–Sep.) 🚌 44, 62, 80, 160

SANTA MARIA MAGGIORE

Santa Maria Maggiore (St. Mary Major) was first built in the fifth century on a site miraculously marked by a summer snow. Much has been added over the years, but it still retains the superb fifth-century mosaics in the nave, while those in the apse represent the best of 13th-century mosaic art. The ceiling is said to be gilded with the first gold to arrive from the New World as a gift from Spain. Pause to reflect that this is Rome's only church where Mass has been celebrated every day since the fifth century.

🔶 D3 ⊠ Piazza di Santa Maria Maggiore
☎ 06 483 195 🕐 Daily 7 a.m.–8 p.m., Apr.–Sep.; 7–7, rest of year 🍴 Agata e Romeo, see page 207
🚇 Termini, Cavour 🚌 16, 70, 75, 105

SANTA MARIA IN TRASTEVERE

If you're exploring the neighborhood of Trastevere, make a point of visiting the church of Santa Maria in Trastevere. A pleasing 18th-century portico fronts the mosaic facade of this ancient church, whose nave columns, like so many in old Roman churches, once supported classical buildings. The Byzantine-style 12th-century mosaics in the apse show the glorification of the Virgin Mary.

🔶 B2 ⊠ Piazza Santa Maria in Trastevere
☎ 06 581 4802 🕐 Daily 7:30–12:30 and 3–6
🚌 44, 60, 170

SCALINATA DI TRINITÀ DEI MONTI

The elegant Scalinata di Trinità dei Monti (Spanish Steps) curve gracefully up from the Piazza di Spagna to the church of Trinità dei Monti, a focal point for Rome's smartest shopping area. Built in 1723, the steps got their name from the piazza, which once housed the Spanish embassy. The poet Keats died in lodgings overlooking the Steps in 1821; it now houses a small museum devoted to Keats and Shelley. The piazza's lovely fountain was built in 1627 to resemble a sunken boat.

🔶 C3 ⊠ Piazza di Spagna 🕐 Museo Keats–Shelley: Mon.–Fri. 9–1 and 3–6 🗡 $$
🚇 Spagna 🚌 116, 119

VIA APPIA ANTICA

A section of the Via Appia Antica (Old Appian Way) still survives just outside the city. It's one of the many roads that fanned out to all corners of the Roman Empire. Built in the fourth century BC to link Rome and Brindisi, today it's a picturesque cobbled way, shaded by pines and lined with tombs and monuments. It was here that St. Paul marched on his way to prison, and Spartacus and his slaves were executed in 71 BC. Nearby, you can visit the catacombs, with their touching mementos of early Christian life.

🔶 D1 ⊠ Via Appia Antica 136 🕐 Catacombs: Mon.–Sat. 8:30–noon and 2:30–5; closed Nov. 🚌 118

VILLA GIULIA

The beautiful Villa Giulia set in peaceful gardens houses one of Italy's great museums devoted to the enigmatic Etruscans. Highlights of this huge collection include the Castellani exhibits with striking Minoan jewelry, fine Greek vases and the seventh-century BC gold and silver from the Barbarini tombs. Most touching of all is the Sarcofago degli Sposi, a sixth-century BC sarcophagus featuring a married couple reclining together on a banqueting couch.

🔶 C4 ⊠ Piazzale di Villa Giulia 9 ☎ 06 322 6571
🕐 Tue.–Sat. 9–7; Sun. 9–2 🚇 Flaminio 🚌 19, 52, 95
🗡 $$ 🛈 English audio-guide available

THE VATICAN

Until Italian unification, the Papacy held territory, known as the Papal States, throughout central Italy. In 1870 these lands became part of the new united Italy and Pope Pius IX retreated to the Vatican as a virtual prisoner. As supreme head of Catholics worldwide, the pontiff clearly needed his own independent sovereign territory to retain his spiritual authority, and in 1929 the Treaty of the Lateran was signed with Mussolini. This established the Vatican State (Città del Vaticano), an area covering 110 acres around the Basilica of St. Peter and the Vatican Palace, today the world's smallest state.

An Independent State

The Vatican has all the appurtenances of an independent state. It has its own judiciary, currency and bank, and retains worldwide diplomatic relations. The ambassadors to the Holy See live throughout Rome. Its daily newspaper is the *Osservatore Romano*, and its broadcasting service is on air 24 hours a day. A branch railroad line runs from the Italian state system into the Vatican itself. Around 200 people actually live within the Vatican, the other 800 or so who work there commute over the "border" daily. They can use the shops and the postal system within the Vatican; the latter is open to anyone and you can send cards home from the post office in the colonnade outside the basilica. Latin is still the official language. The Pope is Europe's sole remaining absolute monarch, with complete power over this tiny state.

The Pope's Army

The Pope's person and the Vatican itself are defended by the Swiss Guard, a 90-strong brigade drawn from Switzerland's four Catholic

Opulent gilded plasterwork decorates the ceiling of the Galleria delle Carte in the Vatican Museums

cantons since 1506. Young men aged 19 to 25 sign up for a term of two to 20 years; their duties are largely ceremonial, but they are highly trained for all contingencies. They wear a picturesque navy-blue uniform. Their instantly recognizable, striped red, yellow and blue dress uniform, said to have been designed by Michelangelo, is reserved for state occasions. The Agenti di Vigilanza, formed in 1816, augment the Swiss Guard.

Seeing the Pope

When he is in Rome, the Pope traditionally gives a midday Sunday blessing from the window of his rooms overlooking the piazza. Since the 1970s, weekly audiences have been held in the vast Aula Paolo VI (Paul VI Hall). Up to 7,000 people attend these moving occasions; tickets are free and obtainable from the Prefetura della Casa Pontifica in the righthand colonnade of the Piazza San Pietro.

Colorful Swiss Guards are responsible for the Pope's safety

Central Italy

WALK: THE BEST OF ROME

Refer to route marked on city map on page 124.

This walk takes you from Papal Rome through medieval Rome to some of the city's Renaissance splendors. You could spend a whole day walking it, stopping for museum visits en route and lunching at one of the cozy neighborhood restaurants near the Pantheon. Or you could just tackle part of it, picking up bus 119 (a minibus that trundles through the narrow streets of the historic center) at the Pantheon or in Piazza di Spagna.

Start at the Castel Sant'Angelo.
The Castel Sant'Angelo was built by the Emperor Hadrian in AD 130 as a mausoleum; it got its present name when Pope Gregory the Great had a vision of an angel on its top in 590. Beginning in the ninth century, it was a Papal fortress linked in 1277 to the Vatican by a passage. After spells as a prison and

The gateway of the Palazzo del Quirinale is the setting for pomp and pageantry barracks, it became a museum with four floors of exhibits tracing its history in 1933.

> *Cross the Ponte Sant'Angelo and walk straight across the Piazza Ponte Sant'Angelo into Via Banco Santo Spirito. Continue left to Largo Tassoni, then turn left onto the busy Corso Vittorio Emanuele. Continue for five blocks, then cross the corso and turn right down the Via Sora, then left onto the Via del Pellegrino. This will bring you to the Campo dei Fiori.*

One of Rome's most alluring squares, the Campo dei Fiori stood at the heart of medieval Rome, surrounded by private palaces, inns and brothels. The statue in the center is the philosopher Giordano Bruno, who was burned here for heresy in the 17th century. The square has a daily fruit, vegetable and fish market, local neighborhood stores abound in the surrounding streets, and it's the perfect place to taste local life and have a *cappuccino*.

> *Turn right down Via Farnesi Gallo to Piazza Farnese, one block south.*

Piazza Farnese is dominated by the Palazzo Farnese, a Renaissance architectural masterpiece partly designed by Michelangelo and begun in 1516. It's now the French Embassy. The beautiful baths forming the fountains are Roman and came from the ruins of the Baths of Caracalla.

> *Retrace your steps to the Campo dei Fiori, cross the square and head down Via Baullari back to the Corso Vittorio Emanuele. Cross the corso and walk past the church of San Pantaleo and down Via Cuccagna into the Piazza Navona (see page 131). After visiting the piazza, go back to where you entered it, face the square and turn right to reach Corso Rinascimento. Cross the road and head up Via Sediari. Turn left at the end onto Via della Scofra, then take the second road on the right to reach the Piazza della Rotonda and the Pantheon (see page 131). With your back to the Pantheon, turn right and walk along Via dei Pastini and Via di Pietro to the Via del Corso; this section is marked with brown pedestrian signs to the Fontana di Trevi (see page 129).*

Via del Corso runs from the Piazza del Popolo to the Piazza Venezia, bisecting the northern half of the city. Partially pedestrian, it's a

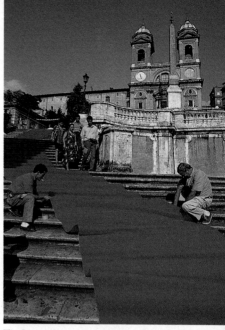
The Spanish Steps are always thronged with visitors

favorite shopping street with a good variety of clothes, shoes and accessories.

> *Cross the Via del Corso and follow Via della Muratte (and the brown signs) to the Fontana di Trevi. Keep the fountain on your left and head up Via Lavatore and Via delle Scuderie, with the bulk of the Quirinale on your right, to branch left to the Via del Tritone with the Palazzo del Quirinale behind you.*

The Palazzo del Quirinale is home to the president of Italy; it was built in the 16th and 17th centuries as the Papal residence. Opposite the palace are the 18th-century Scuderie (Papal Stables), restored and converted in 2000 as an exhibition hall.

> *Cross the Via del Tritone and head straight down the Via Due Macelli to the Piazza di Spagna. Climb the Spanish Steps (see page 132) on your right and turn left at the top of the steps. Follow the Viale della Trinità dei Monti all the way along, keeping the Giardini della Villa Borghese on your right, until you reach Piazzale Napoleone.*

En route, you'll pass the Villa Medici on your right, a gracious 16th-century villa that houses the French Academy. From the Piazzale Napoleone you could visit the Museo Etrusco at the Villa Giulia (see page 132), the Galleria Borghese (see page 130), or enjoy the tranquility of the park.

Central Italy

REGIONAL SIGHTS

Key to symbols

⊞ map coordinates refer to the region map on page 120; sights below are highlighted in yellow on the map

⊠ address or location ☎ telephone number
🕐 opening times 🍴 restaurant on site or nearby
🎫 admission charge: $$$ more than L5,000, $$ L3,000 to L5,000, $ less than L3,000 ℹ️ information

GRAN SASSO D'ITALIA

The highest peak on the Italian peninsula at 9,554 feet is the Gran Sasso d'Italia (Etna on Sicily and some Alpine summits are higher). It rises above the Campo Imperatore, a huge upland plain. This is snow-capped mountain scenery at its best, and the area attracts thousands of hikers and climbers, though drivers can also enjoy some inspiring vistas.

The best access point is the tiny settlement of Fonte Cerreto, where a cable car runs up to the Albergo-Rifugio Campo Imperatore. It was here that Mussolini was imprisoned after the Italian surrender in 1943, only to be lifted out in a daring aerial raid by an ace German pilot dispatched by Hitler.

From the Rifugio, trails lead higher into the massif; take number 10 to Monte della Scindarella (7,326 feet) for a taste of the area – it's a two-hour hike. You could drive farther across the rock-strewn landscape of the Campo Imperatore to explore some of the crumbling and semi-deserted villages that fringe it; Castel del Monte, crowned with a ruined castle and church, and the abandoned settlement of Rocca Caláscio, with its crumbling castle, make interesting stops.

⊞ C3
Tourist information ⊠ Piazza Santa Maria Paganica, L'Aquila ☎ 0862 410 808 🕐 Mon.–Fri. 8–2 and 4–6, Sat. 8–2 ℹ️ For information on hiking in the Gran Sasso massif contact the Italian Alpine Club ⊠ Via XX Settembre, L'Aquila 🕐 Mon.–Fri. 6 a.m.–7 p.m.

L'AQUILA

L'Aquila is the capital of the Abruzzo and a relatively undeveloped and unexplored region on central Italy's east coast. It lies in the shadow of the Gran Sasso Mountain and is a dour stone-built city that proves more attractive on closer inspection, with good shops, a wonderful market and the thriving atmosphere a university brings.

Founded in 1242 by the German Emperor Frederick II, L'Aquila is said to have been created by amalgamating 99 villages; the number remains significant today. The town hall clock chimes 99 times nightly, and the Fontana delle 99 Cannelle (Fountain of the 99 Spouts) is still a major attraction. You'll also want to visit the Museo Nazionale d'Abruzzo (Abruzzo National Museum), housed in the 16th-century castle. The museum is a splendid hodgepodge of exhibits; the main draw is the skeleton of a mammoth discovered nearby in the 1950s. Other sights include the lovely rose-and-white marble church of Santa Maria di Collemaggio and the sumptuous San Bernardino, burial place of St. Bernardino of Siena. The Sienese still come here on the saint's feast, bearing gifts of Tuscan olive oil. Leave time in L'Aquila to visit the daily market, held in the central Piazza del Duomo.

⊞ C3
Tourist information ⊠ Piazza Santa Maria Paganica ☎ 0862 410 808 🕐 Mon.–Fri. 8–2 and 4–6, Sat. 8–2
Museo Nazionale d'Abruzzo ⊠ Viale B Croce ☎ 0862 6331 🕐 Mon.–Sat. 9–2, Sun. 9–1 🎫 $$
Santa Maria di Colllemaggio ⊠ Piazza di Collemaggio 🕐 Daily 8–1 and 3–6
San Bernardino ⊠ Piazza del Teatro 🕐 Daily 8–1 and 3–6

Cattle are released in the early days of spring in the mountains around the Gran Sasso

Left: Preparing for the market in the Piazza del Duomo, the focal point of L'Aquila

The impressive bulk of the Abbey of Montecassino, scene of bitter fighting in World War II

MOLISE

Part of the Abruzzo until 1963, Molise is Italy's newest region, an undeveloped area that has more in common with its neighbors to the south than those to the north. Forty percent of Molise is mountainous; these mountains offer great hiking possibilities, particularly around the lakes, woods and high plains of the Matese chain. From the town of Boiano you can hike up Monte Gallinola, a fabulous two-hour climb that culminates in a coast-to-coast view across the whole Italian peninsula.

Molise's main centers are Isernia and Campobasso, sprawling modern cities surrounded by factories built with northern money. To taste the best of the region, head for the rolling countryside or the coastal resort of Térmoli, with its long sandy beach and medieval heart. Other attractions in Molise include Saepínum, Italy's best-preserved example of a Roman provincial town.

➕ D1–E1

Campobasso tourist information ✉ Piazza Vittoria
☎ 0874 415 662 🕐 Mon.–Sat. 8–2

Isernia tourist information ✉ Via Farinacci 1
☎ 0865 3992 🕐 Mon.–Sat. 8–2

Saepinum ✉ Altilla, 3 kilometers (2 miles) from Sepino 🕐 Museum: Tue.–Sun. 9–1, site always open

MONTECASSINO

Scene of one of World War II's most bitterly fought battles, the Benedictine Abbey of Montecassino was founded in 529 by St. Benedict, who, as legend has it, was led to this impregnable spot by three ravens. It quickly became one of the most important monasteries in Europe, sending monks far and wide to disseminate the Benedictine ideals. Its strategic mountaintop position between Rome and Naples made it a target over the centuries for repeated attacks, and the abbey has been rebuilt many times.

During World War II, the abbey became the German regional headquarters and was besieged by the Allies for more than six months. It was completely destroyed by Allied bombs in May 1944. Its destruction, though vital to the Allies' cause, has caused controversy ever since. The old monastery complex has been faithfully rebuilt and still looms impressively over the valley. The views from the central cloister are as exceptional as ever. The area around and to the south of Montecassino is scattered with much-visited war cemeteries.

➕ D1

Abbazia e Museo di Montecassino ✉ Via Montecassino ☎ 0776 311 529 🕐 Daily 9–noon and

3:30–6:30, Jul.–Aug.; 9–noon and 3:30–5:30, Apr.–Jun.
and Sep.–Oct.; 9–noon and 3:30–5, rest of year 🚹 $

PARCO NAZIONALE D'ABRUZZO

The 99,000 acres of the Parco Nazionale
d'Abruzzo (Abruzzo National Park) make
up one of Europe's great wilderness areas.
If you love the great outdoors, this is a
must-see. Once a royal hunting reserve,
the park was established in 1917 and
comprises a jumble of Apennine
mountain massifs with the Sangro Valley
cutting through its heart.

Here lie the villages of Pescassèroli,
Opi and others, where you can pick up
information on hiking and viewing
wildlife; there are more than 150 well-
marked trails of different standards. It's
likely you'll see the park's chamois, a
subspecies that has developed in the
Abruzzo. Wolves are harder to spot,
though some are kept in reserves near
Pescassèroli. Rarest of all is the Apennine
brown bear; there are 100 in the park and
numbers are increasing. Spring and fall
are probably the best times to explore.
The spring flowers are stunningly
beautiful, while fall sees mountain slopes
glowing with colors.

➕ D2

Information office ✉ Pescassèroli ☎ 0863 91 955
🕐 Daily 9–6, Apr.–Oct.; 9–1 and 3–6, rest of year
ℹ There are smaller summer-only offices at Opi,
Barrea and Civitella Alfedena

TARQUÍNIA

It's hard to realize today that 5,000 years
ago unassuming Tarquínia boasted a
population of more than 100,000 and was
the most important of the 12 Etruscan
cities. Today's town retains its medieval
walls and the 12th-century Romanesque
church of Santa Maria di Castello, but
most visitors are drawn here by the
Etruscan tombs and the superlative
Museo Nazionale Tarquiniense (National
Tarquinian Museum). This museum
houses treasures discovered in the
Etruscan necropolis to the east of town.
There are sarcophagi, ceramics and
delicate gold jewelry, though pride of

Wall paintings in 5,000-year old tombs at
Tarquínia show the firm Etruscan belief in
an afterlife

place must be given to the beautiful pair
of winged terracotta horses, a
breathtakingly sophisticated piece of
decorative sculpture.

The necropolis itself, just outside
town, is an underground honeycomb of
tomb chambers, many of which have
been opened so you can admire the
colorful wall paintings with which they
are adorned. Steps lead down into the
earth to allow you to see lively 5,000-
year-old paintings.

➕ A2

Tourist information ✉ Piazza Cavour 1 ☎ 0766 856
384 🕐 Mon.–Sat. 8:30–2 and 6–8, Apr.–Sep.; 8:30–2
and 4–6, rest of year

Santa Maria di Castello ✉ Piazza Santa Maria di
Castello 🕐 Obtain key from guardian in house next
to church

Museo Nazionale Tarquiniense ✉ Palazzo
Vitelleschi, Piazza Cavour ☎ 0766 856 036
🕐 Tue.–Sun. 9–7; closed Jan. 1, May 1 and Dec. 25
🚹 $$$ ℹ Ticket is also valid for the necropoli in the
Zona Archeologica

Zona Archeologica ✉ Via Ripagretta
☎ 0766 856 308 🕐 Daily 9–1 hour before dusk
🚹 $$$ ℹ The tombs are opened in rotation to help
conserve the paintings and there is no way of
knowing in advance which will be open on any
particular day

Sunlight sparkling on water dazzles the eye in the gardens of the Villa d'Este at Tivoli

TIVOLI

The main attractions of Tivoli, a small town in a lovely wooded position some 30 kilometers (18 miles) from Rome, are the Villa d'Este and the vast classical site of the Villa Adriana (Hadrian's Villa). Both are usually crowded with day trippers from Rome, so come early to appreciate them at their best. The Villa d'Este, built in 1550 and now rather shabby, has superb gardens with terraces, cascades and fountains; wherever you are in its shady green coolness, you'll hear the refreshing splash of falling water. The two Bernini fountains, the elegant Fontana di Biccierone and the Fontana dei Draghi are the most splendid, but make sure you don't miss the breathtaking Viale delle Cento Fontane (Avenue of a Hundred Fountains).

Just outside town are the vast and rambling ruins of the Villa Adriana (Hadrian's Villa), built by the emperor in AD 125 as a retirement home. During his imperial travels, he had been impressed with buildings all over the known world and the villa was designed to incorporate copies of many of these. It eventually covered as much ground as imperial Rome itself. This fascinating place is vast, rambling, green and romantic, and you'll need a map to make sense of it all.

➕ B2

Villa d'Este ✉ Piazza Trento ☎ 0774 312 070
🕐 Tue.–Sun. 9–1 hour before dusk 🍴 Refreshments available in gardens 💷 $$$
Villa Adriana ✉ Via Tiburtina ☎ 0774 530 203
🕐 9–90 minutes before dusk 🍴 Refreshments available in villa site 💷 $$$

VITERBO

Capital of northern Lazio, Viterbo's great days were in medieval times, when it was a favored place for different popes to escape troubles in Rome. Their legacy is a collection of grand palaces and fine churches still enclosed by intact city walls. The entire city has an intensely medieval atmosphere, which you'll best appreciate by exploring the San Pellegrino neighborhood, a tight mass of hilly streets dotted with towers and elevated medieval walkways. The heart of the city is the Piazza del Plebiscito, a fine square circled by 15th- and 16th-century buildings. The decorative lions, which you'll see all over the city, are Viterbo's symbol.

From here, head to Piazza San Lorenzo to see the 13th-century Palazzo dei Papi (Papal Palace) with its Gothic loggia overlooking the green gorge cutting into the city's center. The Duomo (Cathedral) lies opposite, an austere and serene Romanesque church of great beauty. Viterbo has two museums; the Museo Archeologico Nazionale and the Museo Civico, both mainly devoted to exhibits from the surrounding area.

➕ A3

Tourist information ✉ Piazza dei Caduti ☎ 0761 304 795 🕐 Mon.–Sat. 8:30–2:30
Duomo ✉ Piazza San Lorenzo 🕐 Daily 8–1 and 4–7
Museo Archeologico Nazionale ✉ Rocca Albornoz 🕐 Tue.–Sun. 9–6 💷 $$
Museo Civico 🕐 Tue.–Sun. 10–7, May–Sep.; Tue.–Sun. 10–6, rest of year

THE ETRUSCANS

While traveling in Lazio and other parts of central Italy, you'll come across frequent signs of the Etruscans in the shape of monuments, tombs and museums. Who were these enigmatic and mysterious people?

History

The Etruscans step into history's limelight around the fifth century BC. They were a people probably made up of indigenous tribes and seafarers from Asia Minor. Inhabiting an area of central Italy called Etruria and stretching from modern Tuscany down to Rome, they formed a confederacy of 12 cities, built towns, passed laws and traded overseas. They were a lively and imaginative people with sophisticated cultural, political and social systems. That much is clear, but little else of their everyday life is known. This is explained by two factors. First, the Romans so admired them that they absorbed much of Etruscan culture as they rose to power. By the third century BC, the Romans had virtually assimilated the entire nation, together with much of its language, customs and religious beliefs. Secondly, the Etruscans built their cities of wood, not stone, and nothing remains.

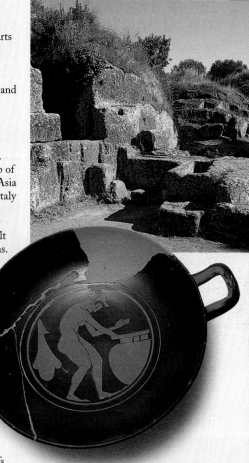

Top: Tombs laid out to form a city for the dead
Inset: Sophisticated Etruscan ceramics

Monuments

We also know that the Etruscans were deeply religious, firmly believing in an afterlife and burying their dead, as did the Egyptians, with all they would need for the future. Their tombs (necropoli), unlike their wooden cities, were permanent, made either of stone or carved out of the soft tufa rock found all over ancient Etruria. Wonderful finds have been made in these tombs – jewelry, vases, sculpture and wall paintings. From these, historians have learned much about the Etruscan way of life. The artifacts from the tombs are preserved in on-site museums, though the finest have gone to the Vatican Museums (see page 130) and the Villa Giulia (see page 132) in Rome.

Wonderful Sites

You can explore Etruscan sites all over central Italy, though the finest and most interesting are found in Lazio. Tarquínia (see page 139) has wonderful painted tombs. Orvieto in Umbria (see page 106) has streets carved from tufa, and Sutri, a 6,000-seat amphitheater carved from the living rock. Cerveteri, north of Rome, is literally a "city of the dead," complete with streets, houses and piazzas; there are more than 5,000 tombs here, though only around 50 have been properly excavated.

Central Italy

DRIVE: THE COAST TO THE ALBAN HILLS

Duration: 4½ to 5 hours

Start this drive in San Felice Circeo, a honey-colored coastal village with a good beach, and an hour's drive south from Rome.

From San Felice, you have access to the Parco Nazionale del Circeo (Monte Circeo National Park), named after the limestone headland of Monte Circeo, which looms above the town. Monte Circeo was reputedly the home of the sorceress Circe, who lured Ulysses with her guiles and siren song. You can drive to the summit for wonderful views up and down the coast. The park, the smallest of Italy's national parks, was set up in 1934 to preserve some of the natural beauty of the neighboring marsh and wetland area, as well as preserve the woodlands and wonderful flora of Monte Circeo itself. It's of special interest to bird enthusiasts as the lakes and lagoons provide marvelous habitats for many water species. With luck, you'll spot herons, storks and fish hawks.

> *Continue north along the coast to Anzio (signposted Sabáudia).*

North of Monte Circeo, the road hugs the coast for more than 32 kilometers (20 miles),

then makes a brief detour inland before hitting the sea again at Nettuno. There's a big, peaceful and beautifully tended World War II cemetery at Nettuno where nearly 8,000 American GIs are buried, killed at the difficult Anzio landings of 1944.

> *At Anzio, take the SS207 (signposted Aprília) and continue for 33 kilometers (20 miles) to Aprília then Pavona. Turn right and follow signs to Castel Gandolfo.*

Castel Gandolfo, set high above Lago Albano (Lake Albano) in the Alban Hills, is best

The Pope's summer palace overlooks
Castél Gandolfo's pretty piazza

Impressive Roman mosaics are one of Òstia Antica's attractions

known as the Pope's summer retreat. Several pontiffs have come here to escape the broiling heat of the Roman summer. It's a pleasant little town, dominated by the Papal Palace, in whose courtyard the Pope traditionally gives a Sunday blessing when he's in residence. Below the town, the picturesque lake is tempting, where you can have a swim or eat at one of the many lakeside restaurants.

Follow signs to Frattócchie, then branch right across country to the SS215 and follow the signs to Frascati.

Frascati is another of the Alban Hill towns; it's the nearest to Rome, so it's often packed with day trippers and Romans who flock here to eat Sunday lunch. It's attractive and picturesque, dominated by the bulk of the majestic Villa Aldobrandi, built in 1598. The villa's gardens today are romantically overgrown. The spectacular fountains are often switched off, but if they're open it's worth going in for the sweeping views from the terrace in front of the house.

White wine has been made in Frascàti since Roman times and is one of the few wines really well known outside Italy. There are plenty of places where you can sample the light and clean-tasting wine and some producers offer tours.

Rejoin the SS215, this time following signs to the Grande Raccordo Annullare

(GRA), Rome's ring road, and turn left. Continue on the GRA for 18 kilometers (11 miles), then exit on the SS8 to Lido di Òstia, Òstia Antica and the coastline.

In Roman times, the coastline lay farther inland than it does today, at the site of the Òstia Antica, the port of ancient Rome. You'll learn far more, in far greater peace, here than in hours spent battling the crowds in the Forum in Rome itself. The site is huge, evocative and dotted with grass-covered mounds and spreading umbrella pines. You could wander for hours (perhaps bringing a picnic with you), but if time is short, head for the Piazzale di Corporazione, the ancient city's commercial center. Ruined shops and offices still line it, and the mosaics in front indicate each building's purpose – ropemakers, grain merchants and chandlers. You can explore private houses (the Casa di Diana with its central courtyard is among the best), walk the streets and visit the Thermopolium, an ancient café.

Parco Nazionale di Circeo information office
✉ Via Carlo Alberti 107, Sabáudia ☎ 0773 511 386 🕐 Mon.–Sat. 9–1 (also 4–7, Apr.–Oct.)
Frascati tourist information ✉ Piazza Marconi ☎ 06 942 0331 🕐 Mon.–Fri. 8–2 and 3:30–6:30, Sat. 8–2
Òstia Antica ☎ 06 5635 8099 🕐 Tue.–Sun. 9–7, Apr.–Sep.; Tue.–Sun. 9–5, rest of year 🏛 $$

THE SOUTH

"IN the deep south, climate, landscape, economy and way of life combine to form a startling contrast to the north."

Clear blue seas surround the famous Faraglioni rocks off the coast of the island of Capri

The South

THE SOUTH

Southern Italy – the Mezzogiorno – starts south of Rome and includes four very different regions, Campania, with its breathtakingly beautiful coastline, the mountainous inland areas of Calabria and Basilicata, the empty flatlands along the Ionian coast and the rolling Apulian (Puglian) seaboard. Its capital is Naples, one of the most vibrant, frustrating and ultimately bewitching cities in Italy. Spiritually a million miles from the dynamic north, Italy's south, remote and little explored, provides a balance to the northern regions and the Renaissance perfection of the central areas.

Echoes of the Past

Invaders poured into the south for more than 2,500 years. Greek, Arab, Norman, German and Spanish conquerors established power bases and each systematically bled the south. They left a superb artistic legacy in temples, churches and palaces. They established a genetic mark on the population and incorporated the rhythm of their speech in the language and dialects, and echoes of their tastes in the intense flavors of southern cuisine. Their absolutist regimes also bequeathed the very elements that kept the south one of the most economically depressed areas of Europe.

Today

Southern Italy is still poor. This is partly the result of centuries of foreign neglect, but it's also due to a policy of

industrializing the north, while using the south as a convenient labor pool to fuel this industry. After World War II, millions of southerners emigrated north to find work, leaving the south increasingly depopulated, its industry and infrastructure undeveloped. The north-south divide is very real and will be only too apparent if you've already explored northern and central Italy.

Despite massive central government and European Union investment in recent years, the southern standard of living still lags far behind the rest of Italy. Organized crime and corruption still exist, though things are improving and the average visitor certainly won't be affected. You will notice the dilapidation and grime of many southern towns, while away from the tourist areas you'll have to bear in mind that you're traveling in the poorer half

The South

Rodi
Gargánico   Péschici
          Vieste
Promontorio del
      Gargano   Monte Sant'Angelo
    San Giovanni Rotondo
          Manfredónia
                      Golfo di
                    Manfredónia   ADRIATIC   SEA
Fóggia
A14
  Orta Nova   Barletta
                  Trani   Bisceglie
Cerignola   Ándria   Molfetta
A16   Bari
       PÚGLIA   Ruvo di Púglia   Mola di Bari
Ófanto   Castel
Melfi   del Monte   Casamássima   Monópoli
4350ft Venosa Spinazzola   Grotte di
                        Acquaviva   Castellana
                        delle Fonti   Fasano
Rionero in   Noci
Vúlture   Altamura   Alberobello
                        Gioia del   Ostuni
                        Colle   Martina   Brindisi
Potenza   Matera   Franca
                Bráddno   Massafra   Mesagne
                Basento   Laterza   Grottáglie   Squinzano
  BASILICATA   Cavone   Francavilla   San Cataldo
Brienza   Táranto   Fontana   Campi   Lecce
     Stigliano   Metaponto   San   Salentina Copertino
Sala Consilina Sáuro   Giórgio Manduria
                                  Iónico
A3   Agri   Sant'   Nardo   Galatina   Otranto
   Mte Sirino   Arcángelo   Policoro   Máglie   Capo
   6578ft   Sinni   Golfo di Táranto Gallipoli   d'Otranto
gonegro   Parco Nazionale   Santa Cesárea
  Rivello Lauria del Pollino Oriolo
   Maratea   7375ft
olfo di Mormanno Mte Pollino   Trebisacce Capo Spúlico   Gagliano del Capo
'castro   Capo Santa Maria
an Nicola   di Léuca
Arcella   Castrovillari
      Spezzano   Corigliano
Diamante Albanese Cráti Cálabro
Belvedere   Rossano
Maríttimo Santa Maria del Pátire
          A3
       CALÁBRIA   Punta Alice
      Sila Grande Parco Nazionale Cirò Marina
Páola Camigliatello della Cálabria
   Cosenza   San Giovanni
            6325ft in Fiore
            Mte Botte   Neto
            Donato
Amantea   5791ft   Crotone
            Mte Gariglione
      La Sila   Isola di
        Nicastro   Capo Rizzuto
         Catanzaro Capo Rizzuto
Golfo di
Sant' Eufémia   Golfo di
                Squillace   IONIAN
      Pizzo
Tropea Vibo Valéntia Soverato   SEA
C Vaticano Mileto Serra San Bruno
            6309ft
         A3   Mte Pecoraro
              Stilo
      Palmi Tauriánova
Scilla   Roccella Iónica
ssina   Gerace Locri
   Aspromonte
   Gambárie 6414ft Bovalino
     Montalto
Réggio di
Calábria
   Mélito di   C Spartivento
   Porto Salvo
         C   D   E

0   20   40   60   80   100 km
0   20   40   60 miles

The South

of the "Two Italys." Persevere; the rewards are tremendous and you'll see a facet of Italy that relatively few visitors experience.

Passionate People

Southern Italians are passionate, volatile and noisy. Seemingly huge altercations may be simply an everyday exchange of news or views. Watch the hand gestures to get some idea of the level of feeling – ill will evaporates as fast as it flares up. Likewise, the offhand reception you may first encounter can turn quickly to overwhelming warmth and friendliness. Spontaneous and open, southerners react quickly, their hearts often ruling their heads.

People are smaller and darker than in the north, though red and blonde hair and blue eyes are the genetic legacy of northern occupation. Society is still male-dominated, particularly in remote areas where it's rare even to see women on the streets. In the country, a large peasant class still exists, and you'll witness archaic agricultural methods still in use.

What To See and Do

With some notable exceptions, the south is less rich in artistic treasures than central and northern Italy. You'll want to visit the classical sites of Pompeii, Paestum and Metaponto, and the ancient city center of Bari with its Arabic echoes. Apulian towns such as Alberobello and Lecce are unique, but it's the coast and landscape of the south that many visitors remember.

South of Naples stretches one of Europe's most stunning coastlines, where you could happily spend a week lolling around the pretty villages and soaking up the sun. If you hanker after less-chic resorts, head farther south and east, where you'll find the homely little resorts of the Ionian coasts and Calabria. Apulia's long beaches and the cliffs of the Gargano strike a happy balance between rural charm and good facilities. Wilderness lovers will find the south's interior everything they could hope for, with great hiking in wonderful mountain scenery. Explore the Sila and Pollino inland areas, where you'll find upland meadows and forests reminiscent of northern landscapes.

Conical-shaped roofs of *trulli* – an architectural oddity found only in Puglia

When To Go

As in the rest of Italy, the best time to visit the south is in spring, early summer and fall. Spring sees the country at its greenest and most beautiful; by May and June it's already warm enough to enjoy the beaches. September and October can be idyllic, with velvet-warm seas and balmy nights. July and August are months to be avoided; the south has a true Mediterranean climate with temperatures climbing into the 90s. These are also the Italian holiday months when coastal resorts are at their most crowded and cities empty of their natives. Many hotels outside the main centers are closed during winter, when daylight hours are short, and it can be wet and windy.

NAPLES

Vibrant Naples (Napoli), the capital of
southern Italy and one of Europe's most
beautiful cities, is light years removed
from the dynamic, work-driven north.
Dirty, ramshackle and confusing,
Naples can feel alien and intimidating,
but visitors are quickly won over by its
exuberance, way of life and people.

Come to Naples with an open mind,
remembering you'll find a big,
sprawling city that suffered huge
damage in World War II.
Indiscriminate construction has
wrecked some of the loveliest outlying
areas, while the 19th-century slum
clearances by no means solved the
problems of overpopulation and social
deprivation. Concentrate instead on the
superb monuments, churches, museums,
galleries and the welcoming charm of
the people. In no other major Italian
city will you find such friendliness.

Getting Around

The horrific traffic makes all
transportation excruciatingly slow, so
it's best to tackle central Naples on foot.
Sites are grouped together in different
areas, so take a bus or cable car to get
there and then walk. Wandering around
is an essential part of the Naples

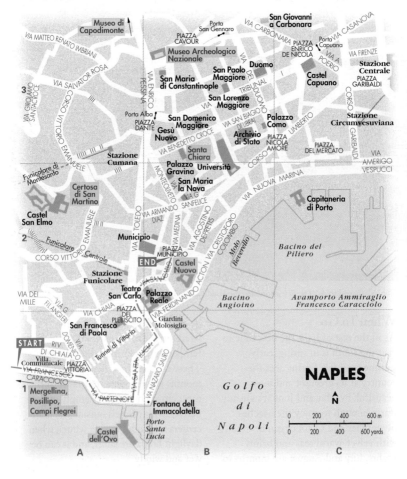

The South

experience, but stick to well-frequented areas. It is wise to avoid the labyrinthine back streets, the docks and the railroad station. Take great care crossing streets; Neapolitan drivers ignore pedestrian crossings, scooters appear to come from nowhere and they frequently use the pavement. The best way to appreciate the beauty of Naples' superb setting on the bay is from the sea; you could combine this with a boat trip to Sorrento (see page 165) or the ravishing islands of Capri (see page 157) and Ischia.

Mediterranean Flavors

Neapolitan cooking ranks among Italy's best, with intense flavors and a strong emphasis on the freshest fish and seafood, and local fruits and vegetables. It is home to thin, crisp pizza, baked in wood-fired ovens. Cakes and pastries, stuffed with *crema* and dripping with liqueurs, come from a *pasticceria*; where you'll often find ice cream, best in summer when it's made with seasonal fruit. Local wines to try are *Lacryma Christi* (Christ's Tears) and *Greco di Tufo*, and be sure to sample *Limoncello*, a lemon-flavored liqueur.

Shopping and Entertainment

Head for the Via Toledo and the Via Chiaia for designer outlets, leather goods, knitwear and accessories; this area is also home to department stores such as la Rinascente and Coin, while the Vomero district has shopping centers at Galleria Vanvitelli and Galleria Scartelli. The San Biagio neighborhood is the place to hunt for coral jewelry and cameo brooches, as well as beautiful traditional nativity figures.

If you like opera and classical music, try to fit in a performance at the San Carlo opera house. Traditional music is easy to find, and many restaurants feature evening serenades.

ESSENTIAL INFORMATION

TOURIST INFORMATION
•Stazione Centrale ☎ 081 26 8779
•Stazione Mergellina ☎ 081 761 2102
•Capodichino Airport ☎ 081 780 5761

URBAN TRANSPORTATION
It's best to walk in traffic-clogged Naples. Longer distances can be covered by the subway, bus and cable car, all of which are slow. There are two types of *Giranapoli* tickets, valid for either 90 minutes or all day; they are interchangeable between the systems and available from tobacconists or newsstands. They must be validated at each stage in the special machines. A new subway line, which will run into the historic center, was scheduled for completion during 2000. The Circumvesuviana railway runs every half-hour from Corso Garibaldi to Sorrento,

an hour's journey. You can also travel to Sorrento by ferry or hydrofoil from either Mergellina or the Molo Beverello docks. The same companies also serve Capri, Ischia and the other islands. There are taxi stands throughout the city, or you can telephone Taxi Napoli (☎ 081 556 4444), Taxi Free (☎ 081 551 5151) or Taxi Partenope (☎ 081 556 0202). Taxis will also take you sightseeing outside Naples for fixed rates.

AIRPORT INFORMATION
Naples Capodichino Airport (☎ 081 789 62 45; 081 789 63 85), with internal and European flights, is northwest of the city center. Airport buses (☎ 081 531 16 46) run at 50-minute intervals to Piazza Municipio, Via Piazza Garibaldi, between 6 p.m. and midnight. Bus 14, every 15 minutes, runs as far as Piazza Garibaldi.

CLIMATE – Average highs and lows

JAN.	FEB.	MAR.	APR.	MAY	JUN.	JUL.	AUG.	SEP.	OCT.	NOV.	DEC.
12°C	13°C	15°C	18°C	22°C	26°C	29°C	29°C	26°C	22°C	17°C	13°C
54°F	55°F	59°F	64°F	72°F	79°F	84°F	84°F	79°F	72°F	63°F	55°F
4°C	5°C	7°C	9°C	13°C	17°C	19°C	19°C	17°C	13°C	8°C	5°C
39°F	41°F	45°F	48°F	55°F	63°F	66°F	66°F	63°F	55°F	46°F	41°F

The South

NAPLES SIGHTS

Key to symbols

✚ map coordinates refer to the Naples map on page 150; sights below are highlighted in yellow on the map

✉ address or location ☎ telephone number

🕐 opening times 🍴 restaurant on site or nearby

Ⓜ nearest subway station

🚌 nearest bus or tram route

💷 admission charge: $$$ more than L5,000, $$ L3,000 to L5,000, $ less than L3,000

ℹ information

CASTEL DELL'OVO

Encircled by the sea, Castel dell'Ovo (Egg Castle) is Naples' oldest castle; it was built between the ninth and 16th centuries. Its name was derived from the story that it was built on top of an egg placed here in Roman times and if the egg breaks, Naples will fall. Run-down and dilapidated by the 1970s, it has now been extensively restored and is used for cultural events.

✚ A1 ✉ Borgo Marinaro 🍴 La Cantinella, see page 209 🚌 R3; tram 1

CASTEL NUOVO

The Castel Nuovo (New Castle), with its five massive towers, dominates the Naples waterfront. First built in 1282, it was enlarged in the 15th century and was later the residence of the Aragonese monarchs. Today, it's the home of the Naples city council. A magnificent Renaissance gateway gives access to the central courtyard, which is surrounded by buildings housing the Museo Civico (Civic Museum), the splendid Gothic Sala dei Baroni (Baron's Hall) and the Cappella Palatina (Palatine Chapel), the only surviving part of an earlier 13th-century building.

Nearby is the huge and imposing Palazzo Reale, a grandiose structure built in 1602 with a flamboyant but strangely dull interior. The famous San Carlo, Italy's largest opera house, is to the east of the castle.

✚ B2 ✉ Piazza Municipio ☎ 081 795 2003 🕐 Mon.–Sat. 9–7 🚌 R2, R3 💷 $$

CERTOSA DI SAN MARTINO

Visible from all over Naples, the hilltop complex of the Certosa di San Martino (St. Martin's Charterhouse) was mainly constructed between the 16th and 18th centuries. You can explore the newly restored Chiostro Grande (Main Cloister), the sumptuous baroque church and the lavishly decorated Quarto del Priore (Prior's Quarters). Don't miss the exhibition of *presepe* (nativity figures), a charming collection of figures, animals and everyday objects fashioned for the great 19th-century Christmas nativity scenes, the highlight of the Certosa. Walk through the monastery to the terrace at the back; attractively planted with shrubs and trees, it commands a sweeping view of the city and Bay of Naples.

✚ A2 ✉ Vomero ☎ 081 578 1769 🕐 Tue.–Sun. 9–2 Ⓜ Montesanto 🚌 V1 💷 $$

MERGELLINA

This waterfront area to the city's west is a popular place to eat. Its harbor is the focal point of the traditional fishermen's quarter, and it's a delightful place to stroll or pause in the main piazza to enjoy ice cream. Fishing boats and island ferries still leave from the harbor.

✚ A1 ✉ Via Mergellina 🍴 Don Salvatore, see page 209 Ⓜ Mergellina 🚌 R3, C21

MUSEO ARCHEOLOGICO NAZIONALE

The Museo Archeologico (Archeological Museum) houses one of the world's most important collections of classical sculpture, mosaics, gems, glass and silver. You'll need two to three hours to do it justice, and buy an English-language guide before you start. The first floor is devoted mainly to sculpture, much from the 17th-century Farnese collections that were largely discovered in Rome. The stars are the muscular *Farnese Hercules*, and the *Farnese Bull*. Dating from 200 BC, this is the largest classical sculptural group to have survived. Many rooms are filled with finds from Pompei and Herculaneum, including charming frescoes and mosaics;

Santa Chiara, one of the best-known churches in the city, stands at the center of historic Naples

don't miss the graceful fresco of Flora scattering spring flowers, and a mosaic of a fierce but friendly dog from a Pompeian front door.

➕ B3 ✉ Piazza Museo ☎ 081 440 166 ◉ Daily 9–7:30 🚌 1, 24, 42 ✋ $$$ ➕ English-language guide books are available at the shop

MUSEO DI CAPODIMONTE

Built in 1738 as the Bourbon King Charles III's palace and surrounded by a wooded park, Capodimonte has been restored and rearranged. You can wander freely through the opulent royal apartments on your way to the majolica and porcelain collection, much of it made by the Capodimonte factory and painted with local scenes. Upstairs is the superb picture gallery, a representative collection spanning the 15th to 17th centuries, with the emphasis on Renaissance paintings. Some rooms are often closed, but with luck you should see Botticelli's *Madonna*, Umbrian pictures by Perugino and Pinturricchio and some sensitive portraits of Pope Paul III by Titian. There's a Raphael portrait of Pope Leo X, contrasting with Sebastiano del Piombo's worldly interpretation of Pope Clement VII.

➕ A3 ✉ Parco di Capodimonte ☎ 081 744 1307 ◉ Tue.–Sat. 10–7, Sun. 9–2 🚌 R4, 24, 110, 161 ✋ $$

POSILLIPO AND THE CAMPI FLEGREI

Posillipo and the Campi Flegrei (literally "Burning Fields," named because of the area's volcanic activity) lie to the west of Naples on what is still a lovely stretch of coast. Dotted with classical ruins, fishing villages, beaches, inlets and grottos, this is an area well worth exploring.

➕ Off the map ✉ Posillipo 🚇 Mergellina, Campi Flegrei

SANTA CHIARA

The great Franciscan church of Santa Chiara is a good starting point for exploring Spaccanapoli, the ebullient heart of historic Naples. Packed with squares and historic buildings, this entire area teems with life, noise and confusion. By contrast, the church is simple and austere. Rebuilt after a fire in 1943, it contains tombs and gives access to the 14th-century cloister with its garden and 17th-century columns and seats. There is a museum and spectacular nativity scene.

➕ B3 ✉ Via Benedetto Croce ☎ 081 552 6209 ◉ Church: daily 7–12:30 and 4–7; cloister: Mon.–Sat. 8:30–12:30 and 3:30–6:30, Sun. 9:30–1; museum Mon.–Sat. 9:30–1 and 3:30–5:30, Sun. 9:30–1 🚌 R1, R4, 110 ✋ Museum: $

The Palazzo Reale, the former Royal Palace

WALK: WATERFRONT NAPLES

Refer to route marked on city map page 150.

This walk beside the sea will take about an hour. Starting from the Villa Communale, it goes through the elegant neighborhood of Chiaia to Santa Lucia and on to Piazza Municipio.

Start on Via Francesco Caracciolo, a pedestrian, waterfront street to the west of the Castel dell'Ovo.

Via Caracciolo was constructed in the late 19th century; its broad elegance will help you to appreciate Naples' glorious location. Views stretch right around the bay from the north headland to Vesuvius in the south.

From Piazza della Repubblica continue along Via Caracciola's walkway. To your left you'll see the green oasis of the Villa Communicale, Naples' central park.

The gardens with steps down to the sea were laid out in 1778 with parallel walks, trees, shrubs and statues; they were enlarged in the 19th century when the promenade was built. The gardens are always crowded on summer evenings, and on the third weekend of every month, when an antiques market takes place in the villa. In the middle of the gardens stands the 19th-century building housing the Aquarium, a rather dreary collection of fish and marine life.

Walk along farther to Piazza Vittoria and continue beside the sea along Via Partenope, a smart street lined with luxury hotels. To your right looms the Castel dell'Ovo (see page 152), which you'll pass on the right as the road swings around to reach the harbor of Santa Lucia.

There's a splendid fish market here in the mornings, while later in the day you can eat a delicious seafood lunch or dinner in one of the restaurants clustered along the waterfront. Every Neapolitan song you've heard seems to feature this area, including the best-known of all, O Sole Mio. Ahead of you stands the flamboyant fountain known as the Immacolatella.

Cross Via Partenope and turn left up Via Santa Lucia.

This area contains some of Naples' most elegant shops, where you'll find outlets for Italian and international designer names, as well as local stores specializing in more traditional Neapolitan products, such as coral necklaces, bracelets and earrings, and delicate cameo brooches.

Via Santa Lucia opens on Via Cesario Console, where you turn left to head up to sweeping Piazza del Plebiscito with the Palazzo Reale to your right. Turn right onto Via San Carlo, which leads past San Carlo opera house and the Castel Nuovo (see page 152) to busy Piazza Municipio, with the grandiose city hall at the top of the square.

There's no best time to visit Naples, although spring and fall are ideal for those who don't enjoy extremes. July and August can be hot, with temperatures well over 95 degrees Fahrenheit (35 degrees Celsius), while winter and spring can be cold and wet. Whenever you visit, you'll find the calendar punctuated by a series of feasts and festivals.

Dressed for the Easter Parade

SEASON BY SEASON

Spring and Summer

Carnival generally falls in February. March 19, the feast of San Giuseppe, is the traditional date for changing to spring clothes, and Good Friday sees religious processions through the streets of many city neighborhoods. This time of grief is followed by the joyous celebrations of Easter Sunday and Monday, affectionately known as *Pasquetta*, when families head to the country for huge feasts.

The first Sunday in May is the first of two annual celebrations of San Gennaro, the patron saint of Naples, when his statue is carried through the streets from the cathedral. Many buildings and churches are opened in May, an inspired idea to encourage locals and visitors to rediscover historic Naples. The *Estate a Napoli* (Summer in Naples) festival, a series of arts events in and around the city, runs from July to September. July 16 is the feast of Madonna del Carmine; a fireworks display commemorates the saving of the church's belltower from fire by the Blessed Virgin Mary. August, the traditional vacation month throughout Italy, is Naples' quietest month, and many restaurants close.

Autumn and Winter

Autumn's biggest feast is on September 19, the feast of the miracle of the blood of San Gennaro. In front of huge crowds in the cathedral, accompanied by cheering and emotional scenes, a phial of the saint's normally solid blood liquidizes. December 8, the feast of the Immaculate Conception, is the start of the Christmas season, when the first of the *presepe* (nativity figures) are made. Christmas itself sees more feasting, while the days before New Year's are marked by fireworks and bagpipers. Children get presents on January 6, the Epiphany, when Befana, a benevolent witch, brings gifts to good kids and "coal" (lumps of black candy) to bad kids.

The South

Costumed processions parade through the streets on Good Friday

Alberobello's beguiling *trulli* are still homes for many local people

REGIONAL SIGHTS

Key to symbols

✚ map coordinates refer to the region map on page 146; sights below are highlighted in yellow on the map
✉ address or location ☎ telephone number
🕐 opening times 🍴 restaurant on site or nearby
⛴ ferry 🖐 admission charge: $$$ more than L5,000, $$ L3,000 to L5,000, $ less than L3,000 🛈 information

ALBEROBELLO

Driving inland south from Bari, you'll start to notice round, stone buildings with conical roofs topped with a stone symbol; these structures are *trulli*, found nowhere else in Europe except in this area of Apulia. Scattered across the landscape, there are more and more to be seen as you approach Alberobello. This little town, a UNESCO World Heritage Site, has more than 1,400 *trulli* in two different areas, the Rione Monti and the Aia Piccola.

The Rione Monti, a series of *trulli*-lined streets running down the hillside, is a tourist heaven. Most of the *trulli* have been turned into craft shops, enabling you to wander through the interiors and even climb on their roofs, where you'll find perfect photo opportunities featuring a forest of these charming structures

Aia Piccola is much more the genuine article; here, the *trulli* are still people's homes. Nobody really knows the origin of this architecture, once thought to have been a form of tax evasion on permanent dwellings. The latest theories link them with ancient Greece or even Syria – Apulia was once part of Magna Graecia – or they could have been introduced by eastern monks or returning Crusaders.
✚ D5
Tourist information ✉ Piazza Ferdinando IV
☎ 080 432 1200 🕐 Mon.–Sat. 9–1:30 and 4–7, Sun. 9–1:30

BARI

Ancient Bari falls into two sections, the grid-plan 19th-century town with its straight avenues and seafront promenade, and the old city, one of southern Italy's most vibrant warrens. Explore the jumble of narrow streets, where vibrant life surges

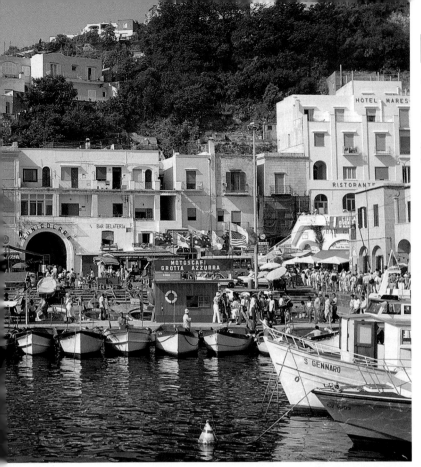

Vacation villas overlook the colorful waterfront of Marina Grande's harbor on Capri

around you: flapping washing, crowded one-room apartments open to the street, women screeching from balconies and roaring scooters.

Here you'll find the great Basilica di San Nicola (St. Nicholas), built between 1087 and 1180 and the stunning prototype for many of Apulia's Romanesque churches. Behind its balanced façade lies a lofty dim interior whose treasures include a 12th-century *ciborio* (altar canopy) and a superb episcopal throne. St. Nicholas is buried in the crypt. Each December, the basilica is the focal point for the exuberant processions and festivities that celebrate the saint's feast. Nearby stands the more austere Cattedrale di San Sabino (St. Sabine's Cathedral), whose simple interior contains an eighth-century icon of the Virgin Mary, said to be a true likeness. Close by you'll find the huge 13th-century bulk of the Castello (Castle), built by Frederick II, which stands on the site of a Roman fort. Pay attention to what's going on around you and make sure your valuables are out of sight; Bari is a tough city with a bad reputation.

✚ C5

Tourist information ✉ Piazza Aldo Moro 33 ☎ 080 524 2244 🕐 Mon.–Sat. 9–2

Basilica di San Nicola ✉ Piazza San Nicola 🕐 Daily 9–1 and 5–7 🎏 Festivities with processions, concerts and fireworks are held during the week of Dec. 6

Cattedrale di San Sabino ✉ Piazza Odegitria 🕐 Daily 8:30–1 and 5–7

Castello ✉ Piazza Federico II de Svevio 2 ☎ 080 521 4361 🕐 Mon.–Sat. 9–1 and 3:30–7 🔖 $

CAPRI

A favorite of Roman emperors, the tiny island of Capri displays spectacular scenery and crystal waters, and is easily reached as a day trip from Naples. The two main settlements are Anacapri and Capri; their white-washed houses and narrow winding streets are jam-packed with tempting boutiques, cafés and restaurants. Many visitors take a boat trip to the Grotta Azzurra (Blue Grotto), a spectacular sea-cave filled with refracted turquoise light.

Another highlight is the beautiful Villa San Michele in Anacapri. Built in the late 19th century by the Swedish physician Axel Munthe, this dream-like villa with its peaceful green garden is filled with classical statues, while from its shady pergola you can enjoy some of the island's loveliest views.

Classical enthusiasts can walk to the ruins of Villa Jovis, Tiberius' clifftop villa, from where he allegedly threw victims into the sea. Another stroll leads to a lookout above the Faraglioni, a cluster of offshore rocks jutting more than 360 feet out of the sea.

⊞ A4

Tourist information ✉ Piazza Umberto 0686 🕐 Mon.–Sat. 8–8, Sun. 8:30–2:30 🚢 Ferry operator: Caremar, from Molo Beverello, Naples (☎ 081 551 5384). Hydrofoil operators: Caremar, from Molo Beverello, Naples (☎ 081 551 3882); NLG, from Molo Beverello, Naples (☎ 081 552 7209); SNAV, from Mergellina, Naples (☎ 081 761 2348)

Blue Grotto ☎ 081 837 0634 🕐 Daily (weather permitting) 9–1 hour before dusk 🚢 From Marina Grande 💰 $$$

Villa San Michele ✉ Anacapri ☎ 081 837 1401 🕐 Daily 9:30–6, May–Sep.; 9:30–5, Apr. and Oct.; 9:30–4:30, Mar.; 10:30–3:30, rest of year 💰 $$

Villa Jovis ✉ Anacapri 🕐 Daily 9–1 hour before dusk 💰 $

CASTEL DEL MONTE

The gentle rolling landscape behind the coast near Bari is dominated by the huge bulk of Castel del Monte. Built of luminous ashlar stone by the Sicily-based German emperor Frederick II in 1240, this mighty building soars up against the blue sky on a windswept, lonely hill. The octagonal castle is built around an octagonal courtyard and is flanked by eight towers, which are also octagonal. This mathematical precision is a mystery,

as is the lack of defensive features normally associated with a medieval castle. Some scholars claim its proportions relate to the movement of the stars. Others think Frederick may have built it as a pilgrim hostel or to imitate a Jerusalem mosque. You can wander around its high, bare, interlinked rooms and look down to the courtyard through the windows and French doors on the upstairs floor. Windows also pierce the outer walls, giving panoramic views of the countryside and sea.

⊞ C5

✉ Andria 🕐 Mon.–Sat. 8:30–7, Sun. 9–1, Apr.–Sep.; Mon.–Sat. 8:30–2, Sun. 9–1, rest of year 🍴 Bar and restaurant outside gates 💰 $$

LECCE

Elegant Lecce is packed with exuberant baroque architecture, the product of 17th-century mercantile money and the zeal of religious orders. Known as Leccese Baroque, the style is opulent, extravagant, yet airy, with churches, palaces and houses all a riot of gambolling *putti*, windswept saints and angels, curlicues, garlands and wreaths. It's a joy to wander, but start with the Basilica di Santa Croce, the apotheosis of the style. It stands next to the wonderful Palazzo dei Celestini, whose restrained courtyard contrasts with its intricate facade. Both were designed by Giuseppe Zimbalo, who was responsible for many of Lecce's most successful buildings. From here, cross Piazza Oronzo, with its Roman amphitheater still used for concerts, and head up Via Vittorio Emanuele to Piazza del Duomo, a spacious and elegant square whose Duomo (Cathedral) is flanked by the lovely Seminario (Seminary) and Palazzo Vescovile (Bishop's Palace).

Lecce's other treasures include more fine churches such as Santa Chiara, the Rosario, the Gesù and the Carmine, Charles V's vast 16th-century castle and the interesting Museo Provinciale.

⊞ E4

Tourist information ✉ Via Vittorio Emanuele 24 ☎ 0832 332 463 🕐 Mon.–Sat. 9–1 and 5–7:30

Basilica di Santa Croce ✉ Via Umberto I 🕐 Daily 8–12:30 and 4–7

A window of Lecce's Basilica di Santa Croce provides a perfect example of the city's flamboyant Baroque architecture

Duomo ✉ Piazza del Duomo ⏰ Daily 8–12:30 and 4–7
Museo Provinciale ✉ Viale Gallipoli 28 ☎ 0832 247 025 ⏰ Mon.–Fri. 8:30–1:30 and 2–7

MARATEA

Pretty Maratea stands on Basilicata's Tyrrhenian coast, where majestic mountains drop to the sea and lovely coves and beaches make a sharp contrast to the flat lands along the Ionian gulf to the east. With its good hotels and restaurants, Maratea makes an ideal stopping point for a few nights if you're traveling south. The old village has a tangle of narrow streets, squares and steps, with some fine old houses and churches. Below lies the port, attractive houses, shops and restaurants, while fine tourist hotels and villas are tucked among the pine trees on either side.

A winding coastal road connects everything and gives access to secluded bays and beaches. High above on Monte San Biagio stands a huge statue of Christ the Redeemer, which was erected in 1965. You can drive up here to visit the

Santuario di San Biagio, built on the site of a pagan temple, and take in the superb views up and down the coast.
➕ B4
Tourist information ✉ Piazza del Gesù ☎ 0973 876 908 ⏰ Daily 9–1 and 3–8, Apr. to mid-Sep.; 9–12:30 and 4–7, rest of year; ✉ Via San Nicola 43 ☎ 0973 876 499 ⏰ Daily 9–1 and 3–8, Apr. to mid-Sep.; 9–12:30 and 4–7, rest of year

The little coastal town of Maratea

The South

DRIVE: THE UNDISCOVERED GARGANO PENINSULA

Duration: 7 to 9 hours

This drive, best enjoyed in spring or early summer, will give you a chance to explore the incredible natural beauty of the Gargano peninsula, as well as take in a couple of its inland and coastal towns. All the roads are steep, twisting and occasionally vertiginous, so don't attempt this if you suffer from travel sickness. It would be a long drive to tackle in a day; both Vieste and Péschici would be good places to spend the night, with excellent swimming and seafood as enticements.

Pilgrims have been visiting Monte Sant'Angelo since the fifth century

The Gargano is the "spur" on the boot of Italy. It's a limestone plateau bordered on the north by beaches and lagoons and on the south by steep pine-clad cliffs and rocky coves. The interior is mountainous with high grassy meadows, intricate agricultural terraces with almonds, olives and grapevines and upland forests of oak and beech trees. The flora and fauna are outstanding, and there are plans to turn the whole area into a national park, a move that would help protect the area from increasing development as more and more summer visitors come to enjoy the lovely coast and clear seas.

Start your drive at Monte Sant'Angelo, reached via the SS89 from Manfredònia on the coast.

Monte Sant'Angelo, one of the oldest Christian shrines in Europe, is dedicated to Archangel Michael. Pilgrims have been journeying here since at least the fifth century to pray at the spot where Michael is said to have appeared. His sanctuary stands on the grotto where he was sighted; you approach through superb 11th-century bronze doors made in Constantinople. The town has some interesting streets of terraced medieval houses and a fine Norman castle, along with hordes of devout pilgrims.

Take the SS272 to the north of town into the valley. At the junction branch right onto the SS528. Follow this until you reach the Foresta Umbra visitor center.

This is an exceptionally

Péschici, just one of the many picturesque seaside towns set in the rocky coastline of the Gargano Peninsula

varied and lovely stretch through woods and meadowland and past ancient terraces. The Foresta Umbra (Forest of Shadows) stretches right across the upland heart of the Gargano. Forest like this, mainly beech and oak, once covered much of Apulia. It's a wonderful wildlife habitat and the home to a wide variety of animals and birds. The woods are rich in wildflowers; spring crocus gives way to numerous different orchids, and in autumn the woodland floor is carpeted with drifts of cyclamen. Foxes, wolves, deer and wild boar inhabit the deep forest, and you could easily spot woodpeckers, hawks and hoopoes. You can learn more at the visitor center, where deer and mouflon are kept in an enclosure. From here, easy hikes lead into the woods past the little lake and its picnic tables.

Turn right onto an unclassified road running northeast and signposted Segheria il Mandrione and Vieste. After 24 kilometers (15 miles), turn right onto the SS89 to Vieste.

Still a small fishing port, Vieste is a jolly and relaxed town with superb beaches and a range of hotels and restaurants. It's not yet swamped by international tourism, and the old center, with its narrow cobbled streets, castle and 11th-century cathedral, is well worth a stop. The coastline to the south is stunningly beautiful, with hidden beaches beneath high limestone cliffs and a series of watery caves and grottoes around the Testa del Gargano headland. You can take a boat trip to view these or venture farther offshore to the beautiful Trémiti islands. Watch for the *trabuco* on Vieste's headland. This huge wooden structure entwined with ropes and winches is for catching mullet; the design is thought to date from Phoenician times.

Explore the road south of Vieste along the coast before retracing your route and heading north on the SS89 to Péschici.

The winding road follows more lovely coast and sandy beaches before you reach Péschici, a picturesque town tumbling down a headland to a sandy beach. It dates from the 10th century when it was built as a defense against Saracen raids, and its claustrophobic labyrinth of alleys has a distinctly Eastern feel. Boats also run from Rodi Garganico, further along the coast to the Trémiti islands.

Vieste tourist information ✉ Piazza Kennedy ☎ 0884 707 495 🕐 Mon.–Fri. 8:30–1:30
Trémiti Islands Ferries ✉ Tickets from Gargano Viaggi, Piazza Roma 7 ☎ 0884 707393 📅 Daily departures from May to Sep.

Atmospheric lighting enhances the fascination of Matera's unique cave houses

MATERA

Matera, a UNESCO World Heritage Site, has been continuously inhabited since Paleolithic times, making it one of the world's oldest settlements. It's a provincial capital with an admirable dose of civic pride, and its *sassi* provide one of Europe's most bizarre urban features. *Sassi* are cave-dwellings dug out of the sides of the ravine over the centuries. Many were inhabited until the 1960s, when the area was cleared and the people rehoused. Today, some *sassi* have been restored and people have moved back, living in very different conditions from 30 years ago, when malaria, trachoma and dysentery were common. A road (Strada Panoramica dei Sassi) has been built through the *sassi* district, but to explore it thoroughly, you'll need to penetrate the maze of tiny streets. Be sure to see the *chiese rupestri* (rock-hewn churches), carved by monks from the eighth to 13th centuries.

Leave time for the rest of the town, which centers around Piazza Vittorio Veneto, a lovely square. From here you can access both the *sassi* and the medieval *civita* area, whose winding streets lead to the 13th-century cathedral. Matera also boasts a superb archeological museum,

housed in the old convent of Santa Chiara. Newly restored, the collection covers local finds from the Paleolithic age to the full flowering of Greek civilization in Magna Graecia.

✚ C4

Tourist information ✉ Via de Viti de Marco 9 ☎ 0835 331 983 🕐 Mon.–Fri. 9–1:30 and 4–7, Sat. 9–1:30 🛈 Guides hold keys to the churches in the *sassi;* apply at the tourist office, or, if approached, make sure it is an official guide wearing a badge

Museo Nazionale Domenico Ridola ✉ Via Ridola 24 ☎ 0835 333 541 🕐 Daily 9–7 💷 $$

METAPONTO

Ancient Metapontum was one of the greatest of the sixth-century BC Greek cities of Magna Graecia. It was a thriving metropolis packed with temples, theaters and public buildings. Today, it's a huge and confusing archeological site where you'll need a lot of imagination to visualize its heyday. Most evocative is the Tavole Paladine, a fifth-century BC temple that is dedicated to Hera and stands alone among flowery grass and oleanders. Metaponto's chief draw is its superb and stylish Museo Archeologico (Archeological Museum), which traces the history of Metapontum from its native pre-Greek civilization to its decline

after Romanization. The jewelry is lovely
– look for the charming headdress of
gilded leaves decorated with berries and
crickets (third century BC) and the gold
bracelets and earrings. The red-and-black
figured vases are very fine, and careful
study of their decoration will tell you
much about everyday Greek life.
➕ C4

Museo Archeologico Nazionale ✉ Via Aristea 21
☎ 0835 745 327 🕐 Daily 9–1 and 3:30–10, Apr.–Sep.;
9–7:30, rest of year 🎫 $$

PARCO NAZIONALE DEL POLLINO

The Parco Nazionale del Pollino (Pollino
National Park), a 494,000-acre area of
wild and unspoiled mountainous
countryside in the southern Apennines,
lies in both Basilicata and Calabria. Its
highest point is Monte Pollino at 7,400
feet, and its landscape varies from high
mountain country through stony steppe
and rich forests to gorges, river valleys,
water meadows and dry river beds. The
park's symbol is the Bosnian pine, a tree
with scaled bark that grows on difficult
terrain up to 6,000 feet; few exist
elsewhere in Europe. Wildlife includes
wolves, wild boar and otter; eagles,
vultures and other raptors are common.

Twisting mountain roads link the
scattered villages within the park, many of
which are becoming popular as bases for
hiking and climbing. The main villages
are Terranova di Pollino, San Severino
Lucano, Carbone, Latronico and
Castellucio. Even if you don't have time to
explore this wonderful area, you can get a
taste of its scenic grandeur from the A3
autostrada; a spectacular section of this
freeway skirts the park's eastern edge.
➕ C4

RÉGGIO DI CALÁBRIA

Calábria's capital, an ancient Greek
foundation, is superbly located facing
Sicily on the Straits of Messina. It's the
only city of any size this far south, with a
vibrancy that belies its reputation.
Repeatedly devastated by earthquakes
over the centuries, dogged by high

The head of a lifesize, fifth-century BC bronze
sculpture, one of the Réggio's treasures

unemployment, and suffering from the
octopus-like embrace of the Calabrian
Mafia, physically it's a ramshackle and
grubby city with a few redeeming
features. But spare time to stroll its superb
seafront with its Roman remains and tree-
shaded garden, before heading down the
main street, Corso Garibaldi, to Réggio's
chief attraction, the Museo Nazionale.
This wonderful collection has material
from all over Calábria and it's well-
presented with plenty of English-
language information. The highlights are
the two antique bronzes known as the
Bronzi di Riace. These two fifth-century
BC sculptures were discovered underwater
off the Riace coast in 1972; after a lengthy
restoration they were returned to Calábria
in 1981. Naked, bearded and tautly
muscled, these superb works are attributed
to Phidias, the greatest sculptor of
antiquity.

Réggio has more shops and better bars
than anywhere else in the region
➕ C1

Tourist information ✉ Corso Garibaldi 329
☎ 0965 892 012 🕐 Mon.–Sat. 8–1:30, 2–8
Museo Nazionale della Magna Graecia ✉ Piazza
de Nava ☎ 0965 812 255 🕐 Mon.–Sat. 9–7 (closed
first and third Mon. of month), Sun. 9 a.m.–10 p.m.,
Apr.–Oct.; 9–7, rest of year 🎫 $$$

The South

RIVIERA CALABRESE

The stretch of coast north from Réggio di Calábria is known as the Riviera Calabrese (Calabrian Riviera). It's a string of small resorts and coastal villages popular with Italian vacationers. Tropea to the north is the prettiest; the lively town is perched above golden beaches. On a clear day there are superb views to the Aeolian Islands and the cone of Stròmboli; summer cruises will take you there.

Don't miss the lovely church of Santa Maria dell'Isola perched on a rocky massif near the sea, or the Norman cathedral in whose walls you can see two unexploded American bombs dating from World War II. Farther south, the coastline is more dramatic with towering cliffs and wide views to Sicily. Tucked down at the shoreline lies Scilla, a picturesque village set round a castle, with a sandy beach that doubles as a fishing port at its foot. This is the ancient Scylla of Homer's *Odyssey*, the lair of one of a pair of sea monsters. Charybdis, home to the other, lies across the Straits on Sicily.

✚ C1

Tropea tourist information ✉ Piazza Ercole
☎ 0963 61 475 🕓 Daily 9:30–12:30 and 5–8, Apr.–Sep.
✉ Via Panoramica ☎ 0965 790 537
🕓 Daily 9:30–12:30 and 5–8, Apr.–Sep.

ROSSANO

Modern Rossano perches on Calábria's east coast. It's a relaxed seaside resort with sandy beaches. Up a twisty road is the old town of Rossano, a shabby and charming hillside town with elegant, if crumbling, 16th-century palazzi and a spacious central square. From the eighth to 11th centuries, Rossano was a great Byzantine center of scholarship and piety, and its greatest treasures date from this time. In its cathedral you can see a ninth-century Byzantine fresco of the Blessed Virgin Mary, while the tiny museum tucked behind contains the famous *Codex Purpureus Rossanensis* (Purple Codex). This is a sixth-century Greek manuscript written on reddish-purple parchment from which it gets its name. The manuscript is illustrated with scenes from the gospels, and you can see how the *Last Supper* was originally depicted. From here, walk to ancient San Marco, a 10th-century Byzantine church, its triple-nave interior topped by five small cupolas. Few other buildings in southern Italy are so evocative.

✚ C3

Tourist information ✉ Piazza del Duomo ☎ 0983 525 263 🕓 Mon.–Sat. 9:30–1 🛈 The tourist office holds keys to the Museo Diocesano and San Marco

Tropea's cathedral dominates the old center of this popular vacation town on the Riviera Calabrese

SORRENTO PENINSULA AND THE AMALFI COAST

One of Europe's most beautiful coastal roads runs around the Sorrento peninsula to the south of Naples. Every twist and turn opens up another spectaular vista of sea and cliffs, while the string of villages it links are among the most attractive and popular on all of Italy's coastline.

Castellammare di Stàbia, nearest to Naples, is an ancient spa-town whose springs still draw people to the therapeutic waters. Sorrento, a good jumping off point for Capri (see page 158), is the first of the truly charming towns along the coast. Its pretty streets, beaches, bars and restaurants have been drawing visitors for the past 200 years, with such diverse figures as Casanova and Goethe also enjoying its delights.

From here, the main road cuts inland and south to emerge on the Amalfi side of the peninsula. Positano, the first town of any size, is a pyramid of color-washed houses tumbling down the cliffs to a beach where sun-worshippers share the space with fishing boats. Tempting shops sell the town's famous brightly colored textiles. Bars and restaurants beckon, and boats sail to otherwise inaccessible swimming coves. East lies Praiano, whose cliff approaches are dotted with opulent private villas. Between here and Amalfi, you can visit the Grotta dello Smeraldo (Emerald Cave), a vividly green sea cave complete with stalagmites and stalactites. Amalfi, tucked between the mountains and the sea, is a cheerful small town whose only clue to its great past as a powerful maritime republic is its wonderful Duomo (Cathedral). Approached up a wide flight of steps, the cathedral was built in the 11th century, its bronze doors cast in Constantinople in 1066. Don't miss the 13th-century cloister known as the Chiostro del Paradiso (Cloister of Paradise), a peaceful enclave with white-washed interlaced arches.

High above the coast east of Amalfi stands Ravello, offering the finest of all views of the coast. The 13th-century cathedral has a splendid pulpit donated by the Rufolo family, who also built the Villa

Colored tiles decorate the belltower of Amalfi's cathedral

Rufolo, where the courtyard and gardens inspired Wagner's *Parsifal*. There are more gardens at the Villa Cimbrone, as well as incomparable views toward the south.

Castellammare di Stàbia ✚ A4
Tourist information ✉ Piazza Matteoti ☎ 081 871 1334 🕐 Mon.–Sat. 9–1:30 and 4:30–7:30
Sorrento ✚ A4
Tourist information ✉ Via Luigi de Maio 35 ☎ 081 877 3397 🕐 Mon.–Sat. 8:30–2 and 4:30–7
Positano ✚ A4
Tourist information ✉ Via Saraceno 4 ☎ 089 875 067 🕐 Daily 8–2
Amalfi ✚ A4
Tourist information ✉ Corso Roma 19 ☎ 089 872 619 🕐 Mon.–Sat. 8–2 and 4–7
Duomo di Sant'Andrea
✉ Piazza del Duomo 🕐 Daily 9–1 and 3–8; Chiostro del Paradiso: daily 9–8, Apr.–Oct.; 10–5, rest of year
Grotta dello Smeraldo
✉ SS 163, 4 kilometers (2.5 miles) from Amalfi 🕐 Daily 9–5, Mar.–Oct.; 10–4, rest of year 💳 $$
Ravello ✚ A4
Tourist information ✉ Piazza Vescovado 1 ☎ 089 857 977 🕐 Mon.–Sat. 8–8, Sun. 8–2
Duomo ✉ Piazza del Duomo 🕐 Daily 8:30–1 and 3–6:30, Mar.–Nov.; 8:30–1 and 3–8, rest of year
Villa Rufolo ✉ Piazza del Duomo ☎ 089 857 675 🕐 Daily 9–8, Apr.–Nov.; 9–6, rest of year 💳 $$
Villa Cimbrone ✉ Via Santa Chiara 26 ☎ 089 857 138 🕐 Daily 9–1 hour before dusk

A forbidding glimpse of the crater on Vesuvius, where the ground is warm even in midwinter

VESUVIUS AND POMPEI

One of the world's best-known volcanoes, Vesuvius rises smoothly to 4,200 feet above the Bay of Naples. It has had more than 100 eruptions since Roman times, the last in 1944. You get a good view of the volcano from the Circumvesuviana railroad. Buses run up to within a half-hour's walk, which is worth it for the spectacular views and odd whisps of steam that come from the deep jumble of reddish rocks that form the crater.

Vesuvius is renowned for its devastating eruption in AD 79, when it engulfed the prosperous Roman city of Pompei (Pompeii) and its neighbor Herculaneum, burying them under a thick layer of pumice and volcanic ash. Pompeii remained buried for more than 1,700 years, perfectly preserved beneath a hard layer of volcanic debris. Excavations started about 1750 and the city gradually emerged. Worth tracking down as you explore the town are the forum, theaters, covered market, bakery, laundry, and numerous taverns advertising bargain prices on the walls outside.

The most interesting buildings are the houses; some are wonderfully preserved and still decorated with wall-paintings in vivid reds and ochres. The House of the Vetii with its lovely garden and frescoed dining room is a highlight, as is the House of the Tragic Poet, whose owners had a portrait mosaic of their dog by the front door with *cave canem* (beware of the dog) carefully inscribed.

Other houses worth seeing are the spacious House of the Faun, House of Menander with its elegant bath and adjoining dressing room, and Villa of the Mysteries. This lies outside Pompeii's walls at the end of the tomb-lined Via dei Sepolcri; its rich frescoes are connected with the Dionysian cult. Magnificent statues and artifacts were found at Pompeii, as were the bodies of those asphyxiated by the fumes; plaster casts of these are scattered throughout the city. Most of Pompeii's artistic treasures were moved; you can see many at the Museo Nazionale Archeologico (see page 152) in Naples.

Vesuvius ✚ A5 🚉 Circumvesuviana railway to Ercolano then bus to stop close to summit
Pompeii ✚ A5 ☎ 081 536 5154 🕐 Daily from 9–1 hour before dusk 🍴 Self-service restaurant and bar outside forum, many in modern Pompeii
🚉 Circumvesuviana railway 🎟 $$$

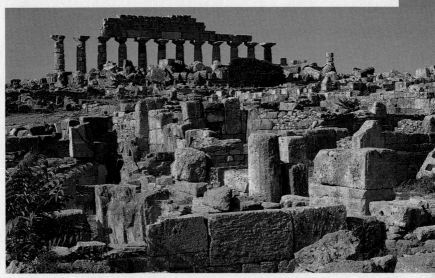

The Acropolis looms above the Greek city of Selinunte, Sicily

MAGNA GRAECIA

Throughout southern Italy and Sicily, you'll see ruins of great Greek temples and cities and a superb array of Greek artistic treasures in archeological museums. Why are they here? Where did they come from?

Greek Arrivals

Greece is mountainous country with little arable land. As the city-states grew in size and influence, they started to trade with parts of Italy and quickly realized that colonization was feasible in this flat and fertile land. Greeks moved into the modern regions of Campania, Basilicata, Calabria and Sicily in the eighth century BC, establishing a network of settlements. They absorbed the cultures and populations of the indigenous tribes and quickly established an efficient and high-yielding agricultural system. Grapes and olives were introduced, the colonies became enormously successful, and cities such as Siracusa, Sybaris, Metapontum and Tarentum were soon richer and more sophisticated than those in Greece. The area was, in every way Magna Graecia – "Greater Greece."

Decline

Like the city-states of mainland Greece, these colonies were split by internal rivalries and internecine war, uniting only when faced with the threat of outside invasion, sometimes from Greece itself. In 415 BC Siracusa and her allies trounced Athens in a great sea battle. The North African power of Carthage, founded by the Phoenicians, posed a continuous threat, often playing one of the Magna Graecia cities against the others. The colonies finally allied in the third century BC against the growing might of Rome. In 400 BC, the Romans razed Sybaris, and in 211 BC the sack of Siracusa marked the effective demise of Magna Graecia.

The Legacy

You can see archeological and historical traces of these city-states all over southern Italy and Sicily. On the mainland, head for the great temples of Paestum, south of Salerno, or Metapuntum with its fabulous archeological museum, or the scattered and sparse ruins of once-voluptuous Sybaris. Sicily is richest of all, with theaters at Taormina and Siracusa and wonderful temples at Segesta, Selinunte and Agrigento. Smaller sites lie everywhere and even somewhat obscure museums have superb collections of stunning Greek vases and sculpture.

SICILY AND SARDINIA

Sicily and Sardinia

" I TALY'S two main islands contribute mountainous interior and beautiful coastline to enhance the rich cultural heritage of the people. "

Snow-capped and smoking, Mount Etna's summit is a fitting backdrop for beautiful Taormina

SICILY AND SARDINIA

Sicily (Sicilia), one of the Mediterranean's largest islands, is also one of its most beautiful, with rugged mountain scenery, woodlands, a diverse coastline, and rich agricultural land producing wheat, olives, vines and citrus fruits. The eastern half is dominated by the graceful cone of Mount Etna, Europe's largest volcano, while the interior pushes north to the coast in the shape of the Monti Madonie. Good beaches are found all round the island, with some internationally renowned resorts on the east and north coasts, while the outlying islands have some of the clearest waters in the Mediterranean. Sardinia (Sardegna) is only a little farther from the African coast of Tunisia than it is from the Italian mainland, making a trip here feasible only if you have plenty of time.

Sicily's Past

A succession of foreign invaders ruled the island from the fifth century BC until the process of Italian unification began in Sicily in 1860. The ancient Greeks, the Carthaginians, the Romans, Arabs, Normans and Spanish all left their marks. These conquerors drained Sicily economically dry, while their rule left a legacy of resentment, oppression and insularity, and an ideal breeding ground for the corruption of organized crime. Marginalized for centuries from mainstream Italy, Sicilians still see themselves as a people apart. Since World War II, aid has poured in from central government and the European Union, but poverty is still widespread.

Sicilians

Sicilians first and Italians second, the island's population is exuberant and outgoing. Tourism is important, and you'll find the people welcoming and friendly, though the levels of accommodations and service may not be what you're used to. English is spoken in the main tourist centers and good hotels, but away from these very few people speak English. You'll notice

Sicily and Sardinia

SARDINIA

in remoter areas that it's rare to see women on the streets or working; society is still male-dominated, with wives and daughters kept at home. Young Sicilian men consider foreign girls fair game, a point for women traveling alone to bear in mind.

When To Visit Sicily

The best time to visit Sicily is the spring, when the island is carpeted in wildflowers and the temperature ideal. Spring comes in late February. July and August can be unbearably hot with sirocco winds blowing in from Africa and little air-conditioning. Winters are mild on the coast, though there's snow in the interior and it can be wet and windy. Few tourists are around from

Sicily and Sardinia

A glimpse of Sardinia's Costa Smeralda, where traditional buildings mingle happily with glitzy resorts

November to March. Many coastal hotels are closed and daylight hours are short in winter.

What To See

You'll want to explore Sicily's diverse landscape, so renting a car is a good idea. Roads are generally uncrowded away from the towns, though the mountain roads can be very twisty. Sightseeing is a major attraction; Sicily has a wealth of ancient monuments including some of the world's finest Greek archeological sites and the museums are excellent. Later architecture is a major draw; this includes Roman mosaics, Norman churches and elegant baroque towns. Many tourists will simply enjoy a beach holiday, with delicious food, hot sun and a relaxed pace of life.

Visiting Sardinia

Sardinia's main attraction is its beautiful coastline and well-organized resorts, which attract the rich and famous from all over Europe. But there's more than that to Sardinia, including archeological traces of its first endemic civilization, fine Romanesque churches built during the Pisan occupancy, a string of fortresses erected by the Genoans and towns that are more Spanish than Italian. The island is increasingly geared to international visitors. Standards of accommodations and service are improving all the time. Spring, early summer and autumn are the best times to visit. If you want a beach vacation, summer is best for its diving, sailing and wind-surfing – be sure to book well in advance as Sardinia is a popular choice with mainland Italians.

Spring carpets inland Sicily with wild flowers

Sicily and Sardinia

PALERMO

Redolent with history and filled with artistic treasures, vibrant Palermo is like no other European city. Unemployment and crime levels are high, and visitors are frequently shocked by the noise, grime and decay. But despite the dirt and chaos, Palermo is full of wonderful things to see. Few other cities have so many rich churches, dating from 12th-century Norman to 17th-century baroque. There are good museums and galleries, a lively arts scene and excellent restaurants.

Discovering Palermo

Pick up a copy of the free monthly *Tourist Information Magazine* from the tourist office. Printed in English, it's packed with useful tips to help make Palermo more accessible, as well as arts, sports and entertainment listings. After dark, avoid the back streets, dock and market areas, and use taxis to travel around the city. It is unwise to drive in Palermo; traffic is chaotic, driving is aggressive and parking spots are almost impossible to find.

The historic core of Palermo can easily be explored on foot. Indeed, to investigate the tangled lanes, walking is the only option, as the streets are too narrow for buses. Taxis are cheap, but agree on a price before your journey starts. Horse-drawn carriages, *carrozze*, ply the main historic center; again, agree on the price before you start.

Shopping

Palermo has a good range of shops, including branches of nationwide department stores such as la Rinascente and Coin, and outlets for the big Italian designer names; these cluster around Via Roma, Via Cavour and Viale della Libertà. Most tourists enjoy browsing in the Mercato delle Pulci (Flea Market), and take time to visit one of Palermo's food markets. Local crafts include ceramics, basketware and wrought iron, still made in the Cala and Via Calderai. Sculpted almond paste confectionery, called *frutta di Martorana*, is a real specialty.

Sicily and Sardinia

Entertainment and Excursions

Palermo's city streets empty early and can feel threatening late at night, though things are livelier in the newer areas. There's an excellent year-round choice of music, opera, theater, dance and open-air movies. The top venue is the Teatro Massimo, beautifully restored and reopened in 1997 after 23 years of closure. The other main theaters are the Politeama and the Golden; both stage classical concerts. Contact tourist information for full details.

The quintessential Palermo entertainment is the puppet theater; you can see a performance at the puppet museum (see page 177) or search out the real thing at Opera dei Pupi. If time is short, you could take a city tour to see Palermo's high points.

Mondello

If the noise and dirt of Palermo starts to get you down, head for Mondello, a charming beach resort that's virtually a city suburb. Lying west of Palermo beneath the bulk of Monte Pellegrino, Mondello has sandy beaches, pleasant walkways, a tiny harbor, a huge range of souvenir and food stalls, and wonderful *gelaterie* (ice cream shops). Restaurants line the front, where you can eat the freshest fish and seafood before heading to the beach for a swim. Mondello buzzes at night, with cruising cars, an animated *passeggiata* (parade) and outdoor discos.

ESSENTIAL INFORMATION

TOURIST INFORMATION
•Piazza Castelnuovo 34 ☎ 091 583 847; fax 091 586 330
•Aeroporto Falcone Borsellino ☎ 091 591 698
•Stazione Centrale, Piazza Giulio Cesare ☎ 091 616 5914
website www.sicily.infcom.it
•City tours: AMAT ☎ 091 350 415; CST ☎ 091 582 294; Touring ☎ 091 942 101
•Opera dei Pupi ✉ Vicola Ragusi 6 ☎ 091 323 400

URBAN TRANSPORTATION
You'll need to use buses to reach sights in the outlying areas; these are run by AMAT (☎ 091 690 2690) and cover every corner of the city. You can buy a single ticket or one valid all day; remember to validate it in the machine at the back of the bus each time you buy a new ticket. Tickets are available at AMAT sales points at the Stazione Centrale and Piazza Verdi where you'll see the sign "Véndita Biglietti AMAT" and all

tobacconists and newsstands. The circular routes served by minibuses, Linea Rossa (Red Line) and Linea Gialla (Yellow Line), cover the main tourist destinations and are useful. Taxis are inexpensive and can be hailed at stands all over the city or you can call Autoradio Taxi (☎ 091 512 727, 513 311, 513 198, 513 374) or Radio Taxi Trinacria (☎ 091 225 455).

AIRPORT INFORMATION
Palermo Falcone Borsellino Airport (☎ 091 702 011, 091 702 3409), with national and international flights, is 19 miles west of the city center at Punta Raisa. There are no direct flights to and from the United States from Palermo or any other Sicilian airport. Buses (☎ 091 580 457) run into Palermo every 30 minutes from 5 a.m. until after the arrival of the last scheduled flight, a journey of 40 minutes. Buses also run twice daily to Agrigento. Taxis are available outside the airport.

CLIMATE – Average highs and lows

JAN.	FEB.	MAR.	APR.	MAY	JUN.	JUL.	AUG.	SEP.	OCT.	NOV.	DEC.
15°C	15°C	16°C	18°C	21°C	25°C	28°C	29°C	27°C	24°C	19°C	16°C
59°F	59°F	61°C	64°F	70°F	77°F	82°F	84°F	81°F	75°F	66°F	61°F
9°C	9°C	11°C	13°C	16°C	20°C	24°C	25°C	22°C	19°C	14°C	12°C
51°F	51°F	52°F	55°F	61°F	68°F	75°F	77°F	72°F	66°F	57°F	54°F

PALERMO SIGHTS

Key to symbols

➕ map coordinates refer to the Palermo map on page 174; sights below are highlighted in yellow on the map

✉ address or location 🕾 telephone number
🕐 opening times 🍴 restaurant on site or nearby
🚇 nearest subway station
🚌 nearest bus or tram route 🚢 ferry
💰 admission charge: $$$ more than L5,000, $$ L3,000 to L5,000, $ less than L3,000 ℹ️ information

CAPPELLA PALATINA

The huge Palazzo dei Normanni (Norman Palace), a ninth-century Arab structure enlarged in the 12th century by the Normans, houses Sicily's regional parliament. On the first floor you'll find Palermo's most beautiful artistic gem, the tiny jewel-like Cappella Palatina, built as a private chapel for the Norman ruler Roger II in the 1130s. The apses, nave and cupola are entirely covered with iridiscent mosaics, glistening under the lights. The work of both Byzantine and local craftsmen, the mosaics show scenes from the Old and New Testaments. The chapel is dominated by a majestic Christ Pantocrator. The intricate marble floor dates from the same era, while the elaborate wooden ceiling is Arabic.

➕ A1 ✉ Piazza Indipendenza 🕾 091 70570 54879
🕐 Mon.–Fri. 9–11:45 and 3–4:45, Sun. 9–10 and noon–1 🚌 103, 105

CATTEDRALE

Palermo's Cattedrale (Cathedral) was founded in 1185 by the English archbishop Roger of the Mill as a private power-base. It wasn't finished for centuries, having been eclipsed by William II's magnificent cathedral at Monreale (see page 182), but the lovely triple-apsed eastern end and matching towers are pure Norman, as are numerous exterior carvings and details. The dome was added in the 18th century when the interior was given a neoclassical facelift. Be sure to see the huge sarcophagi in the chapels on the left of the entrance; here lie Sicily's great Norman rulers – Frederick II, Henry VI and Roger II.

➕ A1 ✉ Corso Vittorio Emanuele 🕾 091 334 376
🕐 Mon.–Sat. 7–7, Sun. 8–1:30 and 4–7 🍴 'A Cuccagna, see page 211 🚇 Linea Rossa

CONVENTO DEI CAPPUCCINI

For hundreds of years, the Capuchin monks of the Convento dei Cappuccini (Capuchin Convent) on the western outskirts of Palermo retained the right to place their dead, and many lay people as well, in the corridors beneath the church. But the bodies weren't buried in coffins; they were embalmed, dressed in clothes such as crumbling silks and dusty top hats that were provided before death, installed in niches and placed in glass cases. It's a bizarre and grotesque collection, some contorted figures fixing you with a basilisk stare, others grinning, while the various states of decomposition can be extremely unnerving.

➕ A1 ✉ Via Cappuccini 1 🕾 091 212 117 🕐 Daily 9–noon and 3–5 🚌 327

GALLERIA REGIONALE SICILIANA

Deep in the notorious Kalsa district stands the 15th-century Palazzo Abatellis, which houses the Galleria Regionale Siciliana (Sicilian Regional Gallery). This is a lovely collection ranging from sculpture and wood-carvings to frescoes, mosaics and paintings. Look for Laurana's serene, white marble bust of Eleanor of Aragon, a clutch of paintings by Sicily's homegrown 15th-century master, Antonello da Messina and some early 13th-century Madonnas. With their wide dark eyes and long-fingered hands, these show clearly the influence of Byzantine art.

➕ C2 ✉ Palazzo Abatellis, Via Alloro 🕾 091 623 0011 🕐 Tue.–Sat. 9–1:30 and 3–7:30, Mon. 9–1:30, Sun. 9–12:30 🚇 Linea Gialla 💰 $$$

LA MARTORANA

The Norman church of La Martorana was built by Roger II's admiral; its name comes from the Spanish convent that later owned it. It's easy to ignore the baroque

Sicily and Sardinia

encrustrations of the 16th-century remodeling inside and concentrate on the superb 12th-century Greek mosaics rioting over the dome and surrounding columns. The figure of Christ is surrounded by angels with splendid wings, their golds and greens highlighted by the sunlight streaming in, while the Virgin Mary and Apostles occupy the side spaces.

🚹 B1 ✉ Piazza Bellini 3 ☎ 091 617 0596
🕐 Mon.–Sat. 8–1 and 3:30–5, Sun. 8:30–1
🍴 'A Cuccagna, see page 211 🚇 Linea Gialla, Linea Rossa

MUSEO ARCHEOLOGICO

A converted church and its cloisters occupy Palermo's Museo Archeologico Regionale (Regional Archeological Museum). This small but excellent collection is essential viewing if you're planning on visiting Sicily's classical sites. Here are preserved the wondrous fifth-century BC lion's-head waterspouts, the metopes (stone carvings) and friezes from the Selinunte temples, as well as artifacts from all the major Neolithic, Carthaginian, Greek and Roman Sicilian sites. A fierce bronze ram, a technical tour-de-force, comes from Siracusa; nearby you'll see Hercules grappling with a stag. Don't miss the fine Roman mosaic pavements; these were excavated from the center of Palermo itself.

🚹 B2 ✉ Piazza Olivella 24 ☎ 091 611 6805
🕐 Mon.–Sat. 9–1:30, Wed. and Fri. 3–6:30, Sun. 9–1:30 🚇 101, 102 💵 $$$

MUSEO DELLE MARIONETTE

Puppet shows are a traditional Sicilian entertainment, usually centering on the exploits of the hero Orlando (Roland) and his struggles against the Saracens. The Museo delle Marionette (Puppet Museum) has Palermo's biggest collection of puppets, costumes and scenery. It also stages summer shows, which are a great antidote to too much culture, even though it's unlikely you'll understand the rich dialect of the performers.

🚹 C2 ✉ Via Butera 1 ☎ 091 329060 🕐 Mon.–Fri. 9–1 and 4–7, Sat. 9–1 🚇 103, 105 💵 $$

SAN CATALDO

The ancient church of San Cataldo, with its red domes, squats amid palm trees in the heart of the city. Built in the 12th century, it was never decorated, and its peaceful plain interior and marble mosaic floor give a sense of spirituality often lacking in some of Palermo's ornate baroque churches.

🚹 B1 ✉ Piazza Bellini 3 🕐 Mon.–Fri. 9–3:30, Sat. 9–12:30, Sun. 9–1 🚇 Linea Gialla, Linea Rossa

SAN GIOVANNI DEGLI EREMITI

To truly appreciate the weight of Palermo's Arab-Norman legacy, visit the deconsecrated church of San Giovanni degli Eremiti (St. John of the Hermits), founded by Roger II and built in 1132. There are distinct Arab overtones in the church's five domes; it was built around an earlier mosque, part of which is still visible. It's an evocative place set amid lemon trees, with a delightful 13th-century cloister; twin columns and pointed arches echo both Arab and Norman architectural styles.

🚹 A1 ✉ Via dei Benedettini ☎ 091 651 5019 🕐 Mon.–Sat. 9–7, Sun. 9–12:30 🚇 103, 105 💵 $

Spooky, fully clothed mummies inhabit the catacombs beneath the Convento dei Cappuccini

Palermo's food markets are among the most exciting in the Mediterranean world

WALK: FROM THE NORMANS TO A VIBRANT CENTER

Refer to route marked on city map page 174.

This walk takes about 2 hours and offers you the chance to see some artistic treasures combined with a taste of Palermo's vibrant street life.

Start at the Porta Nuova (New Gate) at the west end of Corso Vittorio Emanuele.
The New Gate was built in 1535 to commemorate Spain's Charles V's Tunisian campaign; he stopped in Palermo on his way back to Spain, the only visiting Spanish monarch during the 400-year viceregal period.
Visit the Palazzo dei Normanni and the Cappella Palatini (see page 176), then continue east down Via Vittorio Emanuele to the left of the cathedral (see page 176). Continue until you come to the Quattro Canti crossroads (see page 177). Turn right on to Via Maqueda.
The Via Maqueda was constructed in the 16th century to run straight through the old quarters of the Albergheria and the Capo. This area has changed little over the past several hundred years. Behind Maqueda there's a warren of narrow streets, crumbling buildings and tiny squares. You'll see evidence of World War II bomb damage, as well as houses that seem ready for

demolition. Try to ignore these, and concentrate instead on the vibrant street life, surging crowds and intense atmosphere.
Fifty yards along Via Maqueda on the left, you'll see the Piazza Pretoria, recently cleaned and restored. The large building is the Municipio (City Hall) and the huge 16th-century church Santa Caterina. The square's central fountain was designed in the 1500s.
Adjacent to Piazza Pretoria and also on Maqueda, cross Piazza Bellini to visit the churches of La Martorana (see page 176) and San Cataldo (see page 177). Cross the road and turn right a little farther down Via Ponticello, a grubby and run-down street, to reach the glorious church of Il Gesù.
Built in 1564, this church is a Sicilian baroque extravaganza of marble, relief-work and wood inlay, topped by a magnificent green-and-white dome.
Continue down Via Ponticello to lively Piazza Ballarò.
Piazza Ballarò, nearby Piazza del Carmine and the surrounding streets are home to a daily food market, something you shouldn't miss. Palermo markets are among the most raucous in the Mediterranean. The stalls are piled high with a bewildering variety of meat, fish, fruit and vegetables of excellent quality and freshness. You'll find a huge choice of ready-to-go food and tiny eating places where you can lunch on local specialties such as *arancini*, raw sea-urchins or rolls filled with spleen and liver.

Sicily and Sardinia

CUISINES OF PALERMO

Meals in Palermo and Sicily will be a highlight; possibly no other region of Italy has been so influenced by the civilizations that have lived here. Each has left ingredients, flavors and cooking methods that make up one of the most inventive cuisines in the Mediterranean.

Main Meals

Meals follow the standard Italian pattern of *antipasto*, *primo*, *secondo* and *dolce*, and portions are large. The emphasis is on fish, though inland you'll find flavorful meat and game dishes. Pasta dishes include *spaghetti alle vongole* with tiny clams and a hint of spicy *peperoncino* (chili), *pasta con le sarde* with a piquant sardine sauce, and *spaghetti con le seppie*, whose unctuous blackness derives from the ink-sack of the cuttlefish. *Pasta alla Norma* with eggplant, tomatoes and melted cheese is a real Palermo specialty. The main course *(secondo)* is often plain grilled fish, so a squeeze of lemon is all it needs, or a delicate *fritto misto*, deep-fried prawns and calamari. Swordfish and tuna are particularly good. Vegetable dishes are superb; be sure to sample *caponata*, a traditional vegetable stew featuring eggplant, celery, olives and capers, *zucchine in agro-dolce*, an Arab-influenced sweet-sour dish, or anything that includes the huge, tender lime-green cauliflowers, a winter treat.

Snacks and Desserts

Pizza in Palermo makes an excellent snack; paper-thin, crisp and blackened at the edges from the wood-fired oven. It's a revelation to those used to the Americanized version. *Arancini*, another Sicilian special, are rice-balls stuffed with meat-sauce and peas, coated with egg and breadcrumbs, then deep-fried. *Focaccia*, a bread snack with various toppings, also makes a quick lunch. Sicilian desserts show the Arab legacy; heavy use is made of almonds and sugar, and you'll find trays of mouthwatering varieties in every *pasticerria*. *Cannoli* and *cassata Siciliana* both use ricotta cheese, heavily sweetened and studded with candied fruits and chocolate, while Sicilian *gelati* (ice cream) is some of the world's best.

Local Drinks

Wines are straightforward and often served by the carafe. If you want something special, look for the red Corvo, Etna, made from grapes grown on volcanic soil, and Donnafugata from outside Palermo. Settle your dinner with a glass of Sicilian *amaro* (bitters). Averna, found throughout Italy, is made on Sicily, as is Limoncello, a lemon-based liqueur from the east coast.

A typical selection of fish found in Palermo restaurants

The Tempio della Concordia at Agrigento is a reminder of the fifth-century BC golden age on Sicily

SICILY SIGHTS

Key to symbols

✚ map coordinates refer to the region map on page 170; sights below are highlighted in yellow on the map

✉ address or location ☎ telephone number

◷ opening times 🍴 restaurant on site or nearby

🚌 nearest bus or tram route ⛴ ferry

💵 admission charge: $$$ more than L5,000, $$ L3,000 to L5,000, $ less than L3,000 ℹ information

AGRIGENTO

Agrigento's Greek temples and ruins once formed the Hellenistic city of Akragas, founded in the sixth century BC. The ancient city was spread along two ridges above the sea. Modern Agrigento stands on the higher ridge, with the temples known as the Valle dei Templi (Valley of the Temples) strung along the lower a couple of miles down the hill. The site falls into two zones; head first for the eastern zone. Make your way along the path past the Tempio di Ercole (Temple of Hercules) to the superb Tempio della Concordia (Temple of Concord), built around 430 BC and converted to a Christian church in the sixth century, which explains why it is in such an excellent state of preservation.

Farther still stands the half-ruined Tempio di Giunone (Temple of Juno), its masonry still marked by the fire set by the Carthaginians in 406 BC. Down the hill, you can explore the jumble of ruins that comprise the western zone. Here are the so-called Tempio dei Dioscuri (Temple of Castor and Pollux) and the massive remains of the Tempio di Giove (Temple of Jupiter), the largest Doric temple ever, which was supported by huge male figures – one still lies abandoned amid the ruins. From the temples, return back up the hill to visit the Hellenistic-Roman quarter, an excavated section of the original city, and the Museo Nazionale Archeologico (National Archeological Museum), an excellent and varied collection. In its grounds you'll find the third-century BC semi-circular odeum, and the lovely Norman San Nicola, a serene and solid church with a peaceful cloister.

Modern Agrigento is a mix of the medieval and baroque. Via Atanea is the heart of the town and from here narrow alleys and steep stairs follow the Arabic town layout past crumbling palaces to the vast cathedral at the town's highest point.
✚ C2

Tourist information ✉ Via Cesare Battisti 15
☎ 0922 20391 ◷ Mon.–Sat. 9–1:45 and 5–7

⊠ Valle dei Templi (in parking lot) ☎ 0922 26191
🕒 Mon.–Sat. 9–1:45 and 4–7; Sun. 9–1:45
Valle dei Templi ⊠ Via dei Templi 🕒 Daily 8:30–7
🍴 Bar at parking lot (summer only) 💷 Western zone
$; eastern zone free 🚹 Illuminated nightly until 11.
The site can be very hot in summer, and there are
considerable distances to walk
Hellenistic-Roman Quarter ⊠ Via dei Templi
🕒 Daily 9–1 hour before dusk 💷 $
Museo Nazionale Archeologico ⊠ San Nicola, Via
dei Templi ☎ 0922 40111 🕒 Wed.–Sat. 9–1 and
2–5:30, Sun.–Tue. 9–1 💷 $$ 🚹 There is no English
information on any of the exhibits

CATÁNIA

East-coast Catánia, Sicily's second-largest
city, is an ancient settlement crouching in
the shadow of Mount Etna. First
impressions are of a dark and gloomy
place, with sprawling industrial suburbs
and chaotic traffic. Etna's eruptions and
the 1693 earthquake have taken their toll,
leaving a largely 18th-century city center,
with some fine baroque churches and
monuments. The top sites include the
Duomo (Cathedral), fronted by an elegant
piazza, the 18th-century church of San
Nicolò, Sicily's largest church, and the
Museo Civico, housed in the Castello
Ursino. On a less lofty plain, Catánia has
one of Sicily's biggest, liveliest and most
ebullient food markets.
🚩 E2
Tourist information ⊠ Via D Cimarosa 10
☎ 095 730 6211/6233 🕒 Mon.–Sat. 9–7, Sun. 10–6
Duomo ⊠ Piazza del Duomo 🕒 Daily 8–noon
and 5–7
San Nicolò ⊠ Piazza Dante 🕒 Daily 8–noon
🚹 Restoration is ongoing and opening times
may vary
Museo Civico ⊠ Castello Ursino 🕒 Tue.–Sat. 9–1
and 3–6, Sun. 9–1 🚹 Restoration is ongoing and
opening times may vary

CEFALÙ

Cefalù on the north coast is an ancient
port with a strong sense of identity. Its
tangle of medieval streets is built in the
shadow of a huge crag, and it offers good
beaches, a lovely coastline and better-
than-average shops and restaurants.
Spend time exploring the narrow alleys

that lead down to the old port, before
wandering up Corso Ruggero to the
palm-fringed Piazza del Duomo with its
magnificent Duomo (Cathedral). Built by
the Norman Roger II in 1131, this
beautiful building is a fusion of Arab,
Norman and Byzantine styles, the
different architectural elements heavily
influenced by the craftsmen who built it.
As much fortress as cathedral, its twin
towers and honey-colored facade soar
above the historic town. In the shadowy
interior, with its surging columns, your
eye is immediately drawn to the glittering
gold mosaics, dominated by the huge
image of Christ Pantocrator, his right
hand raised in blessing.

For more artistic treasures, head for
the Museo Mandralisca, whose chief
treasure is the fine *Portrait of an Unknown
Man*, painted by Sicilian-born Antonello
da Messina in 1465. Energetic visitors can
climb the brooding outcrop above the
town to enjoy fine views and the ruins of
the fifth-century BC Temple of Diana.
You could also use Cefalù as a base for
exploring the Madonie Mountains, a
magnificent upland area with picturesque
villages, high peaks and excellent hiking.
🚩 C3
Tourist information ⊠ Corso Ruggero 77
☎ 0921 421050 🕒 Mon.–Sat. 8 a.m.–8:30 p.m., Sun.
8–2, Jun.–Sep.; Mon.–Fri. 8–2 and 4–7, Sat. 8–2, rest
of year 🚢 To Aeolian Islands
Duomo ⊠ Piazza del Duomo 🕒 Daily 8–noon
and 3:30–8
Museo Mandralisca ⊠ Via Mandralisca 13
☎ 0921 421547 🕒 Daily 9 a.m.–midnight, Aug.; 9–7,
Easter–Jul. and Sep.; 9–12:30 and 4–7:30, rest of year
💷 $$

ENNA

The ancient mountain stronghold of
Enna stretches along a 3,000-foot high
ridge in the hills of inland Sicily. Just
below the highest point stands the castle,
built by Frederick II in the 14th century, a
massive fortress whose towers give
magnificent views over Enna and the
rugged interior landscape. From here Via
Roma, the main street, runs down the
ridge to Piazza Vittorio Emanuele,
packed with crowds during the evening

Sicily and Sardinia

passeggiata. Enna's Duomo (Cathedral) partly dates from 1307, and you can see its treasures in the Museo Alessi. The nearby Museo Archeologico has some fine Greek vases from the surrounding area. Spend time wandering along the promenade; from here hills stretch out with the tumbling ochre-colored village of Calascibetta in the foreground.

✚ D2

Tourist information ✉ Via Roma 411 ☎ 0935 528288 🕐 Mon.–Fri. 9–1 and 3:30–6:30

Duomo ✉ Piazza Mazzini, Via Roma 🕐 Daily 9–1 and 4–7

Museo Civico Alessi ✉ Piazza Mazzini, Via Roma ☎ 0935 24866 🕐 Tue.–Sun. 9–1 and 4–7 💵 $

Museo Archeologico Varisano ✉ Piazza Mazzini, Via Roma ☎ 0935 24720 🕐 Daily 9–6

ÉRICE

A twisting road winds up to lovely Érice, a tiny hilltop town with sweeping views over the port of Trápani and its surrounding salt-flats to the Isole Égadi (Égadi Islands) off the coast. It's easy to escape the throngs of summer visitors to wander through the pebbled streets and tiny piazzas, pausing to peek at the myriad courtyards bright with flowering tubs.

Érice was ancient Eryx, whose temple of Aphrodite attracted worshippers from all over the Mediterranean. Succeeding waves of Carthaginian, Roman, Arab and Norman invaders came here and built, and you can explore Roger II's Castello di Vénere, built on the site of the ancient temple. There are aged walls, towers and gates, some lovely churches, a 14th-century Duomo (Cathedral), a small museum and a bosky-green public garden, but your chief memories will be of winding alleyways and superb views – a village that is more than the sum of its parts. Have a drink in the pretty Piazza Umberto, where you can also sample some of the almond-based sweetmeats, *dolce di badia*, for which the town is renowned.

✚ A3

Tourist information ✉ Via Conte Pepoli 11 ☎ 0923 869338 🕐 Mon.–Sat. 8–2 and 4–8, Sun. 9–noon, mid-Jul. to Aug.; Mon.–Sat. 8–2, Sun. 9–noon, Jun. to mid-Jul. and Sep.; Mon.–Sat. 8–2, rest of year

Castello di Vénere ✉ Via Castello di Vénere 🕐 Daily 8–2 and 3–6:30, but often closed

Duomo ✉ Piazza Matrice 🕐 Daily 10–noon and 3–6

Museo Comunale ✉ Piazza Umberto 1 ☎ 0923 860048 🕐 Mon.–Sat. 8:30–1:30, Sun. 9–noon

Érice's ancient castle perches above the coastal plain

Sicily and Sardinia

MONREALE

Above the slopes of the Conca d'Oro (Golden Shell) valley, some 8 kilometers (5 miles) from Palermo, stands the small town of Monreale and its Norman Duomo (Cathedral). Here you'll find the world's most extraordinary and accomplished Christian mosaics. The cathedral's ceilings and walls glitter with brilliant splendor. It was built from 1174 to 1184 by the Norman King William II as a direct challenge to Palermo's cathedral, which was erected at the same time by William's powerful rival, the archbishop of Palermo. Completed in only 10 years, the result is an astonishingly homogenous building, its mosaics almost certainly the work of Greek and Byzantine craftsmen. The interior is dominated by the great Christ Pantocrator, while the Madonna and Child, angels and saints are ranked beneath this powerful image. The side apses portray St. Peter and St. Paul and their martyrdoms, while the nave and aisles are covered with gloriously detailed mosaics showing scenes from the Old and New Testaments. Outside the cathedral, a side entrance leads to the superb Chiostro dei Benedettini (Cloisters), part of William's original Benedictine monastery. The elegant arcades are supported by 216 columns, with no two capitals the same.

➕ B3

Duomo ✉ Piazza del Duomo ☉ Daily 8–noon and 3:30–6:30 ⓘ Take plenty of change for the coin-operated light switches. Wear suitable clothes

Chiostro dei Benedettini ✉ Piazza del Duomo ☉ Mon.–Sat. 9–noon and 4–7, Sun. 9–12:30 🎟 $

NOTO

In 1693, a severe earthquake devastated much of eastern Sicily, destroying churches, houses and entire communities. The town of Noto was completely flattened, but within weeks construction had started on what was to become one of Sicily's most perfect baroque townscapes – a new town on a new site. The Sicilian-Spanish aristocrat, Giuseppe Lanza, was in charge of the scheme and it was his vision that produced today's town.

Noto was deliberately planned with the political and religious buildings apart from the residential streets. The Corso Vittorio Emanuele is the finest of the streets; it's lined with graceful *palazzi* with sumptuously decorated facades. This leads to the Piazza del Municipio, a harmonious tree-shaded square lined with fine buildings. It's also the site of the twin-towered cathedral, closed since the collapse of its dome in 1996. West from here, you'll find another of Noto's gems, the eccentrically decorated Palazzo Villadorata with galloping horses and plump cherubs. Spend time wandering the side streets, where you'll find architectural delights at all corners.

➕ E1

Tourist information ✉ Piazza XVI Maggio ☎ 0931 836744 ⓘ Mon.–Sat. 8–2 and 3:30–7, Apr.–Sep.; Mon.–Sat. 9–1:30, rest of year

PIAZZA ARMERINA AND VILLA IMPERIALE

The pleasant town of Piazza Armerina stands in the wooded hills of the southern interior, a mixture of narrow streets and handsome squares, with an elegant cathedral and some attractive, if crumbling, churches and palaces. A few miles southwest of the town in the hamlet of Casale, a wealthy Roman (possibly Maximianus Herculeus, co-emperor with Diocletian) built a vast and grand villa in the heart of the country. The huge early fourth-century, structure was probably designed as a hunting lodge, a theory borne out by the astounding floor mosaics that adorn virtually every floor. These show a wide variety of animals and birds, many from Africa, which tie in neatly with the African-Roman style of the compositions. Round the peristyle (courtyard), there's a wide corridor decorated with a lively hunting scene with tigers, elephants and sea creatures. The high spot is a pavement adorned with 10 bikini-clad girls engaged in sporting activities; the winner, with her triumphant smirk and laurel wreath, is easy to spot.

➕ D2

Villa Imperiale ☎ 0935 680036 ☉ Daily 9–1:30 and 3–7:30 🍴 Cafeteria and bar open May–Oct. 🎟 $$

Slopes beneath the summit of one of the world's most active volcanoes, Mount Etna

DRIVE: THE SLOPES OF MOUNT ETNA

Duration: 5 to 6 hours

This drive takes you on a tour of 10,902-foot Mount Etna, with a chance to ascend as high as possible toward the summit of one of the world's largest and most active volcanoes. You'll drive through countryside decorated with groves of citrus trees and figs, forests of chestnut and oak, and wonderful and ever-changing views of the mountain.

For all its grandeur, Mount Etna is little more than 60,000 years old – a mere stripling in geological terms. Its first recorded eruption was in 475 BC. Since then there have been 90 major eruptions, the worst in 1669, when a fissure opened on the mountain's flank and a stream of magma engulfed Cátania, 40 kilometers (25 miles) away. Ash was thrown as far as 100 kilometers (60 miles), and in places the lava took seven years to cool completely. Etna last erupted in 1991 and was

dangerously active during 1992 when streams of lava destroyed local roads and threatened villages. In early 1999, there was enough activity that planes had to change their flight paths, and January 2000 saw another dramatic eruption.

Start your drive at Taormina (see page 188) and take the SS114 south toward Catánia. Turn right onto the SS120 (signposted Linguaglossa) at Fiumefreddo di Sicilia.

Linguaglossa is the main tourist center on Etna's northern slopes. In winter, it's packed with skiers who base themselves here to use the lifts at Piano Provenzana farther up the mountain. In summer, it's a quiet and attractive town surrounded by pine forests.

Continue on the SS120 to Randazzo, well worth a stop.

As the crow flies, Randazzo is the town closest to Etna's summit and has been frequently threatened by lava flows, though never engulfed. The 1981 eruption came very close, and you can see the flow on the road near the town. Built almost entirely of lava, Randazzo's gloomy medieval heart is, in fact, a reconstruction. The town was one of the

Sicily and Sardinia

main German defensive positions during their 1943 defense of Sicily against the Allies in World War II and was heavily bombed.

A short way outside Randazzo, fork left onto the SS284 toward Bronte.

The road climbs steadily from here, and you'll approach ever closer to the lava flows as you drive through woods of walnuts and chestnuts. Bronte was founded in 1535, and many of its churches date from this time. Today, it's surrounded by pistachio-nut plantations; almost 85 percent of Italy's production comes from around the town.

Continue on the SS284 to Adrano; the road bypasses the town, but you could make a detour to visit the town.

Originally founded by the Greeks, Adrano has a solid medieval castle and a clutch of churches (the nicest is the Chiesa Madre next to the castle).

Continue on the SS284 to the major junction with the SS121 at Paterno. Leave the main road here and take the unclassified road that leads up Etna, signposted Belpasso and Nicolosi.

Nicolosi, another winter ski resort, marks the start of steeper roads leading up toward the summit. The road climbs up grassy slopes

and through woods before emerging into the wierd volcanic landscape. Here, the slopes are dotted with spent craters and smooth black-and-gray mounds of volcanic debris. The road ends at Rifugio Sapienza, 4,600 feet below the summit. There's a place here for overnight stays, as well as restaurants and tacky souvenir shops.

You can continue farther up Etna, either by walking on a rough track (six tough hours), or by taking a cable car and jeep. The cable car runs (weather permitting) as far as Rifugio Montagnola, from where jeeps and a guide take you as far as the Torre del Filósofo. Wear tough shoes or boots and glasses to keep the flying grit out of your eyes, and take plenty of warm and waterproof clothing. At this height, you'll find yourself in a lunar landscape; no vegetation can compete with the folds and craters of black, gray and red lava. Above, the southeast crater of Etna smokes gently, the main crater behind it. At this altitude, you may see gaseous explosions, rock showers and molten lava.

Nicolosi tourist information ✉ Via Garibaldi 63 ☎ 095 911 505 🕐 Daily 8:30–1 and 4–7:30, May–Oct.; 8:30–1, rest of year

The architectural perfection of the Greek temple at Segesta is like a dream from the classical age

SEGESTA

Standing gloriously alone on a windswept hillside, the luminous Greek temple of Segesta is probably the most evocative of all Sicily's great Hellenistic monuments. The city of Segesta flourished as early as the 12th century BC, became Greek in the fifth century BC and spent the following centuries fighting other Greek settlements and allying itself with Carthage. It was eventually overtaken by the city of Selinus to the south. All that remains is its glorious, though unfinished, temple and hillside theater, though excavation work has been ongoing since 1987. From a distance, the temple appears complete, its 36 columns, entablature and pediment all intact. Go closer and you'll see the columns are unfluted and there's no interior *cella* (the area delineated by the outer columns), while the stone building studs have never been removed. Unfinished and romantic, the haunt of birds and lizards, it embodies the classical dream. On a hillside to the east stands the second-century BC theater, a graceful white shell hewn out of the living rock, with breathtaking views across the hills to the sea.

🚩 B3 ⏰ Daily 9–1 hour before dusk
🍴 Bar/cafeteria 🚌 Half-hourly minibus shuttle

service to theater in summer months 🚻 $$
ℹ The Trápani Tourist Board stages classical Greek and Roman drama at the theater during the summer. Further details from Azienda Provinciale Turismo, Via San Francesco d'Assisi 27, Trápani (☎ 0923 29000)

SELINUNTE

The Greek city of Selinus (modern Selinunte), founded in the seventh century BC, reached its peak in the fifth century BC, the era from which the greatest of its temples date. Constantly at loggerheads with its northern neighbor Segesta, it was attacked by Segesta's ally Carthage, which sacked this powerful city in 250 BC. It never really recovered; time and repeated earthquakes did the rest, and today it remains a vast jumble of ruins from which its surviving temples soar. Nobody knows to which gods the temples were dedicated, so they are designated by letters. The site is huge, and you'll need comfortable shoes and stamina to explore it thoroughly. Pick up a plan from the tourist office outside the gates of the archeological park before you start. Temples E, F and G stand amid the wild parsley that gave Selinus its name. The reconstructed columns of E shine against the sky with the sea behind. A mile or so away down by the sea lies the acropolis, with five more temples, stretches of well-preserved streets and massive fifth-century BC walls. Climb to temple C at the highest point; from its 14 standing columns you can gaze over this once-mighty city to the sea.

🚪 B2

Tourist information ✉ Parco Archeologico
☎ 0924 46251 🕐 Daily 8–8, May–Sep.; Mon.–Sat. 9–8, Sun. 9–noon and 3–5, rest of year
Parco Archeologico 🕐 9–1 hour before dusk, May–Sep.; 8–1 hour before dusk, rest of year. Tickets are issued up to two hours before dusk
🎫 $$

SIRACUSA

Ancient and captivating Siracusa (Syracuse) grew up around the eighth-century BC on a coastal island with two natural harbors. By the fifth century BC, it had grown to become the most powerful Greek settlement in the Mediterranean, outshining even Athens. Glorious centuries followed until Syracuse fell to Rome in 214 BC; it later became a prominent early Christian city, only to suffer successive waves of Arab, Norman and Spanish invaders. Much was destroyed in the 1693 earthquake; the subsequent rebuilding shaped the existing glorious city. The main sights fall neatly into two areas: Ortigia, the old town on the island, linked for centuries to the mainland by a bridge, and the archeological zone, with its excavations and museum.

On Ortigia, head first to the Piazza del Duomo, an exquisite elongated square lined with graceful baroque buildings and dominated by the sumptuous facade of the Duomo (Cathedral). Its interior is unique; embedded in the walls you'll see massive columns, the remains of the original Greek temple around which the cathedral was built. No other building gives a better idea of the weight of Syracuse's history. Head next for the Museo Bellomo, housed in a lovely Renaissance palace; highlights include Antonello da Messina's serene *Annunciation* and a vigorous Caravaggio showing the burial of St. Lucy, Syracuse's patron saint.

Other sights on Ortigia include the massive ruins of the Tempio di Apollo and the Fontana di Aretusa (Arethusa's Fountain), the spring which attracted the first citizens to Ortigia. North of the city center lies the Parco Archeologico (Archeological Park), whose star is the Teatro Greco (Greek Theater), the most complete theater in the Greek world. This 15,000-seat auditorium is carved from the living rock, and has sublime views over the city and sea. Wander through the adjacent *latomia* (pits), the quarries which provided the building stone for the ancient city, now a verdant oasis of olive and lemon trees. Here you'll see the oddly shaped cave known as the Orecchio do Dionisio (Dionysius' Ear), while nearby lies the vast Roman amphitheater. Outside the park, take in the Basilica di San Giovanni, which gives access to the underground catacomb system, where Christians were buried from around AD 200. Leave time for the splendid Museo Nazionale Archeologico (National Archeological Museum), where good English labels guide you through the superb, if daunting, collections. Its high point is the *Venus Landolina*, a decadent goddess rising from the sea. Also outstanding are some *kouroi*, fifth-century BC naked athletes.

🚪 E1

Tourist information ✉ Via San Sebastiano 43
☎ 0931 461477 🕐 Mon.–Fri. 8:30–1:30 and 3:30–6:30, Sat. 8:30–1, May–Sep.; Mon.–Sat. 8:30–1:30 (but times are erratic), rest of year ✉ Via Maestranza 33
☎ 0931 464255 🕐 Mon.–Sat. 8:30–2 and 4:30–7:30, Sun. 8:30–2, May–Sep.; Mon.–Sat. 8:30–2 and 4:30–7 (but times are erratic), rest of year
Duomo ✉ Piazza del Duomo 🕐 Daily 8–noon and 4–7 (times may be erratic)
Museo Bellomo ✉ Via Capodieci 14 ☎ 0931 69617 🕐 Mon.–Sat. 9–1:30, Sun. 9–12:30 🎫 $$
Parco Archeologico ✉ Neapolis, Tyche ☎ 0931 66206 🕐 Daily 9–2 hours before dusk 🍴 Bars and cafeterias outside park entrance 🚌 4, 5, 12 from city center 🎫 $$$
Basilica di San Giovanni ✉ Via San Giovanni 🕐 Daily 9–6, guided tours (only) in English, mid-Mar. to mid-Nov.; 9–1 and 3–6, rest of year 🚌 4, 5, 12 from city center 🎫 $$
Museo Nazionale Archeologico ✉ Viale Teocrito 66 ☎ 0931 464022 🕐 Tue.–Sat. 9–1 🎫 $$$

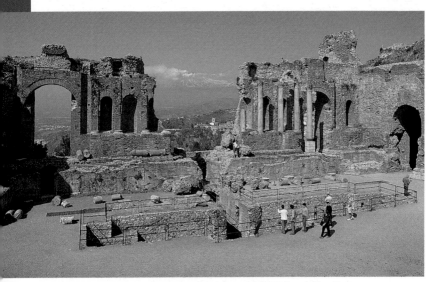

Etna is framed by the stage at the well-preserved Greco-Roman theater at Taormina

TAORMINA

Taormina draws visitors from all over the world. They are attracted by its sublime location, mild climate and excellent facilities. There are more good hotels here than anywhere else in Sicily, plus elegant shops and good restaurants, all adding up to a spectacular resort town.

Taormina tumbles down steep cliffs to a clutch of tiny beaches and enchanting islets and headlands, while to the southwest rises the graceful sweep of smouldering Mount Etna, a fitting backdrop for the town's lush subtropical vegetation, palm trees and cascades of bougainvillea. It's the ideal spot for a stopover, a chance to unwind and experience its charm after the tour buses and day excursions have departed.

The main street, Corso Umberto, runs from one end of the walkable town center to the other. It's lined with 15th- to 19th-century palazzi and punctuated with the cathedral, churches and tiny piazzas. Piazza IX Aprile, halfway down, is a good place to pause at an outdoor café and enjoy the splendid views of Etna and the bay. Farther east, the Corso leads to Via Teatro Greco, giving access to Taormina's main draw, a Greco-Roman theater carved out of the hillside with a superlative backdrop of sea, coast and mountains. The theater dates mainly from first-century Roman adaptations of the original third-century BC Greek construction, and you can climb up and down the tiers of seats and explore the backstage areas.

Down the hill below the theater, don't miss the Villa Comunale (Giardino Trevelyan), a lovely English-inspired park above the sea. Taormina's beaches lie far below the center in outlying Mazzarò; the best way to reach them is to take the *finivia* (cable car) from Via Pirandello at the east end of town.

For the energetic, there are some good hikes around town; you could walk up to the medieval castle above Taormina or hike to the tiny hill-village of Castelmola.
➕ E2

Tourist information ✉ Palazzo Corvaja, Piazza Vittorio Emanuele ☎ 0942 23243 🕐 Mon.–Sat. 8:30–2 and 4–7 (also Sun. 9–1, Apr.–Oct.)

Teatro Greco ✉ Via Teatro Greco 🕐 Daily 9–1 hour before dusk ℹ Contact the tourist office for details of the Jul. and Aug. festivals

Villa Comunale ✉ Via Bagnoli Croce 🕐 Daily dawn–dusk ℹ Contact the tourist office for details of summer events

Funivia ✉ Via L Pirandello ☎ 0942 23906 🕐 Daily 8 a.m.–1 a.m., Apr.–Sep.; 8 a.m.–8:30 p.m., rest of year

Top: The code of silence shrouds Mafia killings
Inset: Lucky Luciano

THE MAFIA

As a tourist in Sicily, you will remain untouched by the tentacles of the Mafia. This mysterious criminal fraternity is inextricably linked with most aspects of Sicilian life, but its members are *uomini d'honore* (men of honor), who live by a code of silence (the *omertà*).

Beginnings

The Mafia goes back hundreds of years to Bourbon times, when ex-bandits were recruited to "police" the interior, taking payments from colleagues and acting as middlemen between landowners and peasants. Bound together by ties of self-interest, they grew rich and powerful and established a semi-formal organization shrouded in secrecy. They filled the gap between Sicilians and authority, whether that authority came from the state, foreign rulers or absentee landowners. "Families" emerged, their members not always blood relations, headed by a *capo* (godfather). Each took its name from the village under its control and formed alliances with other families for the purpose of business.

The 20th Century

During the 1930s, Mussolini was determined to break the power of the Mafia. He might have succeeded but for World War II. Before the Sicilian landings in 1943, the Allies had only one source of intelligence and local support – the American Mafia, formed from among the thousands of Sicilians who had emigrated to America in the early 20th century. American *capi*, such as Lucky Luciano, provided the introductions in Sicily so vitally needed for the invasion, but at the same time succeeded in ensuring the reemergence of the Mafia as a powerful force in the post-war Allied military government. During the second half of the century, the Mafia tentacles spread everywhere – into politics, construction and arms and drug dealing. Immensely rich, the organization dealt brutally with anyone who stood in its way. In 1982 General della Chiesa was murdered, and in 1992 all Italy was shocked by the killings of Giovane Falcone, a respected magistrate, and Judge Paolo Borsellino.

The Future

Recent years have seen arrests of leading *capi*, while former Mafia members such as Tommaso Buscetta have fingered politicians, including Giulio Andreotti and ex-prime minister Silvio Berlusconi. The fight continues, as do the murders, with five people gunned down in a Sicilian bar in early 1999. There is hope that as ordinary Sicilians' attitudes change, the change may finally defeat *la piovra* (the octopus).

Mosaics decorate the cathedral at Cágliari

SARDINIA SIGHTS

Key to symbols

➕ map coordinates refer to the region map on page
171; sights below are highlighted in yellow on the
map

✉ address or location ☎ telephone number
🕐 opening times 🍴 restaurant on site or nearby
⛴ ferry 💳 admission charge: $$$ more than L5,000,
$$ L3,000 to L5,000, $ less than L3,000 ℹ information

CÁGLIARI

Sardinia's capital is situated in the south
of the island. Its hinterland is a bird-rich
network of marshes and lakes, its
foreground the busy Golfo di Cágliari.
Despite the city's quarter-million
inhabitants, Cágliari's center is remarkably
compact, the Castello district containing
all the main sights. This historic area
retains its defensive walls; these include
the Torre del Elefante (Elephant's Tower),
complete with a statue of an elephant on
the facade, and the Torre di San Pancrazio
(St. Pancras' Tower). Both were erected in
1305 by the Pisans after they captured the
city from the Genoese. The best approach
to Castello today is through the Bastione
San Remy; this Spanish-built defensive
wall was transformed in the 1900s into a
wide esplanade, and it's an ideal place to
admire Cágliari's views over the city, port
and lagoons. Walk from here to Piazza
Palazzo, Castello's main square. Here
you'll find the Cattedrale (Cathedral),

first built in the 12th century by the
Pisans. The pulpits and lions guarding the
entrance are Pisan, though the
Romanesque facade was added in the
1930s. The interior contains the tombs of
the princes of the House of Savoy.

Continue north and you'll come to the
Cittadella dei Musei, a modern complex
converted from the old arsenal, which
now houses Cágliari's main museums. The
pick of these must be the Museo
Archeologico (Archeological Museum),
where there's plenty of information on the
enigmatic Nuraghic culture. This
indigenous civilization, traces of which
you'll see all over the island, thrived
between 1500 and 500 BC. The bronze
votive statues depicting warriors, athletes,
workers, animals and many more are the
main source of information about this
culture. The nearby Museo Cardu has a
quirky collection of Oriental art, mainly
Siamese, presented to the city in 1917 by
a Cágliari native who worked at the
Siamese court. More appealing is the
small Pinacoteca Nazionale (National
Gallery) with Italian pictures dating
mainly from the 15th and 16th centuries.
Outside the Castello district, head for the
church of San Saturnino. Recently
restored, this is one of Sardinia's oldest
Christian buildings, dating from the fifth
century and enlarged in the 11th.

Across town are the second-century
Anfiteatro Romano (Roman
Amphitheater) and the Orto Botanico

(Botanical Garden), a lovely green oasis packed with 500 varieties of trees, shrubs and tropical plants.

➕ B1

Tourist information ✉ Piazza Matteoti 9
☎ 070 669 255 🕐 Daily 8–8, Jul.–Aug.; Mon.–Sat. 8–2, rest of year; ✉ Piazza Deffunu 9 ☎ 070 654 811 🕐 Daily 8–8

Cattedrale ✉ Piazza Palazzo 🕐 Daily 8–noon and 4–7

Museo Archeologico ✉ Cittadella dei Musei
☎ 070 655 911 🕐 Tue.–Sun. 9–7 💰 $$

Museo Civico d'Arte Orientale Stefano Cardu
✉ Cittadella dei Musei ☎ 070 490 727 🕐 Tue.–Sun. 9–7 💰 $$

Orto Botanico ✉ Viale Fra Ignazio 13 ☎ 070 6751
🕐 Daily 8:30–1 and 3–6:30 💰 $

Pinacoteca Nazionale ✉ Cittadella dei Musei
☎ 070 670 157 🕐 Daily 9–7:30 💰 $

San Saturnino ✉ Piazza San Cosimo ☎ 070 201 01
🕐 Daily 10–noon

Cala Gonone

East-coast Cala Gonone, until recently only accessible by boat, lies on one of Sardinia's loveliest stretches of mountainous coastline. Since a road was blasted through a mountain to reach the sea, this tiny village has mushroomed and now has plenty of hotels, villas and restaurants. There's still a feeling of seclusion though, and it's a good place to enjoy the spectacular beauty of the area. The maquis-covered white cliffs are pitted with grottoes and sea-caves, while tiny secluded coves offer lovely swimming. Take one of the boat trips to visit the most scenic – Cala Luna and Cala Sisine would be good choices with wonderful views of the deep gorges that cut through the 3,000-foot high mountains en route. Don't miss a trip to the Grotta del Bue Marino, said to be one of the last refuges of the Mediterranean monk seal. The cave itself, a luminous cavern forested with stalactites and stalagmites, is astonishing.

➕ B2

Castelsardo

Castelsardo occupies the hill around the massive castle built in the 13th and 14th centuries by the Genoese, who founded

Elephant Rock, a bizarre natural rock formation

the little town in 1102. Once known as Castelgenovese after its founders, it changed its name again in 1448 to Castelaragonese, after its Spanish conquerors, becoming Castelsardo in 1776.

Visitors are drawn here by its little handicraft and souvenir shops lining the narrow streets – palm-leaf baskets are the local specialty. You can learn more about this traditional handicraft in the Museo dell'Intreccio (Museum of Wickerwork), which occupies the old castle. It's also worth the climb for the lovely views from its terraces, with Corsica visible on a clear day. The town's Cattedrale (Cathedral), perched on the edge of the cliff, dates from the 17th century. Inside you can see the Madonna degli Angeli (Madonna of the Angels), a 15th-century, much-venerated icon created by a local artist. If you're driving, you'll notice the strange rock formation outside town. This is the Roccia dell'Elefante (Elephant Rock), a bizarre block wind-sculpted over the centuries into the shape of an elephant with its trunk raised.

➕ B3

Tourist information ✉ Pro Loco, Castelsardo
☎ 079 471 500 🕐 Mon.–Sat. 8–noon and 3–6, May–Sep. 🚩 The festival, *Lunissanti,* where hooded figures walk slowly through torchlit streets, is held on Easter Mon.

Museo dell'Intreccio ✉ Via Marconi 🕐 Daily 9–1 and 2–5, Apr.–Oct. 💰 $

Cattedrale di Sant'Antonio Abate ✉ Via Seminario
🕐 Daily 8–6

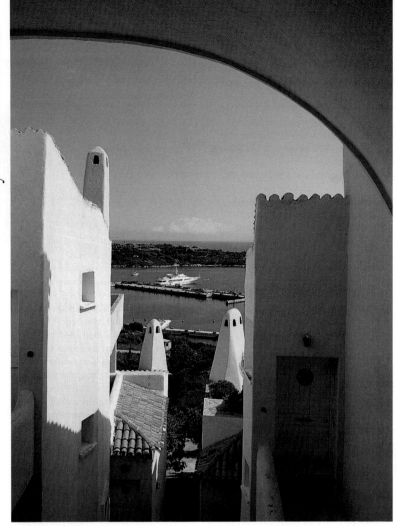

Luxury yachts are an everyday sight from the picturesque streets of the resort of Porto Cervo

COSTA SMERALDA

Until the early 1960s, the north-easternmost corner of Sardinia was a lonely and idyllic stretch of undiscovered coast. In 1962 the Consorzio Costa Smeralda (Emerald Coast Consortium), headed by the Aga Khan, was formed. Its plan was to turn the area into the Mediterranean's smartest playground, complete with luxury hotels, opulent villas, yachting marinas and excellent sporting facilities. Money poured in, hotels, restaurants and designer shops opened, and the rich followed.

Today, the heart of the Emerald Coast is Porto Cervo and Porto Rotondo, two planned villages centered around marinas, where you'll see some of the world's most expensive yachts. Construction is done with local materials, and the buildings combine the different architectural elements found all over the Mediterranean. They are surrounded by indigenous trees and draped in cascades of flowering shrubs. Chic, wealthy and tasteful, the development perfectly fulfills its aim, but loses points on charm and local color. If you plan to stay, it's easy to fall into the sybaritic life and fill your day with gentle strolling and crowd-watching, while swimming and perfecting your tan. There's an excellent golf course and a full summer program of sporting events. For

Sicily and Sardinia

shoppers, the trendy boutiques and designer showrooms of Porto Cervo will be a draw, and there are plenty of expensive and tempting bars and restaurants.

Not all this lovely area is developed though, and you'll find wonderful beaches and laid-back resorts farther along the coast at places such as Santa Teresa Gallura, a small 17th-century town with an active fishing fleet.

Off the north coast lies the archipelago of La Maddalena, a group of seven islands with fabulous beaches. Garibaldi, who played a key role in Italy's unification, lived for many years on the island of Caprera and is buried there. Maddelena and Caprera are joined by a bridge, and a scenic road runs round Maddelena, with views of the other islands and Corsica.

Further east, villages like Cannigione on the Golfo di Arzachena are also still relatively quiet.

La Maddalena ✚ B3
Tourist information ✉ Via XX Settembre 24 ☎ 0789 736 321 🕐 Daily 8–8, May–Oct.; Mon.–Fri. 8–2, rest of year

GENNARGENTU

The Monti del Gennargentu (Gennargentu Mountains) lie at the heart of Sardinia's rugged interior. Now preserved as the Parco Nazionale del Gennargentu, a huge national wilderness

park, it contains Sardinia's highest peak, Punta La Marmora (6,052 feet), which rises above these lonely and unspoiled uplands. Small towns are located throughout the area; isolated and self-contained, these farming villages are home to generous people whose pattern of life has scarcely changed over hundreds of years. These villages still celebrate feast days and festivals with traditional celebrations and are the best places to see traditional dress being worn.

Driving is the only way to explore this fascinating area, basing yourself perhaps at Nuoro, an inland city situated on a plateau beneath Monte Ortobene. From here, you can easily reach the park, which has excellent hiking and superb wildlife – you could see pine martens, wild boar, mouflon, griffon vultures and eagles.
✚ B2
Nuoro tourist information ✉ Piazza Italia 19 ☎ 0784 32 307 🕐 Daily 8–1 and 3–7, May–Oct. ℹ Further information on the park is available from the World Wildlife Fund office, Piazza Santa Maria delle Neve 8, Nuoro (☎ 0784 328 88)

GIARA DI GESTURI

Strange basalt plateaus, known as *giare*, are found all over Sardinia. The Giara di Gesturi is one of the largest. It's an extensive plain more than 12 kilometers (7 miles) across, and its basalt outcrops, covered in maquis and wildflowers, appear

Despite the development, quiet corners can still be found on the Costa Smeralda

amid huge forests of cork oaks. The plateau is home to the tiny native wild horse, which was once found all over Sardinia.

Marshy areas form after rain, making the Giara a favorite feeding ground in spring for migratory birds. To the southeast lies Su Nuraxi, the most extensive and oldest Nuraghic complex in Sardinia. Built by the indigenous population around 1500 BC, the site comprises a fortress structure surrounded by living areas and defensive walls. It was probably inhabited by the Sards and later the Carthaginians for 2,000 years until it was covered with earth at the time of the Roman conquest; a rainstorm washed it clear in 1949. It's excellently preserved, and you can easily identify the different buildings, which include a mill and bakery.

➕ B2

Tourist information ✉ Via Mameli 97, Cágliari ☎ 070 664 195

Su Nuraxi ✉ 1 kilometer (half a mile) east of Barumini ☎ 070 936 8024 ⏰ Daily 9–dusk 🍴 Bar and restaurant nearby 💶 $

NORA

Sardinia's star archeological site lies 40 kilometers (25 miles) south of Cágliari on a narrow spit of land swelling into the sea. Nora was founded by the Phoenicians in the eighth century BC and later settled by the Carthaginians before becoming the Roman capital of Sardinia in AD 238. The city was abandoned around the third century, possibly because of a natural disaster. Some parts are now submerged, and you can see ruins beneath the water, but plenty remains on dry land. The oldest ruin is that of the Carthaginian Temple of Astarte.

Roman remains are plentiful; look for the fourth-century baths decorated with mosaics, the theater, the Forum, and the traces of streets and houses. Many finds from the site are in Cágliari's Archeological Museum (see page 190), including a Punic inscription with the first mention of the name "Sardinia"; other finds are in the museum in nearby Pula. Close by you'll see the Romanesque church of Sant'Efisio, the site of a famous spring procession from Cágliari. The church backs on to a tempting beach with crystal-clear waters, which can be horribly crowded in summer.

➕ A1

✉ 40 kilometers (25 miles) south of Cágliari ☎ 070 920 9138 ⏰ Daily 9–7, Apr.–Oct.; 9–noon and 2–5, rest of year 💶 $ 🎪 Festival of Sant'Efisio May 1–4; commemorates the end of the plague in 1656. The saint's statue is carried through the streets of Cágliari, then taken to Nora on a cart drawn by oxen

Museo Civico Archeologico ✉ Corso Vittorio Emanuele 67 ☎ 070 920 9610 ⏰ Daily 9–1 and 3–6 💶 $

PORTO CONTE

If you're based in the pleasant old port town of Alghero with its strong Spanish influences, you'll be tempted by the lovely beaches near the town known as the Porto Conte. This string of beaches, embraced by two rocky promontories, is part of the Riviera del Corallo (Coral Riviera), from where much of the coral used in the jewelry you'll see on display in Alghero originates from.

The northern arm, Capo Caccia, rears up above the sea with stunning views of Alghero to the south. The Capo is best known for the Grotta di Nettuno (Neptune's Grotto), a spectacular sea-cave extending for more than a mile. Access is either by boat from Alghero, or by descending 654 steps from the Capo above. The steps were built in 1954 and are aptly known as the Escala del Cabriol (Goat's Stairway). Before the steps were built, the only way down was along a dizzying precipitous path. The caves are dramatically and stunningly lit and the narrow corridors hung with stalactites and stalagmites opening into lofty caves. The southern arm of Porto Conte has good beaches and a fine Nuraghi site, the Nuraghi di Palmavera.

➕ A3

Alghero tourist information ✉ Piazza Portaterra 9 ☎ 079 979 054 ⏰ Mon.–Sat. 8–8, May–Sep. (also Sun. 8–noon, Jul.–Aug.); Mon.–Sat. 8–2, rest of year

Grotta di Nettuno ✉ Capa Caccia ⏰ Daily 9–7, Apr.–Sep.; 10–5, Oct.; 9–2, rest of year 🚢 Ferries from Alghero several times daily May–Sep. 💶 $$$

Many visitors are drawn to Sardinia purely for the beauty of its coastline

The waters around Sardinia are among the clearest and cleanest in the Mediterranean, their beaches attracting tens of thousands of visitors who come to enjoy the sun and sea.

THE SARDINIAN COASTLINE

The Beaches

Around the island, beaches range from tiny hidden coves to glorious stretches of golden sands. The Costa Smeralda (the Emerald Coast, see page 192) in the northeast is the most famous stretch, its granite cliffs and turquoise sea providing great diving, snorkeling and sailing. South, the Golfo di Orosei is a paradise for those seeking peace and quiet. Many of its idyllic coves, backed by limestone cliffs, are accessible only by boat or on foot. Poetto, outside Cágliari and south again, provides a lively contrast. Packed with locals and visitors, its 6 kilometers (4 miles) of sandy beaches are well provided with bars and restaurants. The southeast corner at Piscinas has 9 kilometers (6 miles) of sand-dunes covered with feathery tamarisk, juniper and maquis. Some dunes top 165 feet, the highest in Europe. North of here and south of Alghero, you'll find more sandy beaches and clear sea, which give way to the dramatic cliffs to the north and south of Alghero itself. Wind-surfing enthusiasts should head for the north coast, with its guaranteed steady, strong breezes. If you're interested in birdlife, you should see plenty in the cliffs, an ideal nesting habitat. Herring gulls are everywhere, but also look for the rarer Audouin's gull and cormorants fishing from the rocks. Peregrine falcons and kites also use the cliffs as nesting areas.

The Seas

Sardinia's clear azure waters are the cleanest in Italy, with some areas designated international marine reserves. This makes for wonderful diving into waters rich in flora and fauna. Coral grows from 90 to 300 feet down; the mainly red and white Sardinian coral is used in jewelry, while the yellow and white Gorgonian coral can grow to 3 feet in height. Divers will encounter neptune grass, while rocky crevasses make ideal homes for crustaceans and mollusks. If you're offshore, look out for dolphins joyously riding the waves off the northern coast. Sardinia's greatest marine success story is the reestablishment of the monk seal, once thought to be extinct, in the waters of Golfo di Orosei.

Hotels and Restaurants

The hotels and restaurants in this book were selected by local specialists and include establishments in several price ranges. Since price is often the best indication of the level of facilities and quality of service, a three-tiered price guide appears at the beginning of the listings. Because variable rates will affect the amount of foreign currency that can be exchanged for dollars (and thus affect the cost of a room or a meal), price ranges are given in the local currency.

Although price ranges and operating times were accurate at press time, this information is always subject to change without notice. If you're interested in a particular establishment, it is always advisable to call ahead to reserve. The larger and more expensive hotels and the better-known restaurants are more likely to have someone who speaks English on the staff; smaller establishments may not. In such cases it may be better to inquire by fax rather than phone.

Facilities suitable for travelers with disabilities vary greatly, and you are strongly advised to contact an establishment directly to determine whether it will be able to meet your needs. Older buildings may not be adequately designed or equipped for visitors with limited or impaired mobility.

Accommodations
Accommodations have been selected with two considerations in mind: a particularly attractive character or sense of local flavor, or a central location that is convenient for sightseeing. Remember that centrally located hotels fill up quickly, especially during busy summer vacation periods; make reservations well in advance. In-room bathrooms (sometimes referred to as "en-suite facilities") may not be available in smaller budget hotels.

Room rates for European hotels normally include a light breakfast of rolls or croissants and coffee (where this is not the case, the listing description notes that the rate is for "room only"). Some hotels offer a price for overnight accommodations that includes an evening meal.

Eating Out
Listed restaurants range from upscale places suitable for an elegant evening out to small cafés where you can stop and take a leisurely break from a busy day of sightseeing. Some are close to attractions; where this is the case, there is a cross-reference under the attraction listing. Other possibilities for getting a bite to eat are the cafeterias and restaurants on the premises of museums and galleries.

In Italy the different types of restaurant can be confusing. The terms *ristorante, osteria* and *trattoria* are fairly interchangable; *tovola calda* and *pizzeria* imply something a bit more humble.

An elegant Rome hotel – the choice of good accommodations in Italian tourist areas is bewildering

The Northwest and Emilia Romagna

KEY TO SYMBOLS

- ⊞ hotel
- ⊟ restaurant
- ⊠ address
- ☎ telephone number
- 🕒 days/times closed
- Ⓜ nearest subway station
- 🚌 nearby bus/trolley-bus/tram route(s).
- 🚢 ferry
- AE American Express
- CB Carte Blanche
- DI Diners
- MC MasterCard
- VI VISA

Hotels

Price guide: double room with breakfast for two people
- $ up to L200,000
- $$ L200,000–400,000
- $$$ over L400,000

Restaurants

Price guide: dinner per person, excluding drinks
- $ L15,000–30,000
- $$ L30,000–50,000
- $$$ over L500,000

ROOM FOR TWO

Italian hotels charge for the room, not for each person. The price, by law, is displayed on the back of the room door and may vary according to the season (alta/bassa stagione). It may or may not include breakfast. Double beds are far more common than singles; they are generally queen or king size. Single rooms are generally in short supply and cost far more than half that of a double; you are paying for privacy, not space. Many hotels will put another bed in a double room if you request it; the charge for this must also be displayed.

THE NORTHWEST AND EMILIA ROMAGNA

ALBA

⊞ I Castelli $$

This modern hotel has comfortable rooms, a gym and a good restaurant. ⊠ Corso Torino 14/1 ☎ 0173 361 978; fax 0173 361 974   AE, CB, DI, MC, VI

⊟ Il Vicoletto $$

This old restaurant is a good place to try typical regional dishes, which may include truffled pigeon and homemade pasta. You'll be offered a complimentary drink as you arrive. ⊠ Via Bertero 6 ☎ 0173 363 196 🕒 Closed Mon. and 2 weeks Jul.–Aug.   AE, CB, DI, MC, VI

AOSTA

⊞ Europe $$

Room prices vary widely in this traditional hotel. The elegant rooms are quiet and comfortable, and it's only a few minutes stroll to all you'll want to see. ⊠ Piazza Narbonne 8 ☎ 0165 236 363; fax 0165 405 66   AE, CB, DI, MC, VI

⊟ Vecchio Ristoro $

Once an old mill, this cozy restaurant offers a good range of seasonal local dishes. Try the *polenta* as a side dish and delicious mushrooms in autumn. ⊠ Via Tourneuve 4 ☎ 0165 33 238 🕒 Closed Sun., Mon. lunch and 2 weeks in Jun. and Nov.   AE, CB, MC, VI

ASTI

⊟ Gener Neuv $$

A well-established Asti institution where you're sure of a friendly welcome. Sample traditional dishes cooked with the freshest local ingredients. The decor is elegant yet rustic and the wine list formidable. ⊠ Lungotanaro Pescatori 4 ☎ 0141 557 270 🕒 Closed Sun. and Mon. (open for Sun. lunch Sep.–Dec.), Aug. and Dec. 25–Jan. 6 AE, CB, DI, MC, VI

⊞ Reale $$

Located next to the venue for Asti's famous palio, this hotel is a favorite. You'll find well-appointed rooms and a friendly welcome.

⊠ Piazza Alfieri 6 ☎ 0141 530 240; fax 0141 343 57   AE, CB, DI, MC, VI

BÉRGAMO

⊞ Agnello d'Oro $$

This hotel is housed in a 17th-century building with attractive rooms and a nice restaurant, which spills onto the piazza in summer. ⊠ Via Gombito 22 ☎ 0352 49 883; fax 0352 356 12   AE, CB, DI, MC, VI

⊟ Taverna del Colleoni-dell'Angelo $$

Housed in one of Bérgamo's loveliest palaces, this is the place to enjoy sophisticated cooking of the highest order. Choices include sturgeon, truffles, and mushrooms in season, fabulous desserts and a breathtaking wine list. There are tables outside in summer. ⊠ Piazza Vecchia 7 ☎ 0352 32 596 🕒 Closed Mon.   AE, CB, DI, MC, VI

BOLOGNA

⊞ Al Cappello Rosso $$

This wonderful hotel has been in business since the 14th century and still offers a warm welcome, traditional service and modern comfort and facilities. Well-situated in the historic center. ⊠ Via de' Fusari 9 ☎ 051 261 891; fax 051 227 179   AE, CB, DI, MC, VI

⊟ Pappagallo $$

You'll find the best of classical Bolognese cooking at this long-established restaurant in the heart of the old city. Housed in a 14th-century palazzo, the decor and service fully complement the homemade pasta and meat dishes. ⊠ Piazza Mercanzia 3 ☎ 051 231 200 🕒 Closed Sun., also Sat. evening in summer, 2 weeks in Aug.   AE, CB, DI, MC, VI

COMO

⊞ Hotel Como $$

This elegant and comfortable hotel is about 15 minutes from the lake and is in the center of town. Its recently refurbished rooms have excellent facilities and the roof garden has a heated pool. ⊠ Via Mentana 28 ☎ 0312 66 173; fax 0312 660 20 🕒 Closed Dec. and Jan.   AE, CB, DI, MC, VI

¶ Osteria l'Angolo del Silenzio $
One of the oldest buildings in Como, recently modernized, houses this pleasant restaurant offering good local cooking based on fish, mushrooms and game in season. Excellent value. Good wine list.
✉ Viale Lecco 25 ☎ 0313 372 157
🕐 Closed Mon., 2 weeks in Jan. and Aug. AE, CB, DI, MC, VI

CREMONA

🏨 Duomo $
This well-appointed and friendly hotel in the heart of the city offers excellent value, good service, a great location and a restaurant.
✉ Via Gonfalonieri 13 ☎ 0372 35 242; fax 0372 458 392 AE, CB, DI, MC, VI

¶ La Sosta $$
A welcoming restaurant which specializes in local dishes – don't miss the homemade gnocchi or *mostarda di cremona*, the sweet mustard-spiked fruit that accompanies meat here.
✉ Via Sicardo 9 ☎ 0372 456 656
🕐 Closed Sun. evening, Mon. and Aug. AE, CB, DI, MC, VI

FERRARA

🏨 Annunziata $$
This elegant and peaceful midsize hotel is wonderfully located in the city center. The rooms are comfortable and the friendly owners offer free use of bicycles to get around this lovely city.
✉ Piazza Repubblica 5 ☎ 0532 201 111; fax 0532 203 233
🕐 Closed Dec. 25 and Ferragosto (August holiday) AE, CB, DI, MC, VI

¶ La Provvidenza $$
If you want to experience Ferrarese specialties, head here, a pretty restaurant slightly outside the center, to sample truffles and mushrooms in season, homemade pasta and delicious desserts. You can eat in the shady green courtyard in summer.
✉ Corso Ercole I d'Este 92 ☎ 0532 205 187 🕐 Closed Mon. and 2 weeks in Aug. AE, CB, DI, MC, VI

GARDA

🏨 Gabbiano $$
This excellent-value hotel overlooks the lake. Each comfortable room has a balcony, making it an excellent summer choice.
✉ Via dei Cipressi 4 ☎ 0457 256 655; fax 0457 255 363 🕐 Closed Oct.–Mar. CB, MC, VI

¶ Tobago $$
This hotel restaurant is well worth a visit, as much for its pretty location and lovely garden as for the excellent cooking. The menu features a good variety of fish and interesting local dishes.
✉ Via Bellini 1 ☎ 0457 256 340
🕐 Closed Tue. in winter and Jan. 6 to mid-Feb. AE, CB, DI, MC, VI

GENOVA (GENOA)

🏨 Hotel City $$
This modern hotel located in the heart of the city has pleasant bedrooms and good public rooms. It's popular with businessmen for meetings, so reservations are recommended.
✉ Via S Sebastiano 6 ☎ 010 55 451; fax 010 586 301 AE, CB, DI, MC, VI

¶ Rina $$
Genoa's oldest-established restaurant continues to please diners with its fresh fish and other high-quality Ligurian dishes. The surroundings are pleasing and the service excellent.
✉ Mura delle Grazie 3/r ☎ 01 024 66 475 🕐 Closed Mon. and Aug. AE, CB, DI, MC, VI

LEVANTO

¶ Hostaria da Franco $$
Among Lévanto's many good eating places, this establishment stands out for its atmosphere, elegance and excellent food. Fish ranks high, there are constantly changing specialties, and the dining experience when you can eat outside is lovely.
✉ Via privata Olivi 8 ☎ 0187 808 647 🕐 Closed Mon. (except in summer) and Nov. No credit cards

🏨 Stella Maris $$
This pretty hotel not far from the sea is located in an 18th-century palazzo. The dining room and some bedrooms have frescoed ceilings.
✉ Via Marconi 4 ☎ 0187 808 258; fax 0187 807 351 🕐 Closed Nov. AE, CB, DI, MC, VI

MANTOVA

¶ Aquila Nigra $$
A dining experience in this old palace with its frescoed ceilings will be truly memorable. You can enjoy traditional dishes, which vary as the seasons change. Good wine list and professional service.
✉ Vicolo Bonacolsi 4 ☎ 0376 327 180 🕐 Closed Sun. evening (except Apr.–May and Sep.–Oct.), Mon., 2 weeks in Jan. and Aug. AE, CB, DI, MC, VI

🏨 San Lorenzo $$
You'll be within an easy stroll of the Ducal Palace at this lovely hotel in the old center. Antique furnishings blend well with modern comforts, and there is a nice terrace.
✉ Piazza Concordia 14 ☎ 0376 220 500; fax 0376 327 194 AE, CB, DI, MC, VI

MILANO (MILAN)

¶ Aimo e Nadia $$$
This is one of Italy's top restaurants, where you can enjoy the finest of traditional Milanese cooking using the very best ingredients. Creativity, style and flavor are the keynotes, complimented with impeccable service, elegant surroundings and a superb wine list.
✉ Via Montecuccoli 6 ☎ 02 416 886 🕐 Closed Sat. lunch, Sun., throughout Aug. and Jan. 1–6
🚇 Bande Nere AE, CB, DI, MC, VI

¶ Le Bandiere $
This popular restaurant, always packed with locals, offers a wide range of dishes from the north of Italy including delicious risotti and homemade pasta.
✉ Via Palermo 15 ☎ 02 8646 1646 🕐 Closed Sat. lunch, Sun., 2 weeks in Aug. and Dec. 25–Jan. 1
🚇 Lanza, Moscova AE, CB, DI, MC, VI

¶ Bistrot Duomo $$
This restaurant is at the top of the Rinascente building with superlative views over the spires of the cathedral. It offers the best of Lombardy cooking in tasteful surroundings.
✉ Via S Raffaele 2 ☎ 02 877 120
🕐 Closed Sun. and Mon. lunch and 2 weeks in Aug. 🚇 Duomo
AE, CB, DI, MC, VI

The Northwest and Emilia Romagna

KEY TO SYMBOLS
🏨 hotel
🍴 restaurant
✉ address
☎ telephone number
🕐 days/times closed
Ⓜ nearest subway station
🚌 nearby bus/trolley-bus/tram route(s).
⛴ ferry
AE American Express
CB Carte Blanche
DI Diners
MC MasterCard
VI VISA

Hotels
Price guide: double room with breakfast for two people
$ up to L200,000
$$ L200,000–400,000
$$$ over L400,000

Restaurants
Price guide: dinner per person, excluding drinks
$ L15,000–30,000
$$ L30,000–50,000
$$$ over L500,000

WINE AND WATER

Wine and water are the normal accompaniments to Italian meals, except with pizza, which calls for beer. Water is bottled mineral water, *aqua minerale*, and comes with bubbles, *gassata*, or still, *naturale*; it is not expensive. The wine list in cheaper and mid-price restaurants normally has a reasonable selection of local wines, but it's rare to find wine from other Italian areas, let alone foreign wines. All establishments have both red and white carafe wine, *vino della casa*. This may be ordered in one-quarter, one-half or one-liter pitchers. It is quite acceptable to order Coke and other soft drinks, though restaurants do not serve milk.

🏨 Bristol $$
This comfortable hotel is aimed at vacationers and has stylish ambience. The only disadvantage is that it's not right in the center, though transportation is good.
✉ Via Scarlatti 32 ☎ 02 669 4141; fax 02 670 2942 🕐 Closed 2 weeks in Aug. Ⓜ Lima, Centrale AE, CB, DI, MC, VI

🏨 Lloyd $$
Located in the heart of the city and a short walk from the cathedral, this hotel has comfortable rooms and every convenience.
✉ Corso di Porta Romana 48 ☎ 02 5830 3332; fax 02 583 033 65 🕐 Closed 2 weeks in Aug., Dec 25–Jan 6 Ⓜ Crocceta, Missori AE, CB, DI, MC, VI

🏨 London $$
Conveniently located in the historic center close to the Castle Sforzesco, this good-value hotel offers comfortable rooms and attentive service from the English-speaking staff.
✉ Via Rovello 3 ☎ 02 7202 0166; fax 02 805 7037 🕐 Closed Aug., and Dec. 25–Jan. 6 Ⓜ Cadorna, Cairoli CB, MC, VI

🏨 Principe di Savoia $$$
The elegant facade fronts a superbly appointed hotel with excellent service and a good restaurant.
✉ Piazza della Repubblica 17 ☎ 02 62 301; fax 02 659 5838 Ⓜ Repubblica AE, CB, DI, MC, VI

🍴 Savini $$$
This huge and bustling restaurant is a Milanese institution, always busy, always convivial. Rich in atmosphere and tradition, the food covers northern cooking at its best. Try the fixed-price menu for excellent value.
✉ Galleria Vittorio Emanuele II ☎ 02 7200 3433 🕐 Closed Sun., 2 weeks in Aug. and Jan. 1–6 Ⓜ Duomo AE, CB, DI, MC, VI

MODENA

🏨 Centrale $
This is not Módena's smartest hotel, but its location in the old center makes up for a lot. The modernized rooms are comfortable and the service professional.
✉ Via Rismondo 55 ☎ 0592 18 808; fax 0592 382 01 AE, CB, DI, MC, VI

🍴 Fini $$
First opened in 1912, this Módena institution is today an elegant, restrained and upscale restaurant. Enjoy homemade pasta, *fritto misto* and delicious vegetables, all cooked with flair and served with professionalism.
✉ Rua Frati Minori 54 ☎ 0592 23 314 🕐 Closed Mon.–Tue., end of Jul. and Aug., and Dec. 25–Jan. 1 AE, CB, DI, MC, VI

MONTEROSSO

🍴 Miky $$
This friendly, lively restaurant offers everything you'd expect – good pasta dishes, fresh fish, traditional specialties and pizza, which you can enjoy outside on a terrace overlooking the sea.
✉ Via Fegina 104 ☎ 0187 817 608 🕐 Closed Tue. (except in season) and mid-Nov. to mid-Mar. AE, CB, MC, VI

🏨 Pasquale $$
This is a family-run, small hotel right beside the sea, with pleasant and recently refurbished rooms.
✉ Via Fegina 4 ☎ 0187 817 550; fax 0187 817 056 AE, CB, MC, VI

PARMA

🍴 La Greppia $$
This pleasant and welcoming family-run restaurant in the heart of the historic center is a good choice for classic Parma cooking, with home-made pasta and wonderful desserts.
✉ Strada Garibaldi 39/a ☎ 0521 233 686 🕐 Closed Mon.–Tue., Jul. and Dec. 25 AE, CB, DI, MC, VI

🏨 Verdi $$$
Parma's high standard of living is reflected in this elegant hotel overlooking the Parco Ducale. You'll be looked after impeccably. The building dates from the 19th century.
✉ Via Pasini 18 ☎ 0521 293 549; fax 0521 293 559 🕐 Closed 2 weeks in Aug. and Dec. 25 AE, CB, DI, MC, VI

PAVIA

🏨 Ariston $$
This peaceful hotel, within a short stroll of the lovely city center, has been run for many years by the same family. Rooms are simple, functional

The Northeast

and comfortable. Restaurant.
⊠ Via A Scopoli 10/d ☎ 0382 343
34; fax 0382 25 667 Ⓒ Closed Dec.
25 –Jan. 6 AE, CB, DI, MC, VI

🍴 Locanda Vecchia Pavia $$
This high-quality restaurant offers
imaginative dishes using the
freshest of seasonal ingredients.
Excellent service and elegant
surroundings complete the picture.
⊠ Via Cardinal Ribaldi 2 ☎ 0382
304 132 Ⓒ Closed Mon., Wed. lunch
and 2 weeks in Jan. and Aug.
AE, CB, DI, MC, VI

PIACENZA

🍴 Antica Osteria del Teatro $$$
Food guides rate this among the top
restaurants in Italy; an elegant place
housed in a 15th-century palazzo.
The menu has sophisticated
interpretations of classic Emilian
cooking and international dishes,
served with an attentive and
professional service.
⊠ Via Verdi 16 ☎ 0523 323 777
Ⓒ Closed Sun., Mon., Jan. 1–6 and
2 weeks in Aug. AE, CB, DI, MC, VI

🏨 Nazionale $$
This makes a good stopping point.
Rooms are well-equipped and
comfortable, and it's 15 minutes
walk to the city center.
⊠ Via Genova 33 ☎ 0523 712 000;
fax 0523 456 013 AE, CB, DI, MC, VI

🏨 Piccolo Hotel $$$
This charming hotel has access to a
private beach. The pretty rooms
have balconies facing the sea.
⊠ Via Duca degli Abruzzi 31
☎ 0185 269 015; fax 0185 269 621
Ⓒ Closed 2 weeks between Nov.
and Dec. AE, CB, DI, MC, VI

🍴 Puny $$$
Enjoy delicious Ligurian cooking in a
pretty setting overlooking the main
piazza. Try the swordfish, fresh tuna
and homemade desserts.
⊠ Piazza Martiri dell'Olivetta 5
☎ 0185 269 037 Ⓒ Closed Thu.
and mid-Dec. to mid-Feb.
No credit cards

RAVENNA

🏨 Centrale Byron $$
This welcoming and well-furnished
hotel is housed in an old palace close
to the heart of historic Ravenna. The

rooms are large and airy, and it's a
short stroll to everything you'll want
to see.
⊠ Via IV Novembre 14 ☎ 0544
212 225; fax 0544 341 14 Ⓒ Closed
during Christmas period AE, CB, DI,
MC, VI

🍴 Trattoria al Gallo $$
Diners have been well-fed here
since 1909, and you'll enjoy the
simple excellence of the well-
presented dishes. The emphasis is
on fresh local produce, with a good
range of vegetarian dishes and a
comprehensive wine list.
⊠ Via Maggiore 87 ☎ 0544 213
775 Ⓒ Closed Sun. evening,
Mon.–Tue., Easter and Dec. 25
AE, CB, DI, MC, VI

RIMINI

🍴 Acero Rosso $$
This popular restaurant has a wide
range of dishes using meat, fish and
vegetables as a base for light and
tasty meals. Desserts are homemade,
and the wine list is good.
⊠ Viale Tiberio 11 ☎ 0541 53 577
Ⓒ Closed Mon., Sun. evening in
winter, Dec. 25 and 2 weeks
between Jul.–Aug. AE, CB, DI,
MC, VI

🏨 Ambasciatori $$–$$$
Room prices vary tremendously at
this midsize hotel, a few hundred
yards from the beach. It has a pool,
access to a private beach and a
rooftop terrace.
⊠ Viale Vespucci 22 ☎ 0541 55
561; fax 0541 237 90 AE, CB, DI,
MC, VI

STRESA

🏨 Astoria $$
This family-run hotel beside the lake
has modern rooms, a pool and
pleasant terrace restaurant for
summer dining.
⊠ Corso Umberto I 31 ☎ 0323 32
566; fax 0323 933 785 Ⓒ Closed
Nov.–Feb. AE, CB, DI, MC, VI

🍴 Piemontese $$
A pretty and friendly restaurant with
a pergola in the garden for summer
dining. Sample the wide range of
dishes on the *menu degustazione*.
⊠ Via Mazzini 25 ☎ 0323 30 235
Ⓒ Closed Mon., Dec.–Jan. AE, CB,
MC, VI

TORINO (TURIN)

🏨 Conte Biancamano $$
This small and centrally located
hotel is housed in an old palace.
Many of its well-equipped rooms
have wood paneling and there's a
friendly and professional welcome
from its owners.
⊠ Corso Vittorio Emanuele II 73
☎ 011 562 3281; fax 011 562 3789
Ⓒ Closed Dec. 25 –Jan. 1 and Aug.
AE, CB, DI, MC, VI

🍴 Del Cambio $$$
To enjoy Piedmont cooking at its
best, head for this very good
restaurant in an 18th-century
building. High-quality meat is used
in the cooking, the wine list is
excellent, and the service
professional and attentive.
⊠ Piazza Carignano 2 ☎ 011 546
690 Ⓒ Closed Sun., Jan.1–6 and 2
weeks in Aug. AE, CB, DI, MC, VI

THE NORTHEAST

AQUILÉIA

🍴 Colombara $$
This restaurant, popular with local
businessmen, is a good place to find
local dishes, with the emphasis on
fish. Its two rooms are classically
styled and comfortable.
⊠ Via S Zilli 42 ☎ 0431 91 513
Ⓒ Closed Mon. AE, CB, DI, MC, VI

🏨 Patriarchi $$
This comfortable hotel will give you
one of the warmest welcomes you'll
encounter on your travels and a real
sense of personal service.
⊠ Via Giulia Augusta 12 ☎ 0431
919 595; fax 0431 919 596
Ⓒ Closed 2 weeks in Nov. and Dec.
AE, CB, DI, MC, VI

ASOLO

🍴 Ai Due Arche $$
An elegant restaurant with wood-
paneled walls and antique furniture.
Light and refined cooking and
gracious service.
⊠ Via Roma 55 ☎ 0423 952 201
Ⓒ Closed Wed. evening, Thu. and 2
weeks in Jan. AE, CB, DI, MC, VI

🏨 Villa Cipriani $$$
This is a truly world-class luxury hotel
housed in a beautiful 16th-century

The Northeast

KEY TO SYMBOLS

- 🏨 hotel
- 🍴 restaurant
- ✉ address
- ☎ telephone number
- 🕐 days/times closed
- Ⓜ nearest subway station
- 🚌 nearby bus/trolley-bus/tram route(s).
- ⛴ ferry
- AE American Express
- CB Carte Blanche
- DI Diners
- MC MasterCard
- VI VISA

Hotels

Price guide: double room with breakfast for two people
- **$** up to L200,000
- **$$** L200,000–400,000
- **$$$** over L400,000

Restaurants

Price guide: dinner per person, excluding drinks
- **$** L15,000–30,000
- **$$** L30,000–50,000
- **$$$** over L500,000

villa with lovely views over the hills. The clientele is cosmopolitan and often famous, and standards of service are all they would expect.
✉ Via Canova 298 ☎ 0423 523 411; fax 0423 952 095 AE, CB, DI, MC, VI

BOLZANO

🍴 Amadè $$

You'll find the best regional cooking, plus some innovative dishes at this friendly restaurant that concentrates on the freshest market produce. There's a garden for summer dining.
✉ Vicolo Ca' de Bezzi 8 ☎ 0471 971 278 🕐 Closed Sun. AE, CB, DI, MC, VI

🏨 Pircher $$

This friendly and comfortable hotel makes an excellent base for exploring Bolzano's mountains and wine routes. Rooms are well-equipped and there's a welcome pool on the grounds.
✉ Via Merano 52 ☎ 0471 917 513; fax 0471 202 433 AE, CB, MC, VI

CIVIDALE DEL FRIULI

🍴 Alla Frasca $$

This is a traditional trattoria, with good home-cooking and friendly service, where you can eat outside during the summer.
✉ Via de Rubeis 8/a ☎ 0432 731 270 🕐 Closed Mon. and 2 weeks in Jan. AE, CB, MC, VI

🏨 Locanda al Castello $$

This lovely hotel was converted from a convent. Verdant grounds and superb views make up for its position just outside town.
✉ Via del Castello 20 ☎ 0432 733 242; fax 0432 700 901 AE, CB, DI, MC, VI

MERANO

🍴 Grillstube Schloss Maur $$

You'll find plenty of atmosphere in this well-run establishment serving up the special dishes of the region, where Austrian and Italian cooking blends.
✉ Albergo Palace, Via Cavour 2/4 ☎ 0473 271 000 🕐 Evenings only, closed Wed., also mid-Jun.to mid-Jul., mid-Nov. to mid-Dec. AE, CB, DI, MC, VI

🏨 Meranerhof $$

This hotel opposite the thermal baths has been run by the same family for 40 years. They pride themselves on their welcome to regulars, international visitors and families. Two pools.
✉ Via Manzoni 1 ☎ 0473 230 230; fax 0473 233 312 🕐 Closed Jan. 6–Feb. AE, CB, DI, MC, VI

PADOVA (PADUA)

🍴 Antico Brolo $$

A 15th-century building houses this elegant restaurant serving interesting local dishes with an accent on fish. The wine cellar houses a lively pizzeria and there's a pretty garden for outside dining.
✉ Corso Milano 22 ☎ 0496 64 555 🕐 Closed Mon. AE, CB, DI, MC, VI

🏨 Leon Bianco $$

The tranquility is more than you'd expect at this smallish hotel in the historic center of town. Reservations are recommended.
✉ Piazzetta Pedrocchi 12 ☎ 0498 750 814; fax 0498 756 184 AE, CB, DI, MC, VI

TREVISO

🍴 Beccherie $$

One of Treviso's oldest restaurants, the Beccherie is housed in a Venetian-style building with elegant period furniture. Sample the risotto with radicchio, one of Treviso's greatest specialties .
✉ Piazza Ancillotto 10 ☎ 0422 540 871 🕐 Closed Sun. evening, Mon. and part of Jul. AE, CB, DI, MC, VI

🏨 Carlton $$

This recently renovated hotel on the old city walls has good-size rooms, a pleasing decor and good service.
✉ Largo Porta Altinia 15 ☎ 0422 411 661; fax 0422 411 620 AE, CB, DI, MC, VI

TRIESTE

🍴 Antica Trattoria Suban $$

Founded in 1865, this restaurant is still run by the Suban family, who has brought the art of Trieste's middle-European cooking style to great heights with old recipes and traditional flavors.
✉ Via Comici 2 ☎ 0405 43 68

ⓦ Closed Mon., lunch on Tue., 2 weeks in Jan. and 2 weeks in Aug. AE, CB, DI, MC, VI

🏨 Grand Hotel Duchi d'Aosta $$

The style and atmosphere of this impeccably run hotel perfectly encapsulate Trieste's middle-European flavor – somber and restrained elegance with every modern comfort.
✉ Piazza Unità d'Italia 2 ☎ 0407 600 011; fax 0403 660 92   AE, CB, DI, MC, VI

VENÉZIA (VENICE)

🏨 Agli Alboretti $$

This charming hotel, with a pretty courtyard for breakfast, is on a tree-lined street between the Accademia and the Záttere. It's popular with visitors from all over the world, so it makes sense to book well ahead.
✉ Rio Terrà Foscarini, Accademia 884 ☎ 041 523 0058; fax 041 521 01 58 🚤 1, 41, 42 ⓦ Closed 2 weeks in Jan.   AE, CB, DI, MC, VI

🏨 Cipriani $$$

This is one of the world's most famous luxury hotels, with every comfort and impeccable service, beautifully situated in its own gardens on the Giudecca. Every room and suite is different. There's a sense of space you'll find nowhere else in the city.
✉ Fondamenta San Giovanni, Giudecca 10 ☎ 041 520 7744; fax 041 520 39 30 🚤 82 or use hotel's private launch service   AE, CB, DI, MC, VI

🍴 Corte Sconta $$

A famous Venetian fish restaurant tucked away near the Arsenale, with a garden for summer dining. Recipes are truly Venetian, using whatever fish is best in the Rialto market that day. Reservations are essential.
✉ Calle del Pestrin, Castello 3886 ☎ 041 522 7024 ⓦ Closed Sun.–Mon., 2 weeks in Jan. and Feb. and mid-Jul. to mid-Aug. 🚤 82 AE, MC, VI

🏨 Danieli $$$

Generally considered Venice's finest hotel, the Danieli has style, elegance and class, with the advantage of its location in the heart of the city. Be sure to book a room in the older part.

✉ Riva degli Schiavoni, Castello 4196 ☎ 041 522 6480; fax 041 520 0208 🚤 1   AE, CB, DI, MC, VI

🍴 Dona Onesta $

A friendly local restaurant with straightforward Venetian cooking and simple decor. Always busy with visitors and locals alike.
✉ Ponte de la Dona Onesta, Dorsoduro 3922 ☎ 041 710 586 🚤 1   AE, MC, VI

🏨 Europa e Regina $$$

This is probably the best value among Venice's luxury hotels; it's right on the Grand Canal, a stone's throw from St. Mark's and has spacious rooms and a waterside terrace dining area.
✉ Calle Larga XXII Marzo, San Marco 2159 ☎ 041 520 0477; fax 041 523 1533 🚤 1   AE, CB, MC, VI

🍴 Harry's Dolci $$$

This offshoot of the famous Harry's Bar offers equally good food and service with a waterfront terrace for summer dining. All the famous specialties are on the menu, with particularly excellent desserts as a bonus. Reservations are essential.
✉ Fondamenta San Biagio, Giudecca 773 ☎ 041 522 4844 ⓦ Closed mid-Nov. to Mar. and Tue. 🚤 82   AE, CB, DI, MC, VI

🏨 Paganelli $$

Rooms in this quiet, clean and family-run hotel are on the waterfront overlooking St. Mark's Basin – a bonus that other hotels would charge double for.
✉ Riva degle Schiavone, Castello 4182 ☎ 041 522 4324; fax 041 523 9267 🚤 1, 41, 42   AE, CB, MC, VI

🍴 Trattoria alla Madonna $$

This big, noisy fish restaurant, one of the most traditional in Venice, is hugely popular with Venetians and tourists. Service can be slow when they're busy, but the standard of cooking is consistently high.
✉ Calle della Madonna, San Polo 594 ☎ 041 522 3824 ⓦ Closed Wed. and 2 weeks in Jan. and Aug. 🚤 1, 82   AE, MC, VI

VERONA

🍴 Il Desco $$

Verona's best restaurant has everything: service, comfort, antique

decor, a superb wine list and attention to every detail. The cooking is light and creative, using the best seasonal ingredients.
✉ Via Dietro S. Sebastiano 7 ☎ 0455 95 358 ⓦ Closed Sun., Dec. 25–Jan. 6, and 2 weeks in Jun. AE, CB, DI, MC, VI

🏨 Torcolo $$

This friendly hotel is one of the most popular in Verona, so make reservations. It's less than a hundred yards from the Arena.
✉ Vicolo Listone 3 ☎ 0458 007 512; fax 0458 004 058 ⓦ Closed 2 weeks in Jan.   AE, CB, MC, VI

VICENZA

🍴 Antica Trattoria Tre Visi $$

It would be worth eating here for the series of beautifully furnished 15th-century dining rooms. The food is local, with game, mushrooms and mouthwatering desserts.
✉ Corso Palladio 25 ☎ 0444 324 868 ⓦ Closed Sun. evening, Mon. and Jul.   AE, CB, DI, MC, VI

🏨 Campo Marzio $$

Many of Vicenza's more comfortable hotels are outside the center; this is an exception, with good modern rooms and facilities and within an easy stroll of the cathedral.
✉ Viale Roma 21 ☎ 0444 545 700; fax 0444 320 495   AE, CB, MC, VI

TUSCANY, UMBRIA AND THE MARCHE

AREZZO

🍴 Buca di San Francesco $$

Housed in a 14th-century palazzo with original Etruscan paving, this great restaurant follows three rules in its cooking – simplicity, taste and genuine ingredients.
✉ Via San Francesco 1 ☎ 0575 23271 ⓦ Closed Mon. evening, Tue. and 2 weeks in Jul.   AE, CB, DI, MC, VI

🏨 Continentale $$

This spacious and comfortable hotel at the foot of the old center of Arezzo is within easy walking distance of all you'll want to see. Well-furnished rooms and friendly and professional staff.

KEY TO SYMBOLS

- ⊞ hotel
- ⫾ restaurant
- ✉ address
- ☎ telephone number
- Ⓖ days/times closed
- Ⓜ nearest subway station
- 🚌 nearby bus/trolley-bus/tram route(s).
- ⛴ ferry
- AE American Express
- CB Carte Blanche
- DI Diners
- MC MasterCard
- VI VISA

Hotels
Price guide: double room with breakfast for two people
$ up to L200,000
$$ L200,000–400,000
$$$ over L400,000

Restaurants
Price guide: dinner per person, excluding drinks
$ L15,000–30,000
$$ L30,000–50,000
$$$ over L500,000

COFFEE

Italian coffee, *caffè*, comes freshly made and very, very strong. It is perceived as a stimulant, not a drink, hence the tiny cups less than half full – a shot in the arm. For breakfast it is drunk with milk, either as a *cappuccino* or *caffè latte*. For the rest of the day, Italians drink an espresso, known in Italy as *un caffè*. It may have a drop of milk to make it *macchiata* (stained) or a shot of liquor for an extra kick, *caffè corretto*. Decaffeinated coffee is *caffè Hag*. To get anything remotely approaching American coffee, ask for *un caffè americano*, which will be weak and watery.

✉ Piazza Guido Monaco 7 ☎ 057 520 251; fax 057 535 0485 AE, CB, DI, MC, VI

ASCOLI PICENO

⊞ Gioli $$
This is a modern and functional hotel within the old walled center of Ascoli. Warm and welcoming.
✉ Viale De Gasperi 14 ☎ 0736 255 550; fax 0736 255 550 AE, CB, DI, MC, VI

⫾ Tornasacco $
This lovely local restaurant, set on the first floor of an old palazzo in the heart of town, serves typical dishes from the area, with some excellent homemade pasta.
✉ Piazza del Popolo 36 ☎ 0736 254 151 Ⓖ Closed Fri., 2 weeks in Jul. and Dec. 25 AE, CB, DI, MC, VI

ASSISI

⫾ Buca di San Francesco $$
You can enjoy some of Assisi's most delicious pasta dishes and a wide variety of other local specialties in this excellent, rustically elegant restaurant set in a medieval building in the center of town.
✉ Via E Brizi 1 ☎ 0758 122 04 Ⓖ Closed Mon. and throughout Jul. AE, CB, DI, MC, VI

⊞ Subasio $$$
This old-fashioned and historic hotel is within a stone's throw of the Basilica; many famous names have stayed here. The rooms have superb views. Reservations are essential.
✉ Via Frate Elia 2 ☎ 075 812 206; fax 075 816 691 AE, CB, DI, MC, VI

FIRENZE (FLORENCE)

⊞ Aprile $$
This peaceful hotel is housed in a Medici palace with a quiet garden. The bedrooms, with frescoed ceilings and old pictures, have every modern amenity.
✉ Via della Scala 6 ☎ 055 216 237; fax 055 280 947 🚌 2, 17, 22 AE, CB, MC, VI

⊞ Brunelleschi $$$
Book ahead to stay in this comfortable hotel in the heart of Florence. A real sense of tradition and history.
✉ Piazza Sta Elisabetta 3

☎ 055 273 70; fax 055 219 653 🚌 In the pedestrian zone AE, CB, DI, MC, VI

⫾ Cantinetta Antinori $$
Enjoy Tuscan food with superb wine in the 15th-century Palazzo Antinori, the Florence home of this great wine-producing family. The restaurant is furnished with simple elegance in the Florentine style.
✉ Piazza Antinori 3 ☎ 055 292 234 Ⓖ Closed Sat.–Sun., Dec. 25–Jan. 6 and 2 weeks in Aug. 🚌 6, 11, 31 AE, CB, DI, MC, VI

⫾ Dino $$
This uncluttered and airy restaurant housed in three separate rooms in a 14th-century palazzo serves simple and elegant food inspired by centuries-old recipes.
✉ Via Ghibellina 51/r ☎ 055 241 452 Ⓖ Closed Sun. evening and Mon., and 2 weeks in Aug. 🚌 14 AE, CB, DI, MC, VI

⫾ Enoteca Pinchiorri $$$
Considered one of the top five restaurants in Italy, this establishment is set in a 16th-century palazzo with a garden for summer dining. Outstanding and imaginative food, and worth a visit for the wines alone.
✉ Via Ghibellina 87 ☎ 055 242 777 Ⓖ Closed Sun.–Mon., Wed. lunch, and Aug. 🚌 14 AE, CB, DI, MC, VI

⊞ Excelsior $$$
Florence's smartest and most elegant hotel, in a Renaissance-style palazzo in the heart of the historic center, offers every comfort, exceptional service and a roof terrace.
✉ Piazza Ognissanti 3 ☎ 055 264 201; fax 055 210 278 🚌 C AE, CB, DI, MC, VI

⊞ Hermitage $$
You can see the Ponte Vecchio from the fifth-floor public rooms and garden of this comfortable hotel. The well-appointed bedrooms occupy the lower floors.
✉ Vicolo Marzio I, ang. Piazza del Pesce ☎ 055 287 216; fax 055 212 208 🚌 In the pedestrian zone CB, MC, VI

⫾ La Sagrestia $
This excellent-value and typical neighborhood restaurant, just a few

steps from the Ponte Vecchio, serves good Florentine cooking. For real value, go for the fixed-price menu.
✉ Via Guicciardini 27/r ☎ 055 210 003 ⏱ Closed Mon. 🚪 B, 11 AE, CB, DI, MC, VI

GREVE IN CHIANTI

🏨 **Giovanni da Verrazzano $$**
This hotel housed in an old building on the square of this popular Chianti village has well-kept and well-equipped rooms.
✉ Piazza Matteotti 28 ☎ 055 853 189; fax 055 853 648 ⏱ Closed mid-Jan. to mid-Feb. AE, CB, DI, MC, VI

🍴 **Trattoria del Montagliari $$**
It's well worth driving the few miles to Panzano where you'll eat Tuscan meals in a building that's part of a large wine estate. Autumn sees a wide range of mushroom and game specialties appear on the menu.
✉ Via Montagliari 29, Panzano ☎ 0558 52 184 ⏱ Closed Mon. and 2 weeks in Aug. AE, MC, VI

GUBBIO

🏨 **Gattapone $$**
This medieval building in the heart of old Gúbbio has been tastefully converted into a comfortable hotel. Its antique furniture and pretty grounds are bonuses.
✉ Via Ansidei 6 ☎ 075 927 2489; fax 075 927 2417 AE, CB, DI, MC, VI

🍴 **Taverna del Lupo $$**
This big, busy restaurant in a medieval palazzo offers delicious dishes with professional service and a friendly and relaxed atmosphere; truffle dishes in season.
✉ Via Ansidei 6 ☎ 0759 274 368 ⏱ Closed Mon. AE, CB, DI, MC, VI

LUCCA

🍴 **Buca di Sant'Antonio $$**
A series of cozy rooms gives this fine restaurant its special atmosphere. Superb food and wonderful service make it one of Tuscany's top establishments, where traditional dishes are served with a modern twist.
✉ Via della Cervia 3 ☎ 0583 55881 ⏱ Closed Sun. evening, Mon. and 2 weeks in Jul. AE, CB, DI, MC, VI

🏨 **La Luna $$**
One of the very few hotels within the city walls of Lucca. Comfortable rooms. Only a hundred yards from the Piazza Anfiteatro.
✉ Via Fillungo, ang. Corte Compagni 12 ☎ 0583 493 634; 0583 490 021 ⏱ Closed 2 weeks in Jan. AE, CB, DI, MC, VI

MONTALCINO

🏨 **Hotel dei Capitani $$**
This recently converted hotel is in the heart of town. Many of the pretty rooms have lovely views and there's a small pool.
✉ Via Lapini 6 ☎ 0577 847 227; fax 0577 847 239 ⏱ Closed mid-Jan. to Feb. AE, CB, DI, MC, VI

🍴 **Taverna dei Barbi $$**
Drive out to one of Montalcino's finest wine producers to enjoy local specialties served in a converted old farm building. Homemade pasta and game in season.
✉ 5 kilometers (3 miles) from Montalcino at Podernovi ☎ 0577 849 357 ⏱ Closed Tue. evening, Wed. (except in Aug.) and 2 weeks in Jan. AE, CB, DI, MC, VI

MONTEPULCIANO

🍴 **La Grotta $$**
A stroll downhill brings you to this elegantly pretty restaurant on the edge of town. The building was once the home of Sangallo, the Renaissance architect.
✉ Località San Biagio ☎ 0578 757 607 ⏱ Closed Wed. and Jan. 6–end of Feb. AE, CB, DI, MC, VI

🏨 **Hotel il Marzocco $$**
Housed in a 16th-century building, this comfortable hotel just off the main street has been run by the same family for more than 150 years.
✉ Pazza Savonarola 18 ☎ 0578 757 262; fax 0578 757 530 ⏱ Closed mid-Nov. to mid-Dec. AE, CB, DI, MC, VI

NÓRCIA

🍴 **Granaro del Monte $$**
Nórcia's best restaurant. Here you can eat truffle dishes, game in season and meat cooked over a huge open fire. Busy but friendly.
✉ Via Alfieri 12 ☎ 0743 816 513 ⏱ Closed Tue. AE, CB, DI, MC, VI

ORVIETO

🏨 **Maitani $$$**
Less than 200 yards from the cathedral, this elegant and comfortable hotel in a historic building has good-size rooms.
✉ Via Maitani 5 ☎ 0763 342 011; Closed 2 weeks in Jan. AE, CB, DI, MC, VI

🍴 **Trattoria Etrusca $$**
This upscale restaurant in a medieval building is a few paces from the cathedral. Truffles, game and traditional local dishes are featured, and you can visit the wine vaults, carved from the tufa, beneath the dining room.
✉ Via Maitani 10 ☎ 0763 344 016 ⏱ Closed Mon. and 2 weeks in Jan. AE, CB, DI, MC, VI

PASSIGNANO

🏨 **Lido $$**
Right on the edge of Lake Trasimeno, this hotel has airy and spacious rooms and a pretty garden.
✉ Via Roma 1 ☎ 0758 272 19; fax 0758 27 251 ⏱ Closed Dec.–Mar. AE, CB, DI, MC, VI

PERÚGIA

🍴 **Falchetto $$**
This long-established restaurant has kept a tradition of unsophisticated elegance. The cooking is special and features traditional dishes with a modern slant.
✉ Via Bartolo 20 ☎ 075 573 1775 ⏱ Closed Mon. and period between Jan. and Feb. AE, CB, DI, MC, VI

🏨 **Locanda della Posta $$$**
If you want to be in the heart of Perúgia, this is an ideal choice. The excellent rooms are in an old palazzo overlooking the town's main street.
✉ Corso Vannucci 97 ☎ 075 572 8925; fax 075 573 2562 AE, CB, DI, MC, VI

PIENZA

🍴 **Buca delle Fate $**
This big, buzzing restaurant is housed in a 16th-century palazzo and serves straightforward Tuscan cooking, backed up by fine local wines.
✉ Corso Rossellino 38/a ☎ 0578 748 272 ⏱ Closed Mon., 2 weeks in Jan. and Jun. AE, CB, DI, MC, VI

Tuscany, Umbria and the Marche

KEY TO SYMBOLS

🏨 hotel
🍴 restaurant
✉ address
☎ telephone number
🕐 days/times closed
Ⓜ nearest subway station
🚌 nearby bus/trolley-bus/tram route(s).
⛴ ferry
AE American Express
CB Carte Blanche
DI Diners
MC MasterCard
VI VISA

Hotels

Price guide: double room with breakfast for two people
$ up to L200,000
$$ L200,000–400,000
$$$ over L400,000

Restaurants

Price guide: dinner per person, excluding drinks
$ L15,000–30,000
$$ L30,000–50,000
$$$ over L500,000

AGRITURISMO

Agriturismo is accommodations on functioning farms or agricultural estates, giving guests the chance to spend time on the land enjoying home-produced food at its place of origin. The scheme originated as a means of restoring old unused rural properties and agricultural buildings, as well as encouraging traditional crafts and food production methods. Hundreds of lovely old structures have been converted into holiday accommodations, some self-catering, others with simple rooms and dining, some as smart as a good hotel.

🏨 Relais il Chiostro di Pienza $$$

Converted from a 15th-century convent, this is the only hotel within the old town. Frescoed rooms, vaulted ceilings, a garden with a view and a shady cloister.
✉ Corso Rosellino 26 ☎ 0578 748 400; fax 0578 748 440 🕐 Closed Jan. to mid-Mar. AE, CB, DI, MC, VI

PISA

🍴 Ristoro dei Vecchi Macelli $$

You'll find good local cooking and a friendly welcome at this stylish modern restaurant. Fish is recommended and there are interesting vegetable dishes.
✉ Via Volturno 49 ☎ 050 204 24 🕐 Closed Wed., Sun. lunch and 2 weeks in Aug. AE, CB, DI, MC, VI

🏨 Verdi $$

An old palace houses this recently renovated hotel in the heart of the old town and within easy reach of the Piazza dei Miracoli.
✉ Piazza Repubblica 5 ☎ 050 598 947; fax 050 598 944 AE, CB, DI, MC, VI

RADDA IN CHIANTI

🏨 Relais Fattoria Vignale $$$

This 18th-century villa has been transformed into one of Tuscany's luxury hotels. Frescoed ceilings and lovely stonework offset the antique furnishings. There's an excellent restaurant, pool and gardens.
✉ Via Pianigiani 8 ☎ 0577 738 300; fax 0577 738 592 🕐 Open mid-Mar. to Nov. and Dec. 25–Jan. 6 AE, CB, MC, VI

🍴 Vignale $$$

This rustic restaurant housed in an old agricultural building serves local dishes with a twist. It's popular with residents and visitors.
✉ Via XX Settembre 23 ☎ 0577 738 094 🕐 Closed Thu. and Jan. 6 to mid-Mar. AE, CB, DI, MC, VI

SAN GIMIGNANO

🍴 La Griglia $$

You can enjoy eating on the terrace at this well-known 14th-century restaurant in the heart of San Gimignano. There are plenty of local specialties, many of them grilled on the open fire, from which the restaurant gets its name.
✉ Via San Matteo 34/36 ☎ 0577 940 005 🕐 Closed Thu. and mid-Dec. to Feb. AE, CB, DI, MC, VI

🏨 Leon Bianco $$

This tastefully converted, family-run hotel on the town's main square has spacious rooms, lofty vaulted ceilings and a pretty breakfast terrace.
✉ Piazza della Cisterna 13 ☎ 0577 941 294; fax 0577 942 123 🕐 Closed mid-Jan. to mid-Feb. and 2 weeks in Nov.–Dec. AE, CB, DI, MC, VI

SIENA

🏨 Athena $$$

This is a big, modern hotel inside the walls of the old city and 15 minutes from the Campo. Comfortable rooms and professional service.
✉ Via Mascagni 55 ☎ 0577 286 313; fax 0577 481 53 AE, CB, DI, MC, VI

🍴 Marsili $$$

Impeccable service, a wide-ranging wine list, and interesting dishes can be enjoyed in the vaulted elegance of this upscale restaurant.
✉ Via del Castoro 3 ☎ 0577 471 54 🕐 Closed Mon. AE, CB, DI, MC, VI

🍴 Osteria Le Logge $$

This restaurant occupies a medieval apothecary's shop. The cooking is good, with plenty of Sienese dishes and wonderful *porcini* (mushrooms) in autumn.
✉ Via del Porrione 33 ☎ 0577 480 13 🕐 Closed Sun. and 2 weeks in Nov. AE, CB, DI, MC, VI

SPELLO

🍴 Cacciatore $$

If you're looking for perfect terrace dining with a view, head for this restaurant at the top end of town. Umbrian food and good local wines are served in the cozy dining room or under the stars.
✉ Via Giulia 42 ☎ 0742 651 141 🕐 Closed Mon. and 2 weeks between Jun. and Jul. AE, CB, MC, VI

🏨 Palazzo Bocci $$

This 17th-century palazzo was transformed in the mid-1990s into a luxury hotel with a high level of

Central Italy

service and comfort. Vaulted ceilings, terraces and frescoes complete the stylish ambience. ✉ Via Cavour 17 ☎ 0742 301 021; fax 0742 301 464 AE, CB, DI, MC, VI

SPOLETO

🏨 Gattapone $$$
Every room has a view of the gorge and the Ponte delle Torri in this elegant hotel. Good public areas and pretty terraces complete the picture. ✉ Via del Ponte 6 ☎ 0743 223 447; 0743 223 448 AE, CB, DI, MC, VI

🍴 Sabatini $$
Among Spoleto's many excellent restaurants, Sabatini stands out for its lovely garden where you can enjoy imaginative dishes using superb local ingredients. Be sure to try the *antipasto*. ✉ Corso Mazzini 52/54 ☎ 0743 221 831 🕐 Closed Mon. and 2 weeks in Jan. and Aug. AE, CB, DI, MC, VI

TODI

🏨 Fonte Cesia $$
The only hotel in the historic center of Todi, this 18th-century building has retained the original features and has charming rooms furnished in contemporary style. ✉ Via L Leony 3 ☎ 0758 943 737; fax 0758 944 677 AE, CB, DI, MC, VI

🍴 Umbria $$
You can enjoy a warm welcome and excellent home-cooking at this restaurant. The summer terrace has superb views where specialties such as truffle dishes and wild boar are served. Reservations suggested. ✉ Via S Bonaventura 13 ☎ 0758 942 737 🕐 Closed Tue. AE, CB, DI, MC, VI

URBINO

🏨 Bonconte $$
This comfortable hotel lies just inside the city walls, a few minutes walk from the Palazzo Ducale. Avoid the smaller rooms on the top floor. ✉ Via delle Mura 28 ☎ 0722 2463; fax 0722 4782 AE, CB, DI, MC, VI

🍴 Vecchia Urbino $$
A family-run restaurant in the heart of the historic center where you can enjoy truffles, mushrooms and a

superb range of olive oils served in elegant surroundings. ✉ Via dei Vasari 3/5 ☎ 0722 44 47 🕐 Closed Wed. AE, CB, DI, MC, VI

VOLTERRA

🏨 San Lino $$
This comfortable hotel located within the city's walls was once a convent and has been well-converted. It has spacious rooms, and there's a pretty terrace and pool behind the main building. ✉ Via S Lino 26 ☎ 0588 85 250; fax 0588 806 20 🕐 Closed Nov. AE, CB, DI, MC, VI

🍴 Trattoria del Sacco Fiorentino $$
This attractive and friendly restaurant run by an enthusiastic young chef serves Tuscan dishes and some interesting historic recipes rarely found in restaurants. ✉ Piazza XX Settembre 18 ☎ 0588 88 537 🕐 Closed Wed. and 2 weeks in Jan. AE, CB, DI, MC, VI

CENTRAL ITALY

L'AQUILA

🏨 Duomo $$
A converted 19th-century building houses this comfortable hotel. The rooms are functional and it stands in a good location. ✉ Via Dragonetti 6/10 ☎ 0862 410 893; fax 0862 413 058 AE, CB, MC, VI

🍴 Tre Marie $
This restaurant has been run by five generations of the same family. The relaxed and cozy atmosphere makes it an ideal place to sample true Abruzzo dishes. ✉ Via Tre Marie 3 ☎ 0862 413 191 🕐 Closed Sun. evening, Mon. and Dec. 25 No credit cards

MONTECASSINO

🏨 Alba $$
This hotel in the town of Cassino is modern and comfortable. It makes a good stopping point if you want to spend time visiting the monastery. ✉ Via G Di Biasio 53 ☎ 0776 21 873; fax 0776 218 73 AE, CB, DI, MC, VI

🍴 Villa della Meridiana $$
An early 20th-century building houses this pleasant restaurant, where you'll find a good choice of local favorites and plenty of local diners. The garden is lovely for summer dining. ✉ Via S Pasquale 125 ☎ 0776 312 846 🕐 Closed Mon., Ferragosto (August public holiday) and Dec. 25 AE, CB, DI, MC, VI

ROMA (ROME)

🍴 Agata e Romeo $$
This upscale welcoming restaurant near Santa Maria Maggiore offers a wide range of fish dishes in elegant surroundings. ✉ Via Carlo Alberto 45 ☎ 06 446 6115 🕐 Closed Sun. and some holidays 🚇 27, 70, 93 AE, CB, DI, MC, VI

🍴 Alberto Ciarla $$$
One of Rome's finest restaurants, with an elegant atmosphere and fine fish dishes. Family-run, with excellent service and a huge and distinguished wine list. ✉ Piazza San Cosimato 40 ☎ 06 581 8668 🕐 Closed Sun. 🚇 44, 75, 170 AE, CB, DI, MC, VI

🍴 Al Moro $$
This friendly, traditional neighborhood restaurant is tucked away in an alley near the Fontana di Trevi. More sophisticated than it first appears, it's extremely popular and reservations are essential. ✉ Vicolo delle Bollette 13 ☎ 06 678 3495 🕐 Closed Sun. and Aug. 🚇 56, 60, 85 No credit cards

🍴 Checchino dal 1887 $$
A long-established restaurant specializing in traditional Roman dishes – this is the place to try tripe, brains and offal, as well as delicate ricotta and fruit tarts. The decor is cozy and there's an open fire. The wine list is long and interesting. ✉ Via Monte Testaccio 30 ☎ 06 574 6318 🕐 Closed Sun. evening, Mon., Dec. 25–Jan. 1 and Aug. 🚇 13, 23, 57 AE, CB, DI, MC, VI

🏨 Colombus $$
This hotel is just a stone's throw from St. Peter's and is housed in a former Renaissance palace, with many of the original decorative features. The

The South

KEY TO SYMBOLS

🏨	hotel
🍴	restaurant
✉	address
☎	telephone number
🕐	days/times closed
Ⓜ	nearest subway station(s)
🚌	nearby bus/trolley-bus/tram route(s).
⛴	ferry
AE	American Express
CB	Carte Blanche
DI	Diners
MC	MasterCard
VI	VISA

Hotels
Price guide: double room with breakfast for two people
$ up to L200,000
$$ L200,000–400,000
$$$ over L400,000

Restaurants
Price guide: dinner per person, excluding drinks
$ L15,000–30,000
$$ L30,000–50,000
$$$ over L500,000

BARS

Brightly lit and sparklingly clean, bars are open from 6 a.m. until late at night and serve everything from soft drinks, coffee and tea to beer, wine and scotch. You'll usually find a good selection of snack foods and sandwiches, while many double up as *pasticcerie* (pastry shops) or *gelaterie* (ice cream parlors). If you sit down for waiter service, you will pay a premium, whether inside or out. The normal procedure is to pay for what you want first at the cash-desk (*la cassa*), then take the receipt (*lo scontrino*) to the bar and repeat your order. All bars have bathrooms – you may have to ask for the key from the bartender – and provide daily newspapers.

perfect pilgrimage hotel, it's a favorite with visiting prelates.
✉ Via della Conciliazione 33
☎ 06 686 5435; fax 06 686 4874
🚌 23, 64   AE, CB, DI, MC, VI

🍴 El Toulà $$$
Many people consider this elegant restaurant Rome's best. Impeccable service, a menu that includes Venetian international cooking at its best, plus a good wine list make an evening here truly memorable.
✉ Via della Lupa 29/b ☎ 06 687 3750 🕐 Closed Sun., Sat. and Mon. lunch, Aug. and Dec. 25
🚌 81, 90   AE, CB, DI, MC, VI

🏨 Excelsior $$$
If you want the best European hotels have to offer, stay at this world-class luxury hotel. Its opulent decor and high standard of service make a few days here one of Rome's most sybaritic experiences.
✉ Via Vittorio Veneto 125 ☎ 06 47 081; fax 06 482 6205
Ⓜ Barbarini 🚌 52, 53, 95   AE, CB, DI, MC, VI

🏨 Hotel d'Inghilterra $$$
A few minutes walk from the Spanish Steps in the heart of an upscale shopping area, the comfortable rooms of this historic hotel have antique furniture. Excellent service.
✉ Via Bocca di Leone 14 ☎ 06 69 981; fax 06 69 922 243 Ⓜ Spagna
🚌 119, 52, 61   AE, CB, DI, MC, VI

🏨 Portoghesi $$
You'll be within a short walk of Piazza Navona at this old-fashioned and well-known hotel, tucked away on a cobbled street. The rooms have been refurbished and there's a pretty roof terrace.
✉ Via dei Portoghesi 1 ☎ 06 686 4231; fax 06 68 76 976 🚌 70, 81 90
CB, MC, VI

TARQUINIA

🍴 Bersagliere $$
A big, busy restaurant popular with locals and tourists, where you can eat fish dishes as well as good local Lazio cooking. Comfortable but noisy and bustling.
✉ Via B Croce 2 ☎ 0766 856 047 🕐 Closed Mon., Sun. evening, Dec 25–Jan 6 and 2 weeks in Jul.
AE, CB, DI, MC, VI

🏨 Tarconte $$
This hotel is good for visiting this historic Etruscan city. It has friendly and professional service and bright and comfortable rooms.
✉ Via della Tuscia 19 ☎ 0766 856 141; fax 0766 856 585   AE, CB, DI, MC, VI

TIVOLI

🍴 Cinque Statue $
This big restaurant, with many outside tables, attracts Romans visiting Tivoli for the day as well as visitors staying in town. The cooking is simple and robust, with an emphasis on freshness.
✉ Largo S Angelo 1 ☎ 0774 335 366 🕐 Closed Fri., Sun. evening and 2 weeks between Aug. and Sep. AE, CB, DI, MC, VI

🏨 Torre Sant'Angelo $$
You'll find every modern comfort in this beautifully located hotel. It's small enough for truly personal service, with the facilities of many larger hotels, including a restaurant.
✉ Via Quintilio Varo ☎ 0774 332 533; fax 0774 332 533   AE, CB, DI, MC, VI

VITERBO

🍴 Grottino $$
Here you'll find good cooking, home-made bread, a welcoming atmosphere and restrained elegance. It's fairly small, so make reservations.
✉ Via della Cava 7 ☎ 0761 308 188 🕐 Closed Tue.   AE, CB, DI, MC, VI

🏨 Tuscia $$
This family-run hotel is near the medieval city center and within an easy stroll of the commercial area and shops. Rooms are pleasant and comfortable. Good value.
✉ Via Cairoli 41 ☎ 0761 344 400; fax 0761 345 976   AE, CB, DI, MC, VI

THE SOUTH

ALBEROBELLO

🍴 Il Poeta Contadina $$
It's worth the journey to Alberobello to sample the food and outstanding wine list at this pretty restaurant.
✉ Via Indipendenza 21

The South

☎ 0804321 917 Ⓒ Closed Sun. evening and Mon., except in summer, part of Jan. and mid-Jun. to mid-Jul. AE, CB, DI, MC, VI

⌂ Hotel dei Trulli $$

This is the perfect place to stay in Alberobello. It offers peace and quiet, a nice garden, friendly owners and comfortable rooms.
✉ Via Cadore 32 ☎ 080 432 3555; fax 080 432 3560 AE, CB, MC, VI

AMALFI

⌂ La Bussola $$

In the heart of Amalfi, this excellent-value hotel has traditional decor, airy rooms and is located beside the sea.
✉ Lungomare dei Cavalieri 16, ☎ 0898 71 533; fax 0898 71 369 AE, CB, DI, MC, VI

⌘ Da Gemma $$

You can enjoy traditional dishes on a terrace overlooking Amalfi's main square in one of the coast's most popular and best-known restaurants.
✉ Via Fra' Gerardo Sasso 10 ☎ 0898 713 45 Ⓒ Closed Wed. except in summer, also mid-Jan. to mid-Feb. AE, CB, DI, MC, VI

BARI

⌘ Ai 2 Ghiottoni $$

This rustic-style restaurant puts the emphasis firmly on local dishes, with an interesting wine list heavily weighted with Puglian wines.
✉ Via Putignani 11 ☎ 0805 232 240 Ⓒ Closed Sun. and 2 weeks in Aug. AE, CB, DI, MC, VI

⌂ Boston $$

A good mid-range hotel within easy reach of both the historic center and the railroad station. Comfortable and professionally run.
✉ Via Piccinni 155 ☎ 080 521 6633; fax 080 524 6802 AE, CB, DI, MC, VI

CAPRI

⌘ Capannina $$

You can eat either in the pretty dining room or on the green terrace of this well-known establishment, where specialties include imaginative use of fish and vegetable combinations.
✉ Via delle Botteghia 12 bis ☎ 0818 370 732 Ⓒ Open mid-

Mar. to mid-Nov. and one week at New Year's AE, CB, DI, MC, VI

⌘ Da Paolino $$

Try the delicious *antipasto* buffet in this restaurant serving local dishes, where you can eat outside in the shade of a lemon-tree pergola.
✉ Via Palazzo a Mare 11, Marina Grande ☎ 0818 376 102 Ⓒ Open Apr.–Oct., Jul. and Aug. evening only, closed Wed. Apr.–May and Sep.–Oct. AE, CB, DI, MC, VI

⌂ Palatium $$$

An exclusive hotel by the water's edge, this is the only Capri hotel to have access to a beach, with gardens, terrace, salt-water pool, and a good restaurant.
✉ Via Marina Grande 225 ☎ 081 837 6144; fax 081 837 6150 AE, CB, DI, MC, VI

⌂ Syrene $$$

This luxurious and pretty hotel is built in Mediterranean style. The terrace overlooks the cliffs, and the pool stands amid lemon trees.
✉ Via Camerelle 51 ☎ 081 837 0522; fax 081 837 0957 Ⓒ Closed Nov.–Apr. AE, CB, DI, MC, VI

LECCE

⌂ Grand Hotel $$

This splendidly old-fashioned and elegant hotel offers marvelous decor and stucco ceilings. Rooms are simple and comfortable and there's a roof garden and restaurant.
✉ Via O Quarta 28 ☎ 0832 309 405; fax 0832 309 891 AE, CB, DI, MC, VI

⌘ Plaza $

A family-run neighborhood restaurant very near the castle, where you can enjoy local dishes, good value and friendly service.
✉ Via 140 Regg. Fanteria 10 ☎ 0832 305 093 Ⓒ Closed Sun. and 2 weeks in Aug. AE, CB, MC, VI

MARATEA

⌂ Villa del Mare $$

Perched on a rocky headland, this perfect vacation hotel has nice rooms, a pretty terrace and a private elevator down to the hotel's beach.
✉ Acquafredda ☎ 0973 878 007; fax 0973 878 102 Ⓒ Closed Nov.–Apr. AE, CB, DI, MC, VI

⌘ Zà Mariuccia $$

A long-established restaurant in a pretty location, run by the same family for three generations. You can choose your fish from the tank while it's still alive.
✉ Via Grotte 2 ☎ 0973 876 163 Ⓒ Open Mar.–Oct., Jul. and Aug. evenings only, closed Thu. except Jul. and Aug. AE, CB, DI, MC, VI

MATERA

⌂ Italia $$

This comfortable and central hotel in a historic building has a good restaurant and great views over the *sassi* quarter of town.
✉ Via Ridola 5 ☎ 0835 333 561; fax 0835 330 087 AE, CB, DI, MC, VI

⌘ Moro $

This restaurant on the outskirts of the *sassi* quarter overlooking the ravine offers good value, local specialties and friendly service.
✉ Vico IV Capelluti 2 ☎ 0835 332 652 Ⓒ Closed Sun. AE, CB, DI, MC, VI

NÁPOLI (NAPLES)

⌂ Britannique $$

This comfortable hotel in a 19th-century villa has lovely views over the Bay of Naples, a secluded garden and a restaurant.
✉ Corso Vittorio Emanuele 133 ☎ 081 761 4145; fax 081 660 457 ▣ V1 AE, CB, DI, MC, VI

⌘ La Cantinella $$$

This seafront restaurant specializes in creative fish meals, which you can enjoy on the terrace.
✉ Via Cuma 42 ☎ 0817 648 684 Ⓒ Closed Sun., Jun.–Sep. and 2 weeks in Aug. ▣ R3 AE, CB, DI, MC, VI

⌘ Cinquanta tré $$

Naples' oldest restaurant features 17th-century furnishings and an original mosaic pavement, serves great hors d'oeuvres, seafood pasta and Neapolitan desserts.
✉ Piazza Dante 53 ☎ 0815 499 372 ▣ R1, 24 E, CB, DI, MC, VI

⌘ Don Salvatore $$

You'll find very good cooking using the freshest fish and other ingredients in this traditional restaurant, which also doubles as a

KEY TO SYMBOLS
- 🏨 hotel
- 🍴 restaurant
- ✉ address
- ☎ telephone number
- 🕐 days/times closed
- Ⓜ nearest subway station
- 🚌 nearby bus/trolley-bus/tram route(s).
- ⛴ ferry
- AE American Express
- CB Carte Blanche
- DI Diners
- MC MasterCard
- VI VISA

Hotels
Price guide: double room with breakfast for two people
- $ up to L200,000
- $$ L200,000–400,000
- $$$ over L400,000

Restaurants
Price guide: dinner per person, excluding drinks
- $ L15,000–30,000
- $$ L30,000–50,000
- $$$ over L500,000

HOTEL FACILITIES

Outside resorts, mid-range Italian hotels are essentially places to sleep. Top-class hotels have everything you'd expect, but smaller ones will not have every amenity. Many hotels have neither restaurant nor bar, and are unlikely to have lounge areas or other public rooms. Some do not offer breakfast. Rooms will be simple and functional, with tiled floors, limited cupboard space and no easy chairs. Satellite TV is increasing in the north, but is generally limited to hotels catering to business travelers. It is quite normal to ask to see the room before you accept it.

pizzeria. Excellent desserts.
✉ Via Mergellina 5 ☎ 081 681 817 🕐 Closed Wed. Ⓜ Mergellina 🚌 R3,C21 AE, CB, DI, MC, VI

🏨 Excelsior $$$
One of Naples' grandest establishments, located in the elegant Chiaia district. The hotel has period-style rooms and superb views over the bay to Capri.
✉ Via Partenope 48 ☎ 081 764 0111; fax 081 764 9743 🚌 R3 AE, CB, DI, MC, VI

🏨 Grand Hotel Parker's $$
Nineteenth-century decor combines with 21st-century comforts in this hotel. There are lovely views over the city and the rooftop restaurant serves Neapolitan specialties.
✉ Corso Vittorio Emanuele 135 ☎ 081 761 2474; fax 081 663 527 🚌 V1 AE, CB, DI, MC, VI

🍴 Mimì alla Ferrovia $$
A typical Naples restaurant, buzzing and chaotic, where you can enjoy delicious dishes using the freshest ingredients. A local favorite.
✉ Via Alfonso d'Aragona 21 ☎ 081 553 8525 🕐 Closed Sun. and 2 weeks in Aug. 🚌 42, 47, 110 AE, CB, DI, MC, VI

🍴 Taverna dell'Arte $
This characteristic Neapolitan restaurant, with an outside terrace for summer dining, offers traditional dishes made with attention to detail.
✉ Rampe San Giovanni Maggiore 1/A ☎ 081 552 7558 🕐 Closed Sun. and 2 weeks in Jul. 🚌 R1, 42, 47 MC, VI

🏨 Villa Capodimonte $$
This lovely hotel opened in 1995. It's near the park surrounding Capodimonte and offers modern comforts, traditional service and style, a warm welcome and peace and quiet.
✉ Via Moiariello 66 ☎ 081 459 000; fax 081 299 344 🚌 R4, 24 AE, CB, DI, MC, VI

POSITANO

🏨 Buca di Bacco $$
This friendly family-run hotel offers wonderful sea views, comfortable rooms and the bonus of no vehicle access. The hotel will help with luggage. Excellent restaurant.

✉ Via Rampa Teglia 4 ☎ 0898 75 699; fax 0898 75 731 🕐 Closed Nov.–Apr. AE, CB, DI, MC, VI

🍴 Cambusa $$
You can eat right on the main beach on the terrace of this lovely restaurant. The interior decor has a nautical theme.
✉ Piazza A Vespucci 4 ☎ 0898 12 051 AE, CB, DI, MC, VI

REGGIO DI CALABRIA

🍴 Baylik $$
This friendly restaurant is near the harbor and offers imaginative seafood dishes.
✉ Vico Leone 3 ☎ 0965 48 624 🕐 Closed Thu. and 2 weeks in Aug. AE, CB, DI, MC, VI

🏨 Grand Hotel Excelsior $$
Conveniently located hotel for the Museo Nazionale and not far from the ferry port. The rooms offer old-fashioned elegance, modern comforts and good views across the Straits of Messina.
✉ Via Vittorio Veneto 66 ☎ 0965 812 211; fax 0965 893 084 AE, CB, DI, MC, VI

SORRENTO

🍴 Caruso $$
An elegant, refined and award-winning restaurant with excellent and imaginative fish dishes and more than 300 wines.
✉ Via Sant'Antonino 12 ☎ 0818 073 156 AE, CB, DI, MC, VI

🏨 Grand Albergo Excelsior Vittoria $$$
An elegant Edwardian hotel with modern comforts in possibly the finest position in Sorrento. An elevator takes guests to the beach and harbor from the garden.
✉ Piazza T Tasso 34 ☎ 0818 071 044; fax 0818 771 206 AE, CB, DI, MC, VI

TROPEA

🍴 Pimm's $
This small and friendly, good-value restaurant overlooking the sea serves Calabrian dishes and fish grills. Cheap and cheerful.
✉ Largo Migliarese 2 ☎ 0963 666 105 🕐 Closed Mon. and 2 weeks during Jan. and Feb. MC, VI

Sicily

🏨 Rocca Nettuno $$

Many rooms in this big hotel are individual bungalows offering perfect privacy. There's an elevator down to the beach.

✉ Via Annunziata ☎ 096 399 8111; fax 096 360 3513 🅒 Closed Nov. –May AE, CB, DI, MC, VI

VIESTE

🍴 Locanda Dragone $$

Set in a natural cave, this friendly restaurant is in the heart of the old town. Excellent wine list and fish dishes of all sorts.

✉ Via Duomo 8 ☎ 0884 701 212 🅒 Closed mid-Oct. to Apr. and Tue. AE, CB, MC, VI

🏨 Seggio $$

A friendly family-run hotel in the heart of the old center, with excellent restaurant, pool, terrace and steps down to a private beach.

✉ Via Veste 7 ☎ 0884 708 123; fax 0884 708 727 🅒 Closed Nov.–Apr. AE, CB, DI, MC, VI

SICILY

AGRIGENTO

🏨 Hotel della Valle $$

This modern hotel overlooks the archeological zone but is within walking distance of the city center. It has comfortable rooms and a swimming pool.

✉ Via Ugo la Malfa 3 ☎ 092 226 966; fax 092 226 412 AE, CB, DI, MC, VI

🍴 Ruga Reali $

This is a true family restaurant, always busy with locals, right in the heart of the centro storico. Be sure to try the fish.

✉ Cortile Scribani 8 ☎ 0922 20 370 🅒 Closed Wed. except in Aug. AE, CB, DI, MC, VI

CEFALÙ

🏨 Kalura $$

This cliff-top hotel has comfortable rooms overlooking lovely terraces and gardens. There are steps running down to the hotel's private beach.

✉ Via V Cavallaro 13 ☎ 092 142 1354; fax 092 142 3122 AE, CB, DI, MC, VI

🍴 Ostaria del Duomo $$

You can eat outside in the piazza overlooking the cathedral at this restaurant, which specializes in Sicilian dishes. Good wine list.

✉ Via Seminario 5 ☎ 0921 421 838 🅒 Closed Mon. and mid-Nov. to mid-Mar. AE, CB, DI, MC, VI

ENNA

🍴 Centrale $$

This family-run restaurant in the old town serves Sicilian specialties. Try the buffet-style vegetable antipasto.

✉ Piazza VI Dicembre 9 ☎ 0935 500 963 🅒 Closed Sat. in winter. AE, CB, DI, MC, VI

🏨 Grand' Albergo Sicilia $$

Enna's only hotel stands in the heart of the historic center; the interior belies its somewhat soulless appearance with comfortable bedrooms, friendly staff and good reception and lounge areas.

✉ Piazza Colaianni 7 ☎ 093 550 0850; fax 093 550 0488 AE, CB, MC, VI

ERICE

🏨 Moderno $$

Set on one of Érice's prettiest streets, this cozy hotel, housed in an 18th-century building, has an excellent restaurant and attractive terrace.

✉ Via Vittorio Emanuele 63 ☎ 092 386 9300; fax 092 386 9139 AE, CB, DI, MC, VI

🍴 Taverna di Re Aceste $$

Local dishes, particularly fish, are served with flair in this elegant restaurant with a nautical theme. Finish dinner with a traditional dessert from Érice.

✉ Via De Martino 4 ☎ 0923 869 084 🅒 Closed Wed. (except in Aug.) and Nov. AE, CB, DI, MC, VI

PALERMO

🍴 'A Cuccagna $

In the heart of the city, this friendly trattoria, with its cozy ambience, offers classic Sicilian cooking.

✉ Via Principe Granatelli 21/A ☎ 091 587 267 🅒 Closed two weeks in Aug. AE, CB, DI, MC, VI

🍴 Charleston $$$

Head for Palermo's top restaurant to enjoy seafood and Sicilian specialties with excellent service and superb wines in elegant surroundings. The Charleston has a branch restaurant at Mondello during the summer.

✉ Piazzale Ungheria 30 ☎ 091 321 366 🅒 Closed Jun.–Oct. and Sun. AE, CB, DI, MC, VI

🏨 Excelsior Palace $$$

A top-class hotel with gracious and spacious surroundings and period furnishings. The hotel is located within easy reach of Palermo's most popular sights.

✉ Via Marchese Ugo 3 ☎ 091 625 6176; fax 091 342 139 AE, DI, MC, VI

🍴 Friend's Bar $$

You'll find creative Sicilian cooking and excellent fish dishes served at this pretty restaurant with an outdoor seating area for summer dining.

✉ Via Brunelleschi 138 ☎ 091 201 401 🅒 Closed Mon. and 2 weeks in Aug. AE, DI, MC, VI

🏨 Jolly del Foro Italico $$

Standing in the Villa Giulia gardens, this comfortable hotel has high standards of service. The rooms are everything you'd expect from this reputable nationwide chain. Swimming pool.

✉ Foro Italico 22 ☎ 091 616 5090; fax 091 616 1441 AE, DI, MC, VI

🍴 Regine $$

The wonderful display of fish at the entrance gives an idea of the delights that lie in store at this friendly establishment.

✉ Via Trapani 4/a ☎ 091 586 566 🅒 Closed Sun. and Aug. AE, CB, DI, MC, VI

🏨 San Paolo Palace $$

This modern seafront hotel is an ideal choice to escape the city noise and confusion. An elevator takes you to the rooftop pool and restaurant.

✉ Via Messina Marine 91 ☎ 091 621 1112; fax 091 621 5300 AE, DI, MC, VI

🍴 Santandrea $

Ingredients at this popular restaurant come from the nearby Vucceria market. There's no menu, but you can't go wrong from the list the server gives you.

✉ Piazza S Andrea 4 ☎ 091 334 999 🅒 Closed Tue. and 2 weeks in Jan. AE, CB, DI, MC, VI

Sardinia

KEY TO SYMBOLS

- 🏨 hotel
- 🍴 restaurant
- ✉ address
- ☎ telephone number
- 🕐 days/times closed
- Ⓜ nearest subway station
- 🚌 nearby bus/trolley-bus/tram route(s).
- ⛴ ferry
- AE American Express
- CB Carte Blanche
- DI Diners
- MC MasterCard
- VI VISA

Hotels
Price guide: double room with breakfast for two people
$ up to L200,000
$$ L200,000–400,000
$$$ over L400,000

Restaurants
Price guide: dinner per person, excluding drinks
$ L15,000–30,000
$$ L30,000–50,000
$$$ over L500,000

🏨 **Villa Igiea Grand Hotel $$$**
This hotel has an old-fashioned atmosphere and high standards of comfort and service. It stands in a beautiful seafront garden with tennis courts and swimming pool. Considered among Sicily's top hotels.
✉ Salita Belmonte 43 ☎ 091 543 744; fax 091 547 654 AE, DI, MC, VI

SELINUNTE

🏨 **Alceste $$**
This modern hotel is an ideal choice if you want to stay near the classical site; cool, airy rooms and a pretty terrace overlooking the sea.
✉ Via Alceste 21 ☎ 092 446 184; fax 092 446 143 🕐 Closed mid-Jan. to mid-Feb. and mid-Nov. to mid-Dec. AE, CB, DI, MC, VI

🍴 **Pierrot $$**
This Mediterranean-style restaurant has lovely views of the sea and temples, which you can enjoy while sampling freshly caught seafood.
✉ Via Marco Polo 108 ☎ 0924 46 205 🕐 Closed Tue. in winter and Jan. 6–Mar. AE, CB, DI, MC, VI

SIRACUSA

🏨 **Grand Hotel $$$**
This luxurious old hotel on Ortigia in the heart of the old city has been recently renovated. Lovely sea views, elegant furnishings, excellent service and a rooftop restaurant.
✉ Viale Mazzini 12 ☎ 093 146 4600; fax 093 146 4611 AE, CB, DI, MC, VI

🍴 **Jonico-'A Rutta 'E Ciauli $$**
Start with the *antipasto* buffet in Siracusa's best fish restaurant. It has a small museum with 18th-century Sicilian artifacts.
✉ Riviera Dionisio il Grande 194 ☎ 0931 655 40 🕐 Closed Tue., Easter, Ferragosto (August public holiday) and Dec. 25 AE, CB, DI, MC, VI

TAORMINA

🍴 **Ciclope $$**
Right on Taormina's main street, this good-value, family-run restaurant has an outside terrace and serves local specialties.
✉ Corso Umberto ☎ 0942 23 263 🕐 Closed Tue. and mid-Jan. to mid-Feb. AE, CB, DI, MC

🏨 **San Domenico Palace $$$**
A 15th-century convent houses Taormina's most luxurious hotel. Its elegant rooms, impeccable facilities and superb service perfectly complement the stunning views.
✉ Piazza S. Domenico 5 ☎ 094 223 701; fax 094 262 5506 AE, CB, DI, MC, VI

🏨 **Villa Belvedere $$**
There are lovely views of Etna and the sea from this pretty hotel set amid palm trees and olives. Traditional furnishings and a poolside restaurant add to its charm.
✉ Via Bagnoli Croce 79, Messina 98039 ☎ 094 223 791; fax 094 22625 830 🕐 Closed mid-Nov. to mid-Mar. AE, CB, DI, MC, VI

SARDINIA

CAGLIARI

🍴 **Dal Corsaro $$**
This restaurant is a real institution in Cágliari and has Sardinian dishes, with an emphasis on fish, welcoming surroundings and an excellent wine list.
✉ Viale Regina Margherita 28 ☎ 0706 64 318 🕐 Closed Sun., 2 weeks in May and Dec. 25–Jan. 6 AE, CB, DI, MC, VI

🏨 **Sardegna $$**
A quiet and comfortable hotel with good facilities and a restaurant.
✉ Via Lunigiana 50 ☎ 070 286 245; fax 070 290 469 AE, CB, DI, MC, VI

COSTA SMERALDA

🏨 **Green Park $$$**
Located in Porto Rotundo, this is one of the best values on the Costa Smeralda. The hotel offers good service and comfort. Lovely sea view from the terraces.
✉ Località Aldia Manna, Porto Rotondo 07020 ☎ 0789 380 100; fax 0789 380 043 🕐 Closed Nov.–May CB, MC, VI

🍴 **Pescatore $$$**
This is a stylish restaurant to see and be seen in. The terrace has lovely views over Porto Cervo.
✉ Porto Cervo ☎ 0789 931 624 🕐 Open evenings only May–Oct. AE, CB, DI, MC, VI

ESSENTIAL INFORMATION

*"*P*LANNING advice and practical travel tips "*

Italy – Essential Information

BEFORE YOU GO
PASSPORTS
Passport application forms can be obtained by contacting any federal or state court or post office authorized to accept passport applications. U.S. passport agencies have offices in most major cities. You can also request an application form by calling the National Passport Information Center at (888) 362–8668. (Note: There is a credit card charge.) Comprehensive passport information and application forms are available on the U.S. State Department internet site at www.travel.state.gov.
Apply for your passport in good time as processing can take several months from the time of application until it arrives. Rush service is available for an extra charge. Before departure, make sure your passport is valid for at least six months after you are due to travel: some European countries require this.
You may be required to leave your passport with the hotel when you check in; this is to satisfy regulations requiring the hotel to register all foreign visitors with local police authorities. In addition, you must show your passport whenever you cash a traveler's check. Passports also need to be shown whenever national borders are crossed, although in practice border controls have been relaxed between many European Union (E.U.) member countries.
In addition to a passport, some countries require a visa. Travel visas are not necessary to visit Italy, but if you'll be traveling to other nations, check their entry requirements before you leave home.

TRAVEL INSURANCE
Before departing, make sure you are covered by insurance that will reimburse travel expenses if you need to cancel or cut short your trip due to unforeseen circumstances. You'll also need coverage for property loss or theft, emergency health or dental treatment, and emergency evacuation if necessary. Before taking out additional insurance, check to see if your current homeowners or medical coverage already covers you for travel abroad. If you make a claim, your insurance company will need proof of the incident or expenditure. Keep copies of any police report and related documents, or medical bills or statements, to submit with your insurance claim.

ESSENTIAL FOR TRAVELERS

● Required	● Recommended	● Not required	
Passport			●
Visa			●
Travel, medical insurance			●
Round-trip or onward airline ticket			●
Local currency			●
Traveler's checks			●
Credit cards			●
First-aid kit and medicines			●
Health inoculations			●

ESSENTIAL FOR DRIVERS

● Required	● Recommended	● Not required	
Driver's license			●
International Driving Permit			●
Car insurance (for private cars)			●
Car registration (for private cars)			●

*see also DRIVING section

WHEN TO GO
Despite its basically mild winters and warm summers, Italy has a varied and extreme climate. In winter Venice, Turin and Milan can be quite chilly, and you can ski in parts of the country in September. The best months for sightseeing are April, May, June, September and October, although rain and cold linger in northern and mountain areas throughout spring and autumn. July and August are the hottest months everywhere. Winters can be severe, particularly in the Alps and fogbound plains of Lombardy and Emilia-Romagna. European school vacations are another factor in planning when to schedule your trip. Schools in Italy are normally in session from September until early July. This makes May and June good months to visit, both from a weather standpoint and and the fact that there are likely to be fewer crowds at major attractions.

IMPORTANT ADDRESSES
Italian Government Tourist Office
630 Fifth Avenue
Suite 1565
New York, NY 10111
☎ (212) 245-4822
Fax (212) 586-9249

Italian State Tourist Authority
Via Marghera 2
00185 Rome, Italy
☎ 06 49711
Fax 06 446 3379

American Embassy
Via Vittorio Veneto 119a
00187 Rome, Italy
☎ 06 46741
Fax 06 488 2672
Open Mon.– Fri. 8:30–12:30 and 2–4

CUSTOMS

YES

Goods brought into Italy from non-European Union countries limited to:
200 cigarettes or 100 cigarillos or 50 cigars or 250 g. tobacco; 2 L. wine; 1 L. alcohol over 22% volume; 2 L. alcohol under 22% volume; 60 ml. perfume; 250 ml. toilet water; plus any other duty-free goods (including gifts) to the value of L30,000 ($13). There is no limit on the importation of tax-paid goods purchased within the European Union, provided they are for personal use. There are no currency regulations. Returning to the United States, you will be required to complete a customs declaration. You are allowed $400 worth of personal goods; keep sales slips and have them ready for inspection.

NO

No unlicensed drugs, weapons, ammunition, obscene material, pets or other animals, counterfeit money or copied goods, meat or poultry.

MONEY

Italy's currency is the lira (L or Lit; plural lire). The denominations of lira bills are 1,000, 2,000, 5,000, 10,000, 50,000, 100,000 and 500,000. There are coins of 50, 100, 200, 500 and L1,000. Exchange dollars or traveler's checks (assegni touristici) at a bank (banca) or exchange office (ufficio di cambio). Hotels may exchange traveler's checks, but stores do not. ATMs (sportello automatico) are fairly common and accept major credit cards. On Jan. 1, 1999, the euro became the official currency of Italy and the Italian lira became a denomination of the euro. Lira notes and coins continue to be legal tender during a transitional period. Euro bills and coins are likely to be introduced by Jan. 2002. Exchange rate at press time: $1 = L2,250.

TIPS AND GRATUITIES

Restaurants (where service is not included)	10%–15%
Cafés/bars	L200
Taxis	15%
Porters	L2,000
Chambermaids	L3,000 weekly
Restrooms	L100 minimum
Cloakroom attendants	L1,000

COMMUNICATIONS

POST OFFICES

Buy stamps (francobolli) at a post office (ufficio postale) or at a tobacconist (tabaccaio). Mailboxes often have two

slots, one for local mail (città), the other for out-of-town mail (altre destinazione). Mail sent to and from Italy can take up to 3 weeks; to speed delivery send it express (espresso) or registered (raccomandata).

TELEPHONES

Pay phones are usually found in bars and other public places. Coin-operated phones take L100, L200 and L500 coins. Prepaid cards (schede telefoniche) for card-operated

phones are available in values of L5,000, L10,000 and L15,000 from tobacconists, bars, post offices, newsstands, railroad stations and dispensers showing a Telecom Italia (TI) logo. When making international calls use a prepaid card; tear the corner off before using it. Calls from hotel rooms always incur a surcharge.

Phoning inside Italy
All telephone numbers in Italy include an area code that must always be dialed. To call the operator dial 10.

Phoning Italy from abroad
The country code for Italy is 39. Note that Italian numbers in this book do not include the country code; you will need to prefix this number if you are phoning from another country. To call Italy from the United States or Canada dial the prefix 011 39. Include the first zero of the regional code. There is no standard number of digits in Italian numbers. Example: 01 122 3344 becomes 011 39 01 122 3344

Phoning from Italy
To phone the United States or Canada from Italy, prefix the area code and number with 001. Example (111) 222–3333 becomes 001 111 222–3333. To call international information dial 170.

EMERGENCY NUMBERS

Police (polícia) 113 (local), 112 (national)
Fire service (pompieri)   115
Ambulance (ambulanza)   113
Emergency calls are free from phone booths.

Italy – Essential Information

Italy – Essential Information

HOURS OF OPERATION

- Stores Mon.–Sat.
- Museums/monuments
- Offices Mon.–Fri.
- Architectural sites
- Banks Mon.–Fri.
- Churches/pharmacies
- Post offices Mon.–Fri.

| 7 | 8 | 9 | 10 | 11 | 12 | 1 | 2 | 3 | 4 | 5 | 6 | 7 |

Department stores, some grocery stores and stores in tourist areas may not close at lunchtime, and sometimes stay open until later in the evening. Some stores close on Monday morning and may close on Saturday afternoon in summer; most stores close on Sunday.

Some banks close at 2 and do not reopen later in the afternoon.

Many museums are open in the afternoon (usually 5–7), others are open all day, and a few stay open late into the evening. Many museums close early on Sunday (around 1), and most are closed Monday.

Post office times may vary slightly, and they may be open Saturday 8–11:45.

NATIONAL HOLIDAYS

Banks, businesses, and most stores and museums close on these days. Most cities, towns and villages celebrate their patron saint's day, but generally most establishments remain open.

Jan. 1	New Year's Day
Jan. 6	Epiphany
Mar./Apr.	Easter Monday
Apr. 25	Liberation Day 1945
May 1	Labor Day
Aug. 15	Assumption of the Virgin
Nov. 1	All Saints' Day
Dec. 8	Immaculate Conception
Dec. 25	Christmas Day
Dec. 26	St. Stephen's Day

RESTROOMS

Finding a restroom *(gabinetto/bagno/ toletta)* can be difficult away from airports, rail and bus stations, highway service areas and museums. Leave a small tip (about L100) for the attendant. If using the facilities in a bar you will be expected to buy a drink. Some bars have separate restrooms for men *(signori)* and women *(signore)*.

HEALTH ADVICE

MEDICAL SERVICES
Private medical insurance is strongly recommended. Visitors from non-European Union countries can receive treatment in a hospital accident and emergency room, but you will be charged if you are admitted to a bed. A general practitioner *(medico)* can deal with less urgent cases, but also will charge.

DENTAL SERVICES
Emergency dental treatment is available from English-speaking dentists listed in the Yellow Pages *(pagine gialle)*. A fee will be charged, so check that you are covered for treatment on your private medical insurance.

SUN ADVICE

In summer, particularly in July and August, it can be oppressively hot and humid in cities. On sunny days cover head and shoulders and use a sunscreen. Cathedrals and other stone buildings can be refreshingly cool. Take frequent breaks in the shade and drink plenty of fluids.

DRUGS

A pharmacy *(farmacia)* displays a green cross symbol and has staff who can provide prescription medicines and offer advice on minor ailments. Information about the address of the nearest 24-hour facility is normally posted at every pharmacy.

SAFE WATER
In isolated rural areas it is not advisable to drink tap water. However, across most of the country tap water is perfectly safe, although most Italians prefer to drink bottled mineral water *(acqua minerale)*, which is inexpensive and widely available.

PERSONAL SAFETY

Keep valuables (passport, money, checks, credit cards) hidden when you're on the move, and hold bags and cameras across your front – never hung over one shoulder, where they can be easily grabbed. Put money in different places so if one bag is lost you have another source of funds. Tourist attractions and public transportation are prime territory for pickpockets. Avoid lingering

alone after dark, particularly in parks or around railway stations. Contact a police officer if anyone becomes aggressive; police on city streets throughout Italy are usually very approachable and often speak English.

Italy – Essential Information

NATIONAL TRANSPORTATION

AIR *(aeroplano)*
Alitalia, its domestic affiliate ATI and several smaller national carriers offer frequent service between cities and islands. Prices are high, and you will often find it cheaper and more convenient to travel by rail. Students and passengers between 12 and 25 qualify for 25 percent discounts on certain Alitalia flights, and there are 30 percent reductions available on some night flights, as well as 50 percent savings for family groups.

TRAIN *(treno)*
Italian State Railways (Ferrovie dello Stato, or FS) provide an efficient range of services. Regionale, Diretto and Espresso trains are slow for long journeys; InterCity trains, which do not make stops at each station *(stazione)*, cost more but are faster; the Pendolino is the fastest and most expensive. One-way *(andata)* or round-trip *(andata e ritorno)* tickets *(biglietti)* are available in first *(prima)* or second *(seconda)* class. Fares, calculated on a kilometer basis, are some of the cheapest in Europe. Three-day, round-trip tickets are discounted 15 percent on distances up to 250 km (50 km for a 1-day, round-trip ticket). Tickets are valid for 1 day from the day of issue for distances up to 250 km, plus an extra day of validity for each additional 200 km up to a maximum of 6 days. The validity period takes effect from the moment you punch your ticket on the platform machines. Tickets must be used within 2 months of purchase. Stations usually have separate ticket windows for reservations and sleepers *(cucetta)*. Reservations are worth considering for long journeys in summer, when trains can be crowded. The FS issues two main passes. The Chilometrico is valid for 3,000 km of travel over a maximum of 20 journeys. The Italy Railcard is a travel-at-will card available for 8- 15-, 21- and 30-day periods (both first and second class). If you use trains regularly buy the Pozzorario, a biannual timetable that is available in bookshops and at station kiosks.

BUS *(autobus)*
There is no national bus company, but major cities have their own company for short-, medium- and some long-distance bus travel. International Eurolines run from the main Italian cities ☎ 055 215 5151. Ask about services at tourist offices or visit the local bus terminal *(autostazione)*. Tickets must usually be bought beforehand from *tabacchi* (tobacconists) or the bus terminal.

FERRY *(traghetto)*
Genoa and Naples are the main Mediterranean ports, with regular service to Sicily and Sardinia. Naples also has a ferry to Capri and other islands. Many services are reduced off-season, and some are cut. Car ferry bookings for summer travel to Sardinia and Elba should be made serveral months in advance.

PHOTOGRAPHY

The regions of Italy are fascinatingly diverse, each with unique geographical traits, its own cultural identity and a strong sense of individualism. With such diversity the possibility of subject matter is almost endless. From the fishing ports off the coast and the wine-growing regions of Tuscany to the mountains of the Apennines and the sandy beach resorts, you'll find plenty to direct your lens at. If you're interested in architecture there will be much to interest you. In the summer months, most regions will have a good amount of sun and 100asa film should suffice. If you intend to take a few interiors and are cautious about the weather, then pack some 200asa. Film *(pellicola)* and batterries *(batteria)* can be easily found, and if you're visiting a particular tourist attraction there will normally be a kiosk selling a selection of brands. There are developing and printing facilities in most large towns, but these are generally expensive. Don't be concerned about your film and camera going through security equipment at the airport; it is quite safe for film rated up to 1600asa.

MEDIA

Italy's national newspapers *(giornali)* include the authoritative Milan-based *Corriere della Sera*, the Turin-based *La Stampa* and the Rome-based *La Repubblica*. The biggest-selling papers are sports papers. In larger cities, American newspapers (usually previous-day editions) and magazines are available; the most common are *USA Today*, the international edition of the *New York Herald Tribune* and *Time* magazine. They can be purchased at airports and central train stations, as well as at newsstands and tobacconists. Italian radio and television are deregulated and offer a vast range of national and local stations. Standards are low, with local networks geared mainly to advertising, pop music and old films. National stations are better, dividing equally between the three channels of the state RAI network and those founded by Silvio Berlusconi *(Canale 5, Rete 4* and *Italia Uno)*. On the radio you can pick up Voice of America, Radio Canada or BBC broadcasts, and larger hotels often have satellite or cable connections that broadcast BBC channels, the British Sky network or CNN.

ELECTRICITY

Italy has a 220-volt power supply (in some areas, 125 volts). Electrical sockets take plugs with two round pins, or sometimes three pins in a vertical row. American appliances will need a plug adapter and will require a transformer if they do not have a dual-voltage facility.

Italy – Essential Information

DRIVING REGULATIONS

DRIVE ON THE RIGHT
Driving is on the right, and you should yield at intersections to vehicles approaching from your right.

SEAT BELTS
Must be worn in front seats at all times and in the rear seats where fitted.

MINIMUM AGE
The minimum age for driving a car in Italy is 18 (may be higher for some car rental firms).

BLOOD ALCOHOL
The legal blood alcohol limit is 0.08%. Random breath tests are carried out frequently, especially late at night.

TOLLS
You will be issued a ticket on entering nearly every limited-access highway *(autostrada)*: pay on leaving. You can buy prepaid cards at tollbooths, service areas, tourist offices and tobacconists.

ADDITIONAL INFORMATION

An International Driving Permit (IDP) is recommended when driving in Italy. It is a document containing your photograph and confirming that you hold a valid driver's license in your own country. It has a standard translation in several languages and is a useful document to carry; it can speed up formalities if you are involved in an accident.

A Green Card is advised if you are driving a private vehicle overseas to prove that you have liability insurance. For additional information contact your local AAA club.

Dimmed headlights are required by law when passing through tunnels, even if they are well lit.

SPEED LIMITS

REGULATIONS
Police can demand up to a quarter of an imposed fine to be paid on the spot.

Limited-access highways *(autostrada)*
130 k.p.h. (80 m.p.h.)

Main roads
110 k.p.h. (68 m.p.h.)

Urban areas
50 k.p.h (31 m.p.h.)

CAR RENTAL

CAR RENTAL
The leading rental firms have offices at airports, railroad stations and ferry terminals. Hertz offers discounted rates for AAA members. For reservations:

	UNITED STATES	ITALY
Avis	(800) 331-2112	02 715 123
Budget	(800) 527-0700	06 2293 5620
Dollar	(800) 252-897	055 318 609
Hertz	(800) 654-3080	055 307 370

To rent a car you will need a valid U.S. driver's license and preferably an International Driving Permit, and you will probably be asked to show your passport. Depending on which rental company you use, you may be asked for an additional credit card or further proof of identity for renting premium or luxury cars. Most car rental companies will not rent to an individual under 21. If you intend to drive across national borders tell the company, as this will affect both the rate and the type of insurance documentation required.

European cars are generally small, have manual transmissions and rarely offer air-conditioning. Rates vary, but a AAA travel agent should be able to give an accurate estimate. Be sure to inquire about local taxes and find out what insurance coverage is included, and check whether you need a collision damage waiver. AAA travel agencies can reserve a car for you before you leave, provide prepayment arrangements, or reserve a car for you for specified dates and destinations. Rates are lower if reservations are made in the United States prior to departure, and guaranteed in U.S. dollars if you prepay.

FUEL

Gas in Italy is among the most expensive in Europe. It is unleaded *(senza piombo)* and sold in liters. Diesel *(gasolio)* is cheaper. Outside urban areas, stations open daily 7–12:30 and 3–7:30. Gas stations on highways are open 24 hours. Credit cards are not widely accepted away from highways. Self-service and 24-hour pumps which take L10,000 and L50,000 notes are increasingly common.

PARKING

Parking is often difficult in towns: parking lots *(parcheggi)* are invariably full, and most historic centers are partially or fully closed to traffic. Check the signs in the vicinity of your car: Insure there are no restrictions, that you pay for and display a parking sticker if necessary, and check closing times if you use a multistory parking garage. Cars may be towed if illegally parked; contact the local offices of the *Vigili Urbani* to reclaim your vehicle.

AAA

AAA AFFILIATED MOTORING CLUB

Automobile Club D'Italia (ACI)
Via Marsala 8, 00185 Rome
☎ 06 49 981; fax 06 445 2702

If you break down while driving, phone 116 (ACI breakdown service).

Not all automobile clubs offer full services to AAA members.

BREAKDOWNS/ACCIDENTS

There are emergency phones at regular intervals on all highways. If you are involved in an accident, ☎ 118 for emergency medical help, 112 or 113 for police help.

Most car rental firms provide their own free rescue service; if your car is rented, follow the instructions given in the documentation. Use of a car repair service other than those authorized by the rental company may violate your rental agreement.

ROAD SIGNS

Driving in busy Italian cities can be a daunting prospect if you're not used to the signs, driving habits and local regulations. If you are renting a car, be sure to get as much information from the rental company as possible. They will usually provide a chart of common road signs and an area road map. Most road signs in Italy conform to the usual international standards; below is a glossary of terms which may not be familiar to the foreign traveller:

entrada	entrance
incrocio	crossroads
lavori in corso	roadworks ahead
passaggio a livello	level crossing
rallentare	slow down
senso vietato	no entry
sosta vietata	no parking
svolta	bend
uscita	exit

Traffic merges from right

Crossroads

ROAD SIGNS (continued)

Other danger

Steep hill downwards

No overtaking

No entry for vehicular traffic

Dual carriageway ends

Vehicles may pass either side to reach same destination

Ahead only

Keep right

Double bend, first to right

Two-way traffic straight ahead

Italy – Essential Information

Italy – Essential Information

SPEECH

Italian pronunciation is consistent with spelling, and vowels are always silent, but can modify the sound of letters *c* and *g*. As a general rule, accentuate the next-to-last syllable.

c is hard before a, o, u, h	*medico; Chianti*
c is soft before i or e	*ciao* [chow]
g is hard before a, o, u, h	*Gucci, Lamborghini*
g is soft before i or e	*gelati* [jel-ah-tee]
gl as in Amelia	*figlia* [fee-lyah]
gn as in union	*gnocchi* [nyee-ok-kee]
sc before i or e is soft	*prosciutto* [pro-shoot-toh]

Where two consonants appear together, each belongs to a different syllable.

AIRPORT

airport	*aeroporto*
airplane	*aeroplana*
arrivals	*arrivi*
departures	*partenze*
check-in	*accettazione*
information	*informazione*
ticket	*biglietto*
flight	*volo*
baggage	*bagagli*
passport	*passaporto*
window seat	*vicino al finestrino*
first class	*prima classe*
economy class	*classe turistica*
international	*internazionale*

MEETING PEOPLE

good morning	*buon giorno*
excuse me	*scusi*
do you speak English?	*parla inglese?*
yes, no	*si/no*
sorry	*scusami*
please	*per favore*
thank you	*grazie*
your welcome	*prego*
I am American	*sono Americano/-a*
what is your name	*come si chiama*
my name is...	*mi chiamo...*
I don't understand	*non capisco*
pleased to meet you	*piacere di conoscerLa*
how are you?	*com'è va*
okay	*va bene*
goodbye	*arrivederci*
goodnight	*buonanotte*
see you later	*a presto*
have a good trip	*buon viaggio*

HOTEL

the hotel	*l'albergo*
I have a reservation	*ho prenotato*
a room	*camera*
for one/ two nights	*per una/ due notte/-i*
one/ two people	*una/ due persona/-e*
how much does it cost?	*quanto costa?*
key	*una chiave*
shower	*una doccia*
with in-room bathroom	*con bagno*
room service	*il servizio in camera*
porter	*l facchino*

EATING OUT

a table for two	*un tavolo per due*
we've reserved	*abbiamo prenotato*
could we see the menu?	*ci porta il menù*
fixed-price menu	*il menù a prezzo fisso*
first course	*l'antipasto*
main course	*il secondo*
cheese	*formaggio*
dessert	*l dolce*
waiter/ waitress	*cameriere/ cameriera*
wine	*il vino*
mineral water	*acqua minerale*
what's this? (on menu)	*cosa è questo*
I am a vegetarian	*sono vegetariano/a*
bread	*il pane*
beef	*il manzo*
chicken	*il pollo*
ham	*prosciutto*
lamb	*l'agnello*
pork	*il maiale*
seafood	*i frutti di mare*
mussels	*le cozze*
fish	*il pesce*
eggs	*uove*
salad	*insalata*
vegetables	*verdure*
soup	*minestra*
liqueur	*digestivo*
coffee	*il caffè*
hot	*caldo*
cold	*freddo*
good	*buono*
bad	*non è buono*
restroom	*bagno/toiletta*
the check	*il conto*
cover charge	*coperto*

Italy – Essential Information

DIRECTIONS

where is...?	dov'è
turn left/right	a sinistra/destra
straight ahead	sempre diritto
how far is it?	quanto è distante?
near here	qui vicino
far	lontano
facing opposite/	di fronte a
in front of	davanti a
behind	(in) dietro

POST OFFICE

post office	l'ufficio postale
stamp	francobollo
airmail	posta aerea
letter	léttera
postcard	cartolina
package	pacchetto
registered letter	léttera raccoman-.data
mailbox	bucca delle lettere
address	indirizzo

TELEPHONE CALLS

phone booth	telefono pubblico
phone card	scheda telefonica
operator	il/la centralinista
international access code	il prefisso intermnazionale
my number's...	il mio numero...

SHOPPING

baker	panificio
delicatessen	salumeria
fish merchant	pescheria
market	mercato
grocery store	supermercato
bookstore	la libreria
fruit and vegetable	frutta e verdura
butcher	macelleria
do you have?	avete?
how much?	quanto costa
store assistant	commessa/o

PHARMACY

pharmacy	la farmacia
diarrhhoea tablets	astrin-gente
bandage	fascia
tampons	i tamponi
razor blades	le lamette
suntan lotion	olio solare
aspirin	aspirina

EMERGENCIES

police	la polizia
ambulance	un' ambulanza
fire department	i pompieri
doctor	un medico
accident	incidente (m)
first aid	pronto soccorso
where is the nearest hospital?	l'ospedale più vicino?
emergency number	numero d'emergenza
stop thief!	al ladro!
help!	aiuto!

TRANSPORTATION

railroad station	stazione
subway	metropolitana
train	treno
platform	binario
ticket	biglietto
single or two-way	andata o andata e itorno
bus station	la stazione degli autobus
bus	autobus(m)
bus stop	fermata dell' autobus
timetable	orario
non-smoking	vietato fumare
taxi	il taxi

MONEY

credit card	carta di credito
traveler's checks	un traveller cheque
exchange rate	il cambio
bank	banca

NUMBERS

18

1, 2, 3	uno, due, tre
4, 5, 6	quattro, cinque,sei
7, 8, 9	sette, otto, nove
11, 12	undici, dodici
13, 14	tredici, quattordici
15, 16	quindici, sedici
17, 18	diciassette, diciotto
19, 20	diciannove, venti
30, 40	trenta, quaranta
50, 60	cinquanta, sessanta
70, 80	settanta, ottanta
90, 100	novanta, cento
500	cinquecento
1000	mille
2000	duemila
10,000	diecimila

Index

Index

Acknowledgements
The Automobile Association would like to thank the following photographers and libraries for their assistance in the preparation of this title.
JAMES DAVIS TRAVEL PHOTOGRAPHY 75, 157, 192; EYE UBIQUITOUS 42, 43; HULTON GETTY PICTURE COLLECTION
96/97, INTERNATIONAL PHOTOBANK 67, 179; 97; MRI BANKERS GUIDE TO FOREIGN CURRENCY 215; PICTURES COLOUR
LIBRARY 52, 73, 82; REX FEATURES 117; SPECTRUM COLOUR LIBRARY 44, 47, 53a, 144, 154, 162, 167, 182, 184, 191; TOPHAM
PICTUREPOINT 189a, 189b; WORLD PICTURES 53b, 72b 74, 76, 77, 78, 81, 148/149, 156

The remaining photographs are held in the Association's own library (AA PHOTOLIBRARY) and were taken by Clive Sawyer with the exception
of the following:
AA Photolibrary 196; Pete Bennett 20, 48; Eric Meacher 54, 55; Jim Holmes 128, 132a, 134, 135, 215a; Max Jourdan 153, 155a, 155b; Dario
Miterdiri 3, 9; Ken Paterson 10a, 14/15, 16/17, 18/19, 31, 84, 86, 89, 93, 98, 102/103, 103, 104, 106, 107, 112, 113, 114, 115, 116, 139, 141b; Barrie
Smith 215b; Anthony Souter 13, 26, 51, 60/61, 100, 132b, 140, 141aa, 142, 159b, 166; Peter Wilson 118, 121